The Future of Work Series

Series Editor: **Peter Nolan**, Director of the ESRC Future of Work Programme and the Montague Burton Professor of Industrial Relations at Leeds University Business School in the UK.

Few subjects could be judged more vital to current policy and academic debates than the prospects for work and employment. *The Future of Work* series provides the much needed evidence and theoretical advances to enhance our understanding of the critical developments most likely to impact on people's working lives.

Titles include:

Julia Brannen, Peter Moss and Ann Mooney
WORKING AND CARING OVER THE TWENTIETH CENTURY
Change and Continuity in Four Generation Families

Andy Danford, Mike Richardson, Paul Stewart, Stephanie Tailby and Martin Upchurch
PARTNERSHIP AND THE HIGH PERFORMANCE WORKPLACE
Work and Employment Relations in the Aerospace Industry

Geraldine Healy, Edmund Heery, Phil Taylor and William Brown (*editors*)
THE FUTURE OF WORKER REPRESENTATION

Diane Houston (*editor*)
WORK-LIFE BALANCE IN THE 21ST CENTURY

Theo Nichols and Surhan Cam
LABOUR IN A GLOBAL WORLD
Case Studies from the White Goods Industry in Africa, South America, East Asia and Europe

Paul Stewart (*editor*)
GLOBALISATION, THE CHANGING NATURE OF EMPLOYMENT AND THE FUTURE OF WORK
The Experience of Work and Organisational Change

Clare Ungerson and Sue Yeandle (*editors*)
CASH FOR CARE IN DEVELOPED WELFARE STATES

Michael White, Stephen Hill, Colin Mills and Deborah Smeaton
MANAGING TO CHANGE?
British Workplaces and the Future of Work

The Future of Work Series
Series Standing Order ISBN 1–4039–1477–X

You can receive future titles in this series as they are published by placing a standing order. Please contact your bookseller or, in case of difficulty, write to us at the address below with your name and address, the title of the series and one of the ISBNs quoted above.

Customer Services Department, Macmillan Distribution Ltd, Houndmills, Basingstoke, Hampshire RG21 6XS, England

---

Also by Clare Ungerson

WOMEN AND SOCIAL POLICY: A Reader (*edited*)
POLICY IS PERSONAL: Sex, Gender and Informal Care
GENDER AND CARING: Work and Welfare in Britain and Scandinavia (*edited*)

Also by Sue Yeandle

WOMEN'S WORKING LIVES: Patterns and Strategies
YOUTH, UNEMPLOYMENT AND THE FAMILY (*with P. Allatt*)

Cash for Care in Developed Welfare States

Edited by

Clare Ungerson
Emeritus Professor of Social Policy, University of Southampton and Honorary Professor of Social Policy, University of Kent, UK

and

Sue Yeandle
Professor of Sociology, University of Leeds, UK

E·S·R·C
ECONOMIC
& SOCIAL
RESEARCH
COUNCIL

palgrave
macmillan

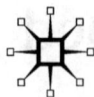

First published 2007 by
PALGRAVE MACMILLAN
Houndmills, Basingstoke, Hampshire RG21 6XS and
175 Fifth Avenue, New York, N.Y. 10010
Companies and representatives throughout the world

PALGRAVE MACMILLAN is the global academic imprint of the Palgrave
Macmillan division of St. Martin's Press, LLC and of Palgrave Macmillan Ltd.
Macmillan® is a registered trademark in the United States, United Kingdom
and other countries. Palgrave is a registered trademark in the European
Union and other countries.

ISBN-13: 978–1–4039–3552–6 hardback
ISBN-10: 1–4039–3552–1 hardback

This book is printed on paper suitable for recycling and made from fully
managed and sustained forest sources.

A catalogue record for this book is available from the British Library.

A catalog record for this book is available from the Library of Congress.

10   9   8   7   6   5   4   3   2   1
16   15   14   13   12   11   10   09   08   07

Printed and bound in Great Britain by
Antony Rowe Ltd, Chippenham and Eastbourne

Contents

Foreword

The public policy issues concerning the provision of care for older people are of great moment. With the age distribution of the population rising in most developed economies, there is an irresistible warrant for careful analysis and debate of the merits and disadvantages of different systems of care provision.

This timely study draws together the latest authoritative findings on the different arrangements for care provision for older people in seven countries: the UK, Austria, France, Italy, the Netherlands, Germany and the USA. Five of the EU country-specific studies formed part of the research project, led by Professor Clare Ungerson and Professor Sue Yeandle, on the Shifting Boundaries between Paid and Unpaid Work that was conducted under the UK Economic and Social Research Council's Future of Work Programme. Launched in 1998, the Programme supported 27 projects and the work of more than one hundred researchers at 22 UK universities. The Programme website is at: www.leeds.ac.uk/esrcfutureofwork

Cash for Care in Developed Welfare States is the eighth research monograph published under the Palgrave Macmillan Future of Work Series. It tackles questions that will become increasingly salient to public policy makers as the developed welfare states come to terms with the costs of maintaining greatly increased numbers of aged people that require care, especially at a time when fewer women of working age remain committed to full time unpaid domestic and caring labour.

Individually and collectively, the national studies examine how the care relationship is being affected by the more widespread introduction of the cash nexus, the process by which care services are increasingly subject to commodification and hence exposure to market forces. The authors scrutinize the complex set of relationships between care users, care givers and care workers and ask to what extent care work can be professionalized. They point to the possibility that commodification may well transform the relationship between carer and the care user where money replaces more traditional state or family-based services.

Writing from a feminist perspective, the authors pose challenging questions about those women that continue to perform unpaid caring roles within the family. How can they gain access to the social and political rights that others take for granted. Cash for care, the authors note, is one way of supporting informal carers, and citizenship rights to them, but it not the only way forward nor necessarily the best route.

These and other pressing issues are discussed authoritatively by an international renowned team of feminist researchers. The book is essential reading for scholars, practitioners and policy makers concerned with the future of care work for the elderly, disabled and children in developed welfare states.

Professor Peter Nolan

List of Figures

List of Tables

Acknowledgements

The publishers and editors would like to acknowledge the use of the figures used in Chapter 9, previously published in Clare Ungerson, 'Whose empowerment and independence? A cross-national perspective on "cash for care" schemes', *Ageing & Society*, volume 24, issue 02, March 2004, pp. 189–212. © Cambridge University Press.

Notes on the Contributors

Blanche Le Bihan is a Researcher in Political Science at LAPSS, National School of Public Health at the University of Rennes, France.

Cristiano Gori is Senior Research Fellow at the Institute for Social Research at the University of Milan-Biocca, Italy.

Elisabeth Hammer is Researcher at the Vienna University of Economics and Business Administration, Austria.

Sharon M. Keigher is Professor in the Department of Social Work at the Helen Bader School of Social Welfare, University of Wisconsin, Milwaukee, USA.

Claude Martin is Senior Researcher at the National Council for Scientific Research and Director of LAPSS, National School of Public Health at the University of Rennes, France.

August Österle is Associate Professor in the Department of Social Policy at the Vienna University of Economics and Business Administration, Austria

Marja Pijl is an independent researcher and gerontologist based in the Netherlands.

Clarie Ramakers is a Research Fellow at the Institute for Applied Social Sciences at Radboud University, The Netherlands

Carlos Reyes is a Researcher in the Department of Social Policy at the Vienna University of Economics and Business Administration, Austria.

Barbara Da Roit has recently completed a PhD on European urban and local studies in the Department of Sociology and Social Research at the University of Milan-Biocca, Italy.

Ulrike Schneider is Professor and Head of the Department of Social Policy at the Vienna University of Economics and Business Administration, Austria.

Bernadette Stiell is Senior Research Fellow at the Centre for Social Inclusion at Sheffield Hallam University, UK.

Clare Ungerson is Emeritus Professor of Social Policy at the University of Southampton and Honorary Professor of Social Policy at the University of Kent, UK.

Sue Yeandle is Professor of Sociology at the University of Leeds, UK.

1
Conceptualizing Cash for Care: The Origins of Contemporary Debates

Sue Yeandle and Clare Ungerson

Theoretical debates and issues

The origins of the work contained within this book lie within feminism rather than gerontology; but the substantive issues tackled within its pages are of considerable interest to gerontologists and to others concerned with the future of care for older people in developed welfare states. The underlying idea of the project to which much of this book relates was a concern with the way in which the boundaries of paid and unpaid work have been shifting in the late twentieth and early twenty-first centuries. The project's background lay in the debates concerning the way in which women's citizenship could be under-written and whether or not 'work' within the domestic domain should be paid (Fraser, 1994; Himmelweit, 1995). Much of this general debate concerning the underpinning of women's citizenship is closely related to a discussion of the way in which the activities of 'care' within the domestic domain can best be recognized and compensated for, such that those in unpaid caring roles – be they parents of small children or providers of caring services to older family members within their own homes – have access to full citizenship, in terms of social rights and in terms of social and political participation (Lister, 1998). The use of cash payments as a form of compensation or wage for the tasks of care undertaken within the home is one of a range of possible solutions to the problem of care and citizenship.

Given these origins, it is in some ways a matter of chance that the focus of this book is on the care of older people. It would have been just as relevant to consider the ways in which cash-for-care schemes are developing for younger disabled people within the domestic domain, and similarly, in some welfare states, to look at the way in which the

1

care of children in their own homes is also increasingly supported by cash supplements directed to their kin who care for them. The focus in this book on the care of older people does, however, give us an empirical basis on which to explore some of the pressing issues surrounding the whole question of the future of long-term care for older people in developed welfare states. The chapters raise questions as to how long-term care can best be funded, consider the relative position of care users, caregivers and care workers in the care relationship, discuss the nature of care work and how far it should and can be professionalized, and debate how informal carers can best be supported. These questions are considered within the overarching framework of the process of care 'commodification' or 'cash-for-care' schemes, where the central idea is that care users are given the opportunity, through cash subvention, to employ their own caring labour directly. In her original typology of cash-for-care schemes, Ungerson (1997) had previously identified one particular form of scheme which she named 'routed wages'. In this type of scheme the payment from the state went to care users who were then allowed, or encouraged, to employ personal assistants to provide them with caring services. It is this form of cash-for-care scheme that is discussed in this book.

Most of the chapters in this book arise from a recent international research study on the *Shifting Boundaries of Paid and Unpaid Work*. The study, directed by the editors of this volume, and forming part of the UK Economic and Social Research Council's Future of Work Programme, explored issues identified in earlier theoretical work on new ways of delivering personal care services to older and disabled people, which Ungerson (1995, 1997) had conceptualized as the 'commodification of care'. This analysis suggested that informal care was becoming commodified through new policies which involved distributing cash allowances to those living independently, but assessed as needing social care, enabling them to pay their care givers to provide them with services. This form of commodification was deemed especially important both because of its potential for 'empowering' care users (in theory, giving them cash rather than services allows care users to decide the nature of the services they receive and to determine who should provide them), and because of its implications for those who provide the services and who are directly 'paid' by care users for the work they do.

A variety of new systems of payments to care users emerged in a number of EU countries and in Canada and parts of the USA during the 1990s. These systems were seen in a number of different types of welfare system, and were developed in countries that were operating differing funding and regulatory regimes. The *Shifting Boundaries* study set out to explore two main issues: first, how the care relationship is affected by the introduction of the cash nexus, and how specific aspects of funding regimes impact on the care relationship; and second, the position of the care givers paid for their work through these systems. The study was, therefore, designed to examine their routes into and out of care work, and to consider the impact of the new funding arrangements on both their labour market attachment and on their work-related social rights.

In the 1990s, the existing literature had begun to explore the position of care users in systems such as these, and to examine their satisfaction with them (Kestenbaum, 1999; Morris, 1993), while other writers had reviewed early policy developments in this field (Glendinning and McLaughlin, 1993; Evers *et al.*, 1994; Weekers and Pijl, 1998). At the European level, the European Foundation for the Improvement of Living and Working Conditions had also undertaken cross-national research on wider aspects of the transfer of classic 'unpaid' work, such as housework, laundry, meal preparation, child care, and the care of older people, to the conventional markets of labour and commerce (Cancedda, 2001; Yeandle, 2002; Yeandle *et al.*, 1999). The *Shifting Boundaries* study was innovative in two main ways. First, it involved conducting a detailed investigation of the position of care givers in this new employment or quasi-employment relationship, and second, the care of older people (rather than disabled people) was chosen as its focus. In particular, it researched the process and impact of the commodification of informal care delivered to older people by kin, neighbours and friends. As anticipated, the study uncovered care relationships, particularly in funding regimes which allow for the payment of relatives, where the carer was neither a giver of care, in the sense of providing classically unpaid informal care, nor a care worker, in the sense of being fully engaged within the conventional labour market, whether 'grey' or fully organized. Thus the study provided the opportunity to explore the hybridity of 'work' and 'care', where carers were motivated both by pecuniary and non-pecuniary impulses.

When the study commenced the existing literature was rather small and the theoretical perspectives underpinning the work were relatively undeveloped. We, therefore, designed the project to be innovative and exploratory, using qualitative methods to uncover processes in the commodification of care that had previously been unexamined. We theorized that the entry of cash into the care relationship was likely to have some impact, and that policy and regulatory difference would lead to different outcomes in terms of who comes forward to provide care for cash, and in terms of the labour market position, both now and in the future, of these care givers. A key difference between the funding regimes explored was that some welfare states allowed for the payment of relatives, while others wholly forbade it; there were also important differences in the regulation of how recipients used the cash payments. These distinctions do have an important impact on both the care relationship and on the type of carers who come forward within these different funding regimes, as various contributors to this book confirm in the chapters that follow.

Policy context

The policy context for the development of commodified care delivery systems, often referred to as 'cash-for-care' or (in the UK) 'direct payments' systems, has a number of important dimensions. As the authors of the country-specific chapters in this volume demonstrate, these issues and concerns have been of differing relative importance, but have been commonly seen in most of the countries examined here.

In the first place, policy on how to provide support for older people has developed in a context of growing awareness of important demographic processes, which began in the twentieth century and are accelerating in the twenty-first. Increased longevity, coupled with falling birth rates and changes in family structure, mean for all developed countries larger numbers of very aged people requiring care, with relatively smaller populations of younger people available to deliver it. In particular, all EU member states, and all parts of North America, have seen increases in the labour force participation of partnered women and mothers, and a diminishing pool of women of working age who are wholly committed to the unpaid performance of domestic and caring labour.

Second, welfare states throughout the developed world have become increasingly conscious of the need to contain the costs of social care, as politicians across the political spectrum have turned away from explicit tax-raising programmes and have tried variously to 'roll back' or at least to contain and control welfare spending. Recent and ongoing debates about the funding of retirement pensions and of how to pay for long-term care have been common concerns widely discussed in all the countries considered in this book.

This has left those responsible for planning, implementing and managing welfare and care policies searching for cost-effective and cheaper means of delivering services, and care services to older people have featured prominently in their deliberations, forming a third important contextual factor. Some have argued that commodified care systems offer a cheaper way of delivering services without compromising the quality of care, principally because they offer the prospect of eliminating layers of welfare bureaucracy. Although this has been strongly disputed by some practitioners, policy makers and academics, it is evident from the later chapters in this book that it is an attitude that still underpins some policy thinking in this field.

Alongside this (and, in the opinion of some, perhaps working at cross-purposes), have been widespread and continuing shifts in the way recipients of welfare and care services themselves view, respond to and make demands of those who support and care for them. Spearheaded by an increasingly organized and vociferous disability movement, especially in the UK and The Netherlands, and by an increasingly politicized older people's movement in North America, recipients of care and their supporters have demanded greater choice, have expressed rising expectations, and have made a powerful case for user empowerment. Further, it is now widely expected that the consumerist rhetoric dominant in the market economies of all the countries studied in this book will have increasing impact on older people's expectations of the services they receive, and that successive generations of older people will want to have a greater say in, and control over, the way they are supported in the future.

Additionally, and connected to this important choice and empowerment agenda, most welfare systems have made some moves towards greater official control of service provision, involving the following key features: a trend towards greater regulation of services (often involving quite complex bureaucratic measures); the establishment of more formal and explicit standards in the provision of care services (usually relating to the quality but also in some cases to the accessibility of these services); the accreditation and statutory checking of standards among service provider organizations; and monitoring, in some cases using registers of approved staff and checks on criminal records, of the individuals authorized to deliver personal care to vulnerable people.

In the UK, this complex set of policy concerns, developments and contexts has been encapsulated in the expressed political objective of 'modernizing social services', the title given to a major policy initiative set in train by the incoming New Labour government in 1997. Far from a unique UK approach, however, the policy has reflected developments at the level of both the EU and its individual member states, as well as experience in parts of the USA, as contributors to this volume confirm.

The five-nation comparative study of commodified care systems

The *Shifting Boundaries* project received funding from the UK's Economic and Social Research Council sufficient to support new empirical invest-igations in five EU Member States: the UK, Austria, France, Italy and The Netherlands. The project, led and directed by the editors of this book, involved directly comparable exploratory qualitative work in each of the five countries. The study design and detailed methodology have been described elsewhere (Ungerson, 2004). The local research teams also explored the policy origins and context for the development of cash-for-care schemes in their own country, and this work forms the basis for Chapters 2 to 6 in the present volume. It involved analysis of existing research data and statistical evidence, and discussion of the history and likely future development of cash-for-care schemes in the countries concerned. The following chapters also draw to varying degrees on the new empirical data collected specifically for the *Shifting Boundaries* study.

The *Shifting Boundaries* study aimed to assess the impact of policy change on employer/employee (carer/care recipient) relations within the domestic domain, and to explore how older care users managed risk in recruiting and organizing their caring labour. It also sought to identify the main effects of cash-for-care schemes on care workers in the labour market, in particular assessing their impact on informal economic activity, and on workers' social rights. The research was thus designed to contribute to policy debates on the management and organization of 'direct payment' and 'cash-for-care' systems, and to explore how far devolved employer/employee relations can and should be regulated by state organization and prescription.

The five national reports outlining the policy context within which the commodified care relationships were undertaken have been used in preparing five of the chapters in this volume. Two additional chapters have also been written especially for this volume, contributed by experts in the field whose work relates to Germany and the USA, countries not included in the original study. The book thus offers a comparative perspective, based in analysis, of seven different countries, although only five EU states were in the original ESRC-sponsored study.

How the book is organized

This book is organized so that the reader can gain detailed understanding of how care for older people has become commodified in recent years in seven different developed countries. In the past decade or so, these countries have all adopted policies that offer some elderly care users the opportunity to receive cash payments instead of services, although in each case the policies have been designed and implemented in different ways, with the intention of achieving some very different, as well as some shared objectives.

Chapters 2 to 8 explore the policy background, demographic circumstances, implementation arrangements and rules and regulations applied in each of the seven countries studied. Some chapters also include evidence from the authors' recent empirical investigations of how commodification of care has affected both care users and care givers, and about how the implementation of cash-for-care policies plays out in practice. Where possible, contributors include the perspectives of care workers/care providers as well as those of older people who are care users. The book suggests that, in designing or reshaping social care policies to enable older people needing care to receive it in their own homes from people they themselves choose to employ, policy makers need to understand, and to take responsibility for, the new workforce issues that arise, albeit in the almost universally welcomed context of care users' enhanced control over their own lives.

In Chapter 2 Österle and Hammer draw attention to the increased importance of the market sector in the Austrian system. Their chapter confirms that the introduction in Austria of cash-for-care arrangements (in the form of the *Pflegegeld* system) has increased the purchasing power of care recipients. The system involves largely unregulated payments, and as such tends to be spent by recipients in three main ways: purchasing care from social service organizations; paying individual, privately employed care workers; and paying family or friends for the care they have previously given, or would otherwise deliver, unpaid. This chapter shows that cash-for-care systems of particular kinds can set up considerable vulnerability for care workers, and indeed may create an environment in which a grey or unofficial migrant labour market in the delivery of domiciliary care can expand and flourish.

Chapter 3, by Martin and Le Bihan, deals with developments in the French system. The chapter considers a range of policy developments and experiments introduced in France in the past decade, and explores some of the tensions that have arisen between national policy design and local implementation. Here some of the key policy developments have been strongly linked to attempts to combat unemployment and to create new jobs. The authors of this chapter show that in France the developments initially destabilized existing qualified jobs in domiciliary care and created additional unskilled and casualized employment. Subsequent refinements to the schemes have gradually produced more indirect employment of care workers, whose contracts are often with local authorities or with not-for-profit providers, and various changes designed to maintain and develop the professionalization and accreditation of caring labour are discussed. This chapter thus focuses on a key issue for promoters of consumer choice and of cash-for-care systems: how far caring labour ought to, or should, be professionalized. Through its focus on reforms to the original French scheme, the *'Prestation Spécifique Dépendence'*, including those designed to raise the skill levels and qualifications of care workers, the chapter highlights an important dilemma. Allowing, or encouraging, those requiring care to employ their own labour raises critical questions about how more skilled caring labour can remain affordable and can be paid for through systems of cash payments to individuals in need of support.

In their consideration of the Italian case, Gori and da Roit examine the *'indennita di accompagnamento'*. They emphasize that the social care market in Italy is a virtually unstructured economic sector, and point out that most care workers remunerated through the cash-for-care system are individual workers employed directly by families, rather than by care organizations. As in Austria, unofficial migrant labour features strongly, although in Italy the sources of caring labour appear to be further flung, including examples from South America. These workers have absolutely minimal social rights, although as Gori and da Roit point out, even in the regular Italian care market, working conditions, social rights, minimum wages and labour costs are highly variable. As the authors observe, many of these care workers have few other options in the labour market, and in some cases caring work is their job of last resort. Even in this unregulated context, some experiments, often developed in the voluntary (third) sector, are nevertheless under way to increase the quality of care and to afford stakeholders greater safety. The authors conclude their analysis with the challenging observation that, in Italy, recourse to grey labour and the availability of cheap migrant labour are the very features that have enabled the care market to expand, permitting families to outsource some of the caring and other domestic labour traditionally provided by women within the family setting.

Pijl and Ramakers, in their chapter on The Netherlands, describe how the Dutch, in the 1990s, developed an elaborate system of 'personal budgets', given to care users which, under strict regulation and payment by an outside body, allowed them to 'employ' their relatives, friends and neighbours; and many of them did so. The authors use empirical data from the *Shifting Boundaries* project to demonstrate how satisfactory this system was, both to care users and their employed caregivers. However, the subsequent shift of the Dutch national government towards the right has focused attention on the apparently high costs of the personal budget scheme and the fact that relatives are being paid to undertake care which they had previously provided 'free'. As a result, Dutch policy in this area is changing rapidly. The authors note that at the time of writing their chapter, the provision of unpaid care by relatives was becoming a formal expectation of the agencies that allocate support to care users.

Yeandle and Stiell's chapter (Chapter 6) focuses on the background to the development of Direct Payments for older people in England, and offers detailed insight into the way the scheme was initially implemented in one English city. The chapter explores the origins of the scheme in demand for user empowerment, considers some of the effects of the scheme's specific disbarment on care users which prevents them from using Direct Payments to pay their relatives, and notes the generally sluggish take-up of the scheme for older people. This chapter presents details of the contractual and other arrangements put in place to support and protect care users, and to give them control over the services they receive. While these seem mostly to be welcomed by care users, the limited availability of caring labour, and the difficulty of finding employees, restrict the benefit of these arrangements. The chapter also draws attention to a lack of effective arrangements to protect and support individual care workers, especially those who are directly employed as the personal employees of people in whose private homes they carry out their work. Concerns about job insecurity, health and safety, and the emotionally demanding nature of work in this field, as well as about the content and boundaries of the job and the relationships between the care worker and the care recipient are all highlighted in this contribution.

In the chapter on Germany contributed by Schneider and Reyes, the authors discuss the introduction in 1994 of a two-tier system for funding long-term care through compulsory contributions, noting both its context and its consequences. They stress that while additional job creation was an expected outcome of the changes, the main political arguments presented at the time related to the incentives to family caring which the changes would bring, as cash benefits were passed to family carers. The chapter shows how the German system requires care users to take responsibility for the 'service mix' they require, pointing out that opting for cash rather than services implies accepting responsibility for one's own care management. The authors claim that the choices made have important effects on employment in the care sector. The German system allows clients to opt for a benefit package which includes cash benefits and which can be passed to family carers. Schneider and Reyes argue that this development has not been positive in employment terms, and effectively 'traps' carers, most of whom are women, in the care situation. Other elements of the German system are also seen to place pressure on women to assume traditional housekeeping and caring roles. Although, for these authors, the margin for reform measures is slender, they note some recent innovations and policy adjustments, including the experimental introduction of individualized, cash managed budgets. In one example, scheme rules aim to prevent encouragement of the grey economy, and cash benefits may not be passed to family carers. Schneider and Reyes conclude that over a decade of change, much programme spending has been absorbed in private households without improving the situation in the formal care labour market, while even the more recent innovations may have created increased demand only for low skilled caring labour.

The final country chapter focuses on the USA. Here Keigher examines dilemmas in what Americans term 'consumer-directed care', and suggests some of the challenges that arise when personal and private preference become the basis for public policy on long-term care. Drawing her examples from several different US states, Keigher points to evidence that the supply of care workers increases when people are allowed to employ their relatives, but notes that those needing care who lack close family or friends may become further disadvantaged as a result. In a telling observation, Keigher notes that poorer older people requiring care come to depend on the cheapest and lowest skilled available caring labour, comprising those with least choice in the labour market who may themselves be struggling to secure a living wage. In this situation, the risk is that older care users may become both 'accomplices to exploitation' and 'prey for unscrupulous workers'. This chapter highlights a worrying risk associated with cash-for-care arrangements: the potential downward spiral in which the quality of care, the quality of care work, and the social rights of caregivers are all poor and deteriorating.

In Chapter 9, the book offers the editors' reflections and conclusions arising from the different cultural settings, welfare regimes and policy mixes considered in the book. We present a diagrammatic method of understanding the variations between the different schemes. These diagrams also begin to demonstrate the way in which the different funding regimes impact on certain aspects of the care relationship, particularly the time available to care 'workers' to care for individual older people. The main question considered in this chapter is how far these schemes are sustainable and which factors are likely to drive similarities and further differences cross nationally in the future. We consider ways in which many welfare states are attempting to strike a balance between providing better quality care based on training and credentialism while, at the same time, trying to maintain cost containment in the field of long-term care. Such a balance poses fundamental questions about cash-for-care schemes, because many of them appear designed to draw cheap and untrained labour into care occupations. There are also issues surrounding the use of undocumented and informally employed care labour and how far the use of labour which is outside both fiscal and social rights regimes is sustainable in the long run.

These opening comments on the cash-for-care arrangements and policies in the seven countries discussed in this book already indicate the range of important issues faced by governments, social care professionals and citizens in a twenty-first century characterized by developed economies all of which have ageing populations. In the chapters that follow, the authors reveal the complexity, variety and importance of both workforce and policy design issues. In all cases, demand for domiciliary care in support of independent living by older people is rising, and in coming years huge numbers of older people and of care workers will potentially be affected by these developments. Budgetary considerations loom large in most countries, as does the need for urgent attention to the future sourcing of an adequate supply of caring labour. As this book reveals, international migration, both regulated and illegal, is already contributing to the supply of caring labour in some countries. In others the emphasis is on measures to professionalize care work and to upskill and revalue caring labour, with a view to making employment in this field more attractive.

This book is of interest to all those concerned with the future of work, paid conventionally, unpaid, and commodified, and with the welfare of ageing populations. As we indicate in the concluding chapter, we seek to unpick the complexity of the politics of, and development of, cash-for-care schemes, rather than to assume that they are necessarily a panacea for an over bureaucratic and, some would argue, an over professionalized welfare state. Using comparative analysis, we have aimed to develop a better understanding of the implications of this important development in the delivery of long-term care.

References

Cancedda, A. (2001) *Employment in Household Services*, Dublin: European Foundation for the Improvement of Living and Working Conditions.

Evers, A., Pijl. M. and Ungerson, C. (eds) (1994) *Payments for Care: A Comparative Overview*, Avebury.

Fraser, N. (1994) 'After the Family Wage: Gender Equity and the Welfare State', *Political Theory*, 22(4), 591–618.

Glendinning, C. and McLaughlin, E. (1993) *Paying for Care – Lessons from Europe*, London: HMSO.

Himmelweit, S. (1995) 'The Discovery of "Unpaid Work": The Social Consequences of the Expansion of "Work" ', *Feminist Economics*, 1(2), 1–19.

Kestenbaum, A. (1999) *What Price Independence? Independent Living and People with High Support Needs*, York: Joseph Rowntree Foundation.

Lister, R. (1998) *Citizenship: Feminist Perspectives*, Basingstoke: Macmillan.

Morris, J. (1993) *Independent Lives? Community Care and Disabled People*, Basingstoke: Macmillan.

Ungerson, C. (1995) 'Gender, Cash and Informal Care: European Perspectives and Dilemmas', *Journal of Social Policy*, 24(1), 31–52.

Ungerson, C. (1997) 'Social Politics and the Commodification of Care', *Social Politics*, 4(3), 362–81.

Ungerson, C. (2004) 'Whose Empowerment and Independence? A Cross-national Perspective on "Cash for Care" Schemes', *Ageing & Society*, 24(1), 1–24.

Weekers, S. and Pijl, M. (1998) *Home Care and Care Allowances in the European Union*, Utrecht: Netherlands Institute of Care and Welfare (NIZW).

Yeandle, S., Gore, T., Pickford, H. and Stiell, B. (1999) *Employment in Household Services in the UK*, Dublin, European Foundation for the Improvement of Living and Working Conditions.

Yeandle, S. (2002) 'Developments in Household Services in Europe: Working Conditions and Labour Relations', *Transfer: European Review of Labour and Research*, Special Issues, No. 3.

2
Care Allowances and the Formalization of Care Arrangements: The Austrian Experience

August Österle and Elisabeth Hammer

Austria's payment for care scheme is the cornerstone of its welfare state in the field of long-term care. Eligibility for this cash benefit (*Pflegegeld*), which is designed as a contribution to the costs of care, is determined by the need for care. It is not means-tested, not limited to specific age-groups and not pre-determined regarding the actual use of the benefit. This highly unregulated – regarding use – benefit scheme was introduced for a range of reasons which include supporting informal care work and a market-driven development of the social service sector. This chapter explores the conditions and implications of the Austrian payment for care programme as it affects the development and the characteristics of formal employment relations in the care sector. The concept of routed wages as a particular type of commodification is applied as the analytical framework (see the introduction to this volume). Routed wages are understood as a form of commodification where payments are made to care recipients in the expectation that they will use these benefits to employ their own caring labour. Whether and how payments for care operate as routed wages is determined by the design of the payments, the individual care setting at the micro-level, and the way the scheme is embedded in the overall welfare state structure.

After presenting the welfare state context and the demographic, social and economic background in Austria, the chapter details the payment for care programme and long-term care policies in this country. Then new empirical data is used to show how payments for care are used by care recipients. Generally the options available are: buying care work in the social service market; employing care workers in 'grey care markets'; and employing care workers from family networks. Finally we present some general conclusions about the Austrian long-term care allowance scheme as a routed wages scheme and about the informal carers' role in the Austrian context.

The Austrian welfare state context

In comparative welfare state research, Austria is described as a corporatist conservative welfare state or as a social insurance type welfare state (e.g., Esping-Andersen, 1990). Various characteristics underpin this classification: major social risks are covered in a social insurance system; social partners play a significant role in social policy making; key actors in the actual provision of welfare are the state, the family and the non-profit sector; strong links exist between social protection and employment participation; social assistance is the second pillar in the social security system; and welfare state responsibilities are shared between the federal level and the provinces (*Länder*) level (Badelt and Österle, 2001; Unger and Heitzmann, 2003).

Rather as in Germany, social rights in Austria are linked to class and status through a variety of social insurance schemes which mirror the divisions and differentials prevailing in the (labour) market. From a gender-sensitive point of view, Austria serves as a perfect example of a male breadwinner state (Lewis, 1992), drawing a firm dividing line between public and private responsibilities. Women typically acquire social rights by virtue of their dependent status within the family as wives, and are expected to undertake caring work at home with only limited support from the state. Additionally, the principle of subsidiarity plays an important part in limiting the influence of the state (Esping-Andersen, 1990). The normative context of the Austrian welfare state gives priority to cash benefits and reinforces family relations by a limited provision of social services. Thus the welfare state context in Austria tends to underpin both class stratification, through its employment centredness, and gender divisions, through its centredness around the family (Hammer and Österle, 2003).

With regard to social expenditure, Austria ranks slightly above the European average (28.4 per cent compared to 27.5 per cent as a share of GDP in 2001; Eurostat, 2004). About 85 per cent of social expenditure is spent on old age pensions and survivors' pensions, health care and family benefits (BMSG, 2004b). Risks related to old age, illness, occupational accidents and unemployment are covered in a social insurance scheme, with a variety of bodies in charge of the actual administration of these schemes. The financing of social insurance is mainly through contributions made by employers and employees. In parts of the system, the federal state contributes from tax funds to cover deficits or to finance specific benefits or services. In the provision of benefits and services, the insurance principle is stronger in social pension insurance, social insurance for occupational diseases and injuries and unemployment insurance. For example, pensions are determined by previous income (the contribution base) and length of the contributory period. Public pensions without individual contributions only exist as widow(er)'s and orphan's pensions. In health care, by contrast, coverage through social health insurance is extended to most population groups making need the key criteria for access and, hence, offering almost universal access to services. Historically, social policies in Austria were characterized by expanding the personal and material scope of programmes up until the 1980s, and to some extent until the mid 1990s, but became increasingly restrictive after that time (Unger and Heitzmann, 2003). Hence, social protection expenditure (as a percentage of GDP) has increased up until the mid 1990s (to almost 30 per cent) and has since fallen back, to 28.4 per cent in 2001.

Developments have been quite different in long-term care. As in many European countries, long-term care was not even considered as a separate social risk for most of the twentieth century. In Austria, until 1993, long-term care was delivered in a very fragmented way, with benefit levels comparatively low, strict means-testing of benefits in social assistance schemes, and enormous variations between, and even within, the Austrian provinces with regard to in-kind services. The 1993 long-term care reform began a process of clarifying both public and private responsibilities, and the division of responsibilities between federal and provincial agencies (see below).

Recent welfare state reforms in Europe have been shaped by a variety of factors. These changes, including demographic developments, changing economic paradigms and increasingly clearly articulated limitations of financing the welfare state, are of particular importance for long-term care. Austria shares the demographic challenge with all other European countries. In 2001, about 3.6 per cent (292,000 people) of the Austrian population was over 80 years of age. This age group, the most likely to need long-term care, will represent 4.8 per cent in 2010 (396,000 people) and 7.0 per cent in 2030 (590,000) (Statistik Austria, 2004). Apart from age structure, dependency forecasts have to take into account how dependency ratios will change over time. An earlier Austrian study pointed out that, with an unchanged morbidity structure, the number of elderly people in need of long-term care would increase by 65 per cent between 1990 and 2030. That increase, however, could be as 'low' as +30 per cent, in the case of better health, or as high as +95 per cent, in the case of increased morbidity (Badelt et al, 1996). The European Economic Policy Committee (2001) has estimated that long-term care expenditure in Austria, as a proportion of GDP, will more than double between 2000 and 2050. Mindful of these concerns, and in the context of shifting paradigms in economic policy, policy makers emphasize the importance of cost containment and the restructuring of welfare schemes. Policy discourses accordingly focus on concepts such as freedom, empowerment, autonomy and choice. In the field of care, cash benefits (and thus the possibility of exercising purchasing power) are seen as the prime instruments capable of delivering these concepts at the individual level. How long-term care policies in Austria have taken these ideas into account, and with what implications for care arrangements, will be discussed in the following sections.

Payments for care and the provision and finance of long-term care

The 1993 long-term care reform in Austria represented a major social policy innovation. Since then, the long-term care system has built on three main pillars: a tax-financed cash benefit scheme directing payments to those in need of permanent long-term care; a state-provinces treaty setting general conditions regarding federal and provincial responsibilities for service provision; and provincial regulations about the provision and financing of services. At the core of the new system is a cash benefit scheme (*Pflegegeld*). The main explicit objectives of the allowance programme were: to make a contribution towards care-related additional expenses (and thus to support people in need of care); to ensure access to personal services and assistance; to offer free choice with regard to care provision; to provide an incentive for informal care within the family and other primary networks; and to enable people to be cared for in their homes and to remain in their own communities. Last but not least, this type of benefit was seen as a long-term care approach that could also offer cost containment advantages (Hammer and Österle, 2003; Österle, 2001).

Long-term care allowances are intended for people in need of permanent long-term care due to physical, mental or psychic disability or a sensory disability that is expected to last at least six months. Allowances are paid at seven levels (see below); are not means-tested, and are paid directly to care recipients 12 times a year. Recipients are free to spend the money as they wish. They may pay for care-related expenses such as adaptations in the house or specific dietary requirements, they may buy social services and/or pay family members, or even hire them as care workers. Only in the case of residential care is the benefit directly transferred – apart from some pocket money – to the accounts of the residential home.

Administration of long-term care allowances is linked to that of other benefits, most importantly social pensions, accident insurance schemes and federal or provincial civil service pensions. A physician appointed by the respective body assesses care needs via a medical certificate, using standardized procedures covering medical, household and personal requirements. Eligibility requirements state that needs must exceed 50 hours per month. Whereas dependency levels 1 to 3 take account simply of the quantitative amount of care and assistance required, dependency levels 4 to 7 also include qualitative aspects. In addition, assessments have to recognize care documentation (where it exists). Furthermore, potential recipients are entitled to be examined and interviewed in the presence of a person of their choice. The amount of the long-term care allowance is, therefore, determined by both the degree of need and the level of dependency. Decisions on applications are made through an official notification, against which it is possible to appeal to the Labour and Social Tribunal. (BMAGS, 1999b)

Nearly 55 per cent of care recipients awarded care allowances are at levels 1 and 2 of the benefit scheme, with care needs ranging between 50 and 120 hours per month (see Table 2.1). For about 13 per cent of beneficiaries, care needs exceed 180 hours per month. About two thirds of care recipients are women. Greater age is accompanied by a higher risk of morbidity and chronic illness. About 45 per cent of care recipients are over 80 years old, and another 37 per cent between 60 and 80 years of age. Overall, beneficiaries of the scheme represent 4 per cent of the Austrian population. The overall number has steadily increased since 1997 and at a more significant rate in the most recent years, which cannot be attributed to changes in assessment procedures. Changes in the distribution among the seven benefit levels have occurred mainly as a consequence of administrative changes, but a more significant increase in the number of beneficiaries has occurred in dependency levels 6 and 7. An investigation into the causes, however, has not yet been made. It is plausible that this is a result of ageing populations and a reflection of the previously mentioned increase in morbidity.

Table 2.1 The Austrian long-term care allowance

Level	Benefit (per month) 2004 – €	Care needs (per month)	Beneficiairies (1 Jan 2003)	
1	€145.40	> 50 hours	69,136	19.4%
2	€268.00	> 75 hours	126,449	35.4%
3	€413.50	> 120 hours	62,634	17.6%
4	€620.30	> 160 hours	52,584	14.7%
5	€842.40	> 180 hours, need for an unusually high level of care	29,510	8.3%
6	€1,148.70	> 180 hours, need for regular care-related measures during the day and at night or permanent attendance during the day and at night because of the risk that the person in need of care endangers themselves or others	10,093	2.8%
7	€1,531.50	> 180 hours of care, inability systematically to move arms or legs, or comparable conditions	6,391	1.8%

Source: BMSG (2004a).

Apart from some amendments to the assessment procedure, a reduction of minimum requirements for level 4, and a reduction of benefit rates in level 1, the long-term care allowance scheme has remained unchanged since 1993. However, as part of cost containment measures in the Austrian welfare system, no increases in benefit levels have been made since 1995. By 2004, this represented a 'loss' of roughly 16 per cent (Österle and Hammer, 2004).

The Austrian long-term care allowance scheme is among the most unregulated in Europe (see Ungerson, 2003 and other chapters in this volume). For the Austrian welfare state, the allowance represents a new type of benefit distinct from social insurance benefits and distinct from social assistance. Unlike most social insurance schemes, it takes no account of causality. Nor does it refer to other benefits or to the income of (potential) beneficiaries, as in social assistance schemes. In addition, it is explicitly defined as a contribution to long-term care costs, leaving care-related expenses to be covered from individual and family resources or, in the last resort, from social assistance. Thus any discussion of the implications of this specific cash benefit scheme has to recognize how access to residential care, social services and other forms of care work is organized and financed (Österle, 2001).

Historically, residential care was the major public response to long-term care for those who did not have access to family care. Currently, about 41,000 nursing beds are available in public, non-profit and for-profit homes (Rubisch, 1998), i.e. 514 beds per 100,000 inhabitants or 26 beds per 1,000 people above 60 years of age. More recent attempts to reduce acute beds in hospitals, and at the same time to strengthen community care, have led to an increase in the proportion of more severely disabled people living in residential care settings, without significant changes in the total number of places. Financing residential care is based on fees per day levied differentially according to levels of care need. Pensions as well as long-term care allowances are directly transferred to the accounts of the homes, leaving only 'pocket money' to the residents. Costs which cannot be covered through clients' contributions are paid by provinces or communities according to social assistance legislation in the nine provinces. These payments can subsequently be recovered from residents' savings or from the income of close family members. The regulations, as well as the actual decisions, vary considerably across the nine provinces (Barta and Ganner, 1998). Overall, with the introduction of payments for care, an important inter-governmental redistribution of financial responsibilities took place, reducing the proportion of residential care costs to be covered by social assistance.

The 1993 long-term care treaty between the central government and the nine provinces obliged provinces to develop a comprehensive community care system covering residential, semi-residential and domiciliary services by 2010. In the respective plans of the nine provinces it is estimated that adequate coverage will require the number of nurses and helpers (on a full-time basis) in 2010 to be at least twice as high as in 1996 (BMAGS, 1999a). In fact, social service provision has increased considerably since the 1990s, both as a result of these plans and as a result of the payment for care programme (see below). But supply structures are still characterized by a lack of diversified services, a lack of service provision overnight or at weekends, and by regional inequalities in service supply. As the long-term care allowances have become available, competition among providers, most of them in the non-profit sector, has increased in some provinces, although in many areas specific organizations still work in an almost monopolistic position. There is no nation-wide approach to coordination between the different service sectors and service providers, although a number of models have evolved all over the country since the 1990s (Leichsenring and Alaszewski, 2004). Eligibility criteria and access to services are also highly variable, although some provinces use standardized forms for assessing needs. In the case of home nursing by qualified nurses, a referral from a physician is needed for reimbursement by the social health insurance fund. But reimbursement is based on quite strict criteria covering only medical expenses, such as administering injections or dressing wounds. Otherwise, home nursing, as well as home help and other types of relevant services, are funded by a combination of payments by provinces and municipalities (as a general subsidy or related to specific services for clients) as well as clients' co-payments. These are mostly means-tested and increasingly related to the amount of the cash benefit. In general, co-payments became more widespread, and have increased substantially, since the introduction of the long-term care allowance scheme (BMSG, 2004a).

The informal sector still plays a key role in long-term care, even if this remains largely unrecognized. Close family members, above all partners, daughters and daughters in law, are the main care-givers in Austria. About 90 per cent of those receiving long-term care allowances are cared for at home. Given the availability and accessibility of home nursing and home help services, this leaves close family members as the main care givers. About 80 per cent of informal care givers are women. More than 60 per cent of informal care givers are of working age and, hence, face questions about combining or not combining paid and unpaid work, work in the regular labour market and care work within the family or other informal networks, and, as a result, have to bear all the consequences of any decisions they take. This affects mainly women, as the number of male informal carers below 60 years of age is very small. Whereas labour force participation among all women between 15 and 65 years of age is 63 per cent in Austria, it is just 37 per cent among those who also work as informal carers (Badelt *et al.*, 1997). Whether and how the situation of informal carers has changed with the introduction of long-term care allowances is discussed in the following sections.

Different ways of formalizing care arrangements – varieties and similarities

The Austrian long-term care allowance represents a type of benefit that provides financial support for a social risk (long-term care), directs the payment to the care recipient and leaves decisions about how to make use of the benefit to the care recipient (or those who are formally or informally in charge of acting for the care recipient). Apart from covering expenditure for appliances or aids, the intention of the benefit scheme is that payments will be used to buy caring labour or to provide financial support for informal care. If long-term care allowances are used to buy caring labour this can be done in three different ways: paying for care provided by social service organizations; paying individual care workers outside social service organizations; or paying informal carers. In contracting care workers outside social service organizations, cash benefits are a means of setting up direct employer–employee relationships constituting a form of 'routed wages', be they in regular or irregular labour markets. On the other hand, cash benefits can also be used to pass on 'symbolic payments' to caring kin, friends and neighbours, thereby supporting informal care without establishing employer–employee relationships (Ungerson, 1997).

Paying for social services

The establishment of an unregulated cash system has increased the purchasing power of care recipients, but does not necessarily increase service consumption. Generally, social service consumption is – apart from individual ideas about adequate care arrangements – co-determined by the availability of such services and the relative cost of services. As mentioned already, until the 1990s services were very limited in many regions. The introduction of long-term care allowances can be seen (and was thought of as) an incentive to find alternatives to the traditional family care arrangement and care provided in residential care settings. Nursing homes have, in fact, seen a change in the composition of their client group. Apart from efforts to reduce the length of stay in hospitals, this arises from attempts by residential care homes themselves to transfer people with lower levels of need back to community care, as well as from the choices of care recipients or their families, who have increased purchasing power to search for community-based care arrangements.

However, increased purchasing power among care recipients, and hence an increasing ability to purchase social services, has partly been outweighed by a considerable increase in the co-payments that have to be made by those receiving social services (BMSG, 2004a). Using long hours of professional care from social service providers rapidly creates a considerable financial burden, even when it only partly covers care needs (Österle and Hammer, 2004). This can either reinforce the family care arrangement, or encourage care recipients (or family members of care recipients) to search for 'cost-effective' alternative care arrangements.

Paying for migrant care

After the introduction of the long-term care allowance scheme, Austria saw a considerable increase in care work provided by migrant workers from neighbouring central and eastern European countries. Care workers from these countries are increasingly employed by social service providers, but to a large extent they also operate in grey care markets. The development of these grey care markets (which are the focus of this section) is caused by increasingly open borders to the east, and by wage differentials between the countries, as well as by a new understanding among care recipients about how they can employ their own care workers.

Socio-economic circumstances in the countries of origin of migrant workers are characterized by higher unemployment rates and lower wage levels. Average gross earnings in, for example, Hungary and the Czech Republic are about 30 per cent of median gross earnings in Austria, and even less in Slovakia. The same applies to wage levels in care-related sectors, which are below average earnings in all these countries (Statistik Austria, 2004; wiiw, 2003). Apart from wages, the general labour market situation and unemployment in particular may work as an additional 'push' factor, creating incentives for migration. This certainly is the case for Slovakia, where the unemployment rate is 17.1 per cent, which is almost twice the rate of the EU 25 average (9.1 per cent) and far beyond the Austrian unemployment rate (4.1 per cent). Unemployment rates in the Czech Republic (7.8 per cent) and in Hungary (5.8 per cent) are between the Austrian and the EU average rate. Still, as there are considerable regional variations regarding labour markets within countries, regional differences in the latter countries may still operate as an important incentive for work migration.

Before EU enlargement, many migrant workers in grey care markets from central and eastern European countries were officially entering Austria as tourists. Care arrangements, therefore, were organized in a way that ensured legal entry into and legal stay in Austria, for example by arranging fortnightly shifts with two care workers for one care recipient. Whereas historically this type of migrant work arrangement was more widespread in cleaning services, it became an important issue for long-term care after the mid 1990s. There are only very rough estimates available on the number of care workers, ranging from 10,000 to 40,000 care workers (Streissler, 2004). The organization of this kind of care work takes different forms. On the one hand, agencies established either in Austria or in the neighbouring countries arrange contacts between those looking for a care-giving 'job' in Austria and those looking for support in caring for a person in need of care. The existence of grey care markets is well known among professionals in the health and care sectors (for example, among GPs, social workers or in nursing homes) who may give hints regarding the existence of these grey care markets. On the other hand, there are also ethnic networks of migrants arranging care jobs for each other or people who are advertising these 'jobs' in newspapers in Austria or in neighbouring countries. A care worker coming from Hungary describes her experience with recruitment into the routed wage system in Austria:

> I read about it in an advertisement in the newspaper – at home in Hungary. I then telephoned. We spoke about it once, then again, finally for a second and third time. He said that, if it was possible, I ought to come to see what it was all about. It was a Friday and then I stayed there. I was here for a week along with the other girl and then on my own for a second week. It was hard at first as everything was new and strange. However, now it's no problem.

Mostly, this type of irregular employment does not replace regular employment of Austrians or already established foreign workers, but creates 'new jobs' that would not exist under regular conditions of labour and social law. Given the private cost of care provided in residential care settings or by social services, this form of care work forms an alternative to informal care that fits with both the ability and the willingness to pay of 'employers'. Workers in the grey market are willing to work for wages much lower than those fixed as the agreed minimum, and without any social protection. Care workers 'come providing "needed" labour services for employers unwilling or unable to offer higher wages and more attractive job opportunities to those with legal rights to work or to reduce their demand for low-skilled labour' (Chiswick, 2000, p. 173).

Those who manage the 'employment relationship' are either care recipients themselves or close relatives. For them, the main reason for 'employing' people in this grey market is the relative price of care and the possibility of 'employing' someone for long hours. The 'job description' often includes not only care but also different kinds of services, such as housework, gardening, and so on. Buying professional care at market prices or contributing with co-payments to the costs of professional care soon exceeds the ability to pay of most. This would leave them in a situation where an enormous amount of care has to be provided on a purely informal basis. Care bought in the grey market offers access to cheaper care. Thus, it expands the opportunities for many people to reduce their time spent on care-giving and/or to reduce expenditure on care provided from outside the family.

For those offering care in the grey market, this kind of work in Austria often gives them a higher income than they could achieve in their home country. As a carer from Hungary remarks on her pay: 'I can't say it's too little. For I have two full weeks off. I find it's quite good – besides, he couldn't pay me more. I don't ask for any more either.'

In general, the care workers' orientation towards caring is pragmatic and instrumental. Seeing this kind of work in Austria as a first step into the Austrian labour market, or an opportunity to improve language skills, supports the view that the establishment of transnational grey care markets is seen, instrumentally, as labour force participation: 'Well, it's a job, isn't it?. . . I do it somehow.' Nevertheless, the nature of the employer–employee relationship seems to have considerable influence on the care workers' orientation towards caring as well as on individual job satisfaction: 'I do everything that I have to do. That's my job. If the family is pleasant, it isn't difficult for me to have to do everything.'

When care workers are asked about their experiences in current and previous care jobs it also becomes obvious that the concept of the employer–employee relationship varies considerably: 'I was much happier in X. The family there was really nice. I only had to look after the wife, who had Alzheimer's – it was more difficult to handle, but I didn't have to do the housework. They had their own cleaner, who always came in. They did their own cooking – there really was nothing to do. I was treated as one of the family. . . Where I am working now, I'm just a foreigner – nothing more than that. That's the difference.'

Delivering caring labour with the care worker living in the same household involves the development of a personal relationship. This can then make it harder to end a relationship. Asking a care worker about having to say 'I'm not coming any more', she responds: 'That's a bit of a problem. . . If someone needs me, saying No is very difficult for me.' In general, the negative implications and consequences of these care jobs are often neglected. Employer–employee relationships in the field of grey care tend to be fragile and are characterized by an imbalance of power, to the disadvantage of the care workers. This imbalance of power not only concerns basic working conditions, but also more personal ways of arranging the care relationship. One care worker coming from Hungary describes this imbalance of power as follows: 'It [the work] isn't bad, but there are a lot of things I could change and mustn't. I'm talking about in the apartment and with the caring. A larger apartment wouldn't be so bad. However, I am only here for a week at a time, so I can put up with it. We answered an advertisement to come here and said that we needed a larger room. (pauses). He has many habits that mean a lot to him. But they do make work.' On how she reacts to these habits, the care worker adds: 'I do it as he'd like it done. If he thinks that it's better that way. I'm happier doing it that way – I've no stomach for a fight. It's better that way. He is my boss to a certain extent.'

The particular status of working in a grey market, and thus, the marginalization of foreign care workers become apparent when it comes to the perception of social rights, which are accepted as basic entitlements in mainstream employment: 'I've never been ill. I still come to work if I am ill, if I have temperature, a cold, or a cough.'

With no social rights granted whatsoever, a great deal of individual empowerment seems to be needed in order to handle the structural imbalance of power in situations, for example, of illness. Asking a care worker about if she would still come to 'work' when she was ill, she responds: 'No (emphatically). I came once when I was ill. That was when the wife died. I was running a temperature and couldn't sleep a wink, so I slept for two hours that afternoon. The daughter then said that I had been asleep the whole day – I mean just that. I certainly wouldn't do it again.'

With the diffusion of grey-care markets a variety of effects arise at the macro-level. Cheaper work in grey markets influences the value of professional care work in regular markets. In particular, low-skilled workers will find it more difficult to find jobs at regular levels of wages and social security when a substitute is available at considerably lower prices. Also, quality assurance is more difficult in grey care markets. Whereas professional providers are obliged to follow certain guidelines regarding quality, for example the qualification of their staff, no such guidelines are applicable in grey markets. With no professional care alongside grey care there is no systematic contact with the professional health and social care system. Today, the existence of grey care is well known among those providing professional care, among those searching for care, as well as among decision makers in social policy. However, there has not yet been any response regarding the implications and risks arising from this form of care work.

Payments for care and informal care

Long-term care is strongly based on unpaid female work within family networks. The long-term care allowance scheme in Austria has been introduced with the intention of supporting informal care via these payments, without specifying precisely how this support should take place. Empirical data suggest that a variety of monetary transfers between care recipients and family carers have developed, but only in very few of them has this created employment arrangements that accord with the formal requirements of labour and social security law. Monetary transfers, in the form of regular payments to the carer, payments for covering carers' expenses and monetary or in-kind gifts, are all reported by a quarter of informal carers. A third of informal carers report that there is no explicit financial arrangement and 30 per cent report that long-term care allowances are part of common housekeeping arrangements. The latter arrangement occurs in particular with partners caring for each other (Badelt *et al.*, 1997).

Even if there is some form of monetary flow between care recipients and carers, this cannot necessarily be seen as a form of income or income replacement, because payments from care recipients have to be used to cover extra expenses for care and in general do not even completely cover these extra expenses (Badelt *et al.*, 1997). This points to the concept of 'symbolic payments' rather than 'routed wages', where payments are made to caring kin, friends and neighbours without establishing employer–employee relationships. Payments are seen as a financial recognition for care work that is considered to be a family responsibility, or as an individual responsibility towards the care recipient.

In the Badelt *et al.* study in 1997 just 16 out of 1,320 respondents (informal carers) reported that regular employment contracts had been established in previously informal care arrangements. Apart from these isolated cases, one Austrian province (Salzburg) has for some time promoted a more systematic approach of establishing regular employment contracts. A non-profit organization, rather than the care recipient, acted as employer, and previously informal carers (family or non-family carers) became employees. Representing the formal employer, a social worker supervised the caring relationships at regular intervals and supported the informal carers in all care-related matters. As long-term care allowances would have been too small to allow for regular employment contracts, wages were subsidized by the province. The pilot project slowly came to an end when the informal carers' access to the social pension insurance system was gradually improved at the end of the 1990s (see below). Then, the province ceased to subsidize wages and the caring relationships had to be managed – once again – autonomously, lacking any support and/or counselling from a social worker. With no financial support from the province, all employment relationships were transformed into informal caring arrangements and not one regular employment relationship was established.

Asked about this care arrangement, and whether the care recipient (in this case the mother) is the boss, the care worker describes the relationship as follows: 'No. X [the non-profit-organization] is the boss and my mother is the company (laughs). It's like a marriage – those who can't get on get divorced and others achieve a working relationship.' When asked about the duration of this relationship ('married to her mother'), the carer responded: 'Oh, as a small child – ever since I was born. [. . .] I've more or less always lived the life of a carer.'

Even if formal relationships have been established, relationships are still strongly determined by the family bond. Some of the carers, therefore, prefer to talk about compensation or recognition, rather than wage: 'It was an acknowledgement for me. For years I had no money of my own, and suddenly everything was very comfortable.' Another care worker also regards the wage as compensation and points to her feelings of responsibility towards her mother: 'Well, now and again I feel uncomfortable that I was earning money here. I don't really want money. That's why I treat this as compensation and I sometimes buy her something. Then I can calm down again. I calm myself down and think of myself as simply being employed here. You would do it anyway; I am her daughter. Without being paid.'

For another carer, the establishment of a care work contract within the family was an alternative to unemployment in the 'outside' labour market: 'I was 43 at the time. I had numerous interviews, but nobody would take me on any more. It's still practically the same [. . .] At the moment – the outlook is pretty grim. Mummy died in October last year.' For one carer, the establishment of a regular care work contract resulted in an overall improvement of her employment status: 'I earn more than I did in the factory. I was very surprised. On top of that, I am in a proper employee relationship here, and in the factory I was just another poorly paid worker.'

The employment relationships established by the non-profit organization may also be superior to a 'normal' working contract. One carer, who lives with her son and her dependent mother, points to this fact and reports:

The plus side is that I can always be with my son, because he is ill an amazing amount, just as I was as a child. I don't have to get into trouble with an employer because I'm automatically at home. Of course I'm employed in the sense that I'm earning money and my son is insured. If I was employed in a firm, I wouldn't always be able to take time off. My son was sick twice in January – no employer would have given me time off. Then I would lose my job.

In contrast, to what happens in migrant care, the Salzburg model has formalized caring arrangements in accordance with labour and social regulations. However, similar to migrant care, actual take-up of social rights regarding holidays remains difficult. Two care workers report:

> Officially, of course, I was entitled to holidays, but I was always at home with her.

> You can never be ill, but of course I am ill myself sometimes. If I'm ill, I just do what is absolutely necessary – just looking after my mother. I certainly can't do any additional work. I basically just do the essentials. I do something really quick for mealtimes – that way, I can get through. I simply must not be ill – and I never have been. I've never been ill.

The combination of care work contract and family relationship makes exit from care work especially difficult, even when the health problems of the carer become quite evident:

> It's getting worse. If I had known that she was going to develop this way, I would never have done it. I would have looked out an old people's home for her somewhere [. . .] She thinks only of herself; my health is of no concern to her. Who will take me on after she's gone? She may live for another 2–3 years, and then I will be over 40. Who is going to take me on then? I already have a slipped disc in my neck.

This form of regular employment of formerly informal carers has been abolished in the meantime for financial reasons. Now the care recipients may compensate the carers directly using their care allowance. But one formerly employed carer phrases the difference as follows: 'The care allowance – it certainly isn't my income.'

Without additional public support, long-term care allowances are too small to allow for formal employer–employee relationships. Only if care recipients are able to considerably top up long-term care allowances are they in a position to establish such contracts. In general, therefore, payments between care recipients and informal carers have to be seen as symbolic payments. Thus, carers remain in a rather precarious situation, as additional measures to directly support informal care are quite limited. In 1998, an option to choose cover through the social pension insurance system at a lower rate for family carers was introduced, and has been extended since. Carers have access to the scheme if they have given up regular employment in order to care for a close relative in need of care according to benefit level 3 or higher. Because of the financial contribution still to be made for this, and due to lack of information and awareness, take up is very small. There are also leave arrangements for family carers, but these are limited to one to two weeks per year. Take up of a newly introduced hospice care leave programme (offering hospice care leave up to six months) is very small. Apart from that, any direct forms of supporting informal carers – via, for example, systematic social protection, leave arrangements or respite schemes – are still absent in Austria (Österle and Hammer, 2004).

Discussion

The long-term care allowance programme together with the state–provinces treaty, signified an extension and clarification of state involvement in an area where the role of the public sector was formerly mainly of the social assistance type. With the reform, the public sector took on more financial responsibility, by implementing a new universal benefit scheme and attempting an extension of social services. Involvement of the public sector via a 'contribution to care-related additional expenses' brought into effect the concept of choice by increasing purchasing power on the part of care recipients, and this has increased the importance of the market sector in long-term care (Hammer and Österle, 2003).

The Austrian case supports Ungerson's (1995, 1997) findings that the dualism of paid and unpaid care is dissolving in the process of implementing payment for care schemes. The scheme, and its context, increases purchasing power among care recipients and thus allows for some commodification of care. In an increasing number of care arrangements, care work is partly organized as paid work. For others, long-term care allowances are a way of recognizing care work financially. At the same time, these arrangements remain highly unregulated. For Austria, our analysis has identified three different means of using the money: first, money is used to pay for aids and services delivered by social service providers. Because of an increase in co-payments, these services became more expensive in absolute and in relative terms. Considerable limitations in availability and affordability of these services make alternative options a necessity. Hence, second, cash benefits are used as a means of setting up direct employer–employee relationships, which constitute a form of 'routed wages'. Taking affordability into consideration, migrant care work became an increasingly attractive solution. Employer–employee relationships can be seen as a form of marketization in the Austrian long-term care sector, however, without being recognized in either employment law or social security legislation. The third way of using the money is to pass on 'symbolic payments' to caring kin, friends and neighbours. Whereas these payments are widely appreciated as a financial recognition of care work undertaken within family networks, our interviews have also highlighted that these payments have become an integral part of supporting traditional forms of providing care and, thus, of reinforcing traditional gender divisions in the provision of family care.

References

Badelt, C. and Österle, A. (2001) *Grundzüge der Sozialpolitik. Sozialpolitik in Österreich*, Wien: Manz.
Badelt, C., Holzmann, A., Matul, C. and Österle, A. (1996) *Kosten der Pflegesicherung. Strukturen und Entwicklungstrends der Altenbetreuung.* 2nd edn, Wien: Böhlau.
Badelt, C., Holzmann-Jenkins, A., Matul, C. and Österle, A. (1997) *Analyse der Auswirkungen des Pflegevorsorgesystems*, Wien: BMAGS.
Barta, H. and Ganner M. (eds) (1998) *Alter, Recht und Gesellschaft. Rechtliche Rahmenbedingungen der Alten- und Pflegebetreuung*, Wien: WUV-Universitätsverlag.
BMAGS (Federal Ministry for Labour, Health and Social Affairs) (1999a) *Dienste und Einrichtungen für pflegebedürftige Menschen in Österreich. Übersicht über die Bedarfs- und Entwicklungspläne der Länder*, Wien: BMAGS.
BMAGS (Federal Ministry for Labour, Health and Social Affairs) (1999b) *Pflegevorsorge. Provision for Long-term Care. Prevention dependence*, Wien: BMAGS.
BMSG (Federal Ministry of Social Security and Generations) (2004a) *Bericht des Arbeitskreises für Pflegevorsorge 2002*, Wien: BMSG.
BMSG (Federal Ministry of Social Security and Generations) (2004b) *Sozialstatistik* (http//:www.bmsg.gv.at), Wien: BMSG.
Chiswick, B. R. (2000) 'The Economics of Illegal Migration for the Host Economy', in: Çinar, D., Gächter, A. and Waldrauch, H. (eds), 'Irregular Migration: Dynamics, Impact, Policy Options', *Eurosocial Reports*, vol. 67, Vienna.
Economic Policy Committee (2001) *Budgetary Challenges Posed by Ageing Populations* (http//:europe.eu.int/comm/economy_finance/epc_en.htm), Brussels.
Esping-Andersen, G. (1990) *The Three Worlds of Welfare Capitalism*, Cambridge: Polity Press.
Eurostat (2004) *European Social Statistics. Social Protection Expenditure and Receipts*, Luxembourg: European Communities.
Hammer, E. and Österle, A. (2003) 'Welfare State Policy and Informal Long-term Care Giving in Austria: Old Gender Divisions and New Stratification Processes Among Women', *Journal of Social Policy*, 32:1, 37–53.
Leichsenring, K. and Alaszewski, A. M. (eds) (2004) *Providing Integrated Health and Social Care for Older Persons. A European Overview of Issues at Stake*, Aldershot: Ashgate.

Lewis, J. (1992) Gender and the Development of Welfare Regimes, *Journal of European Social Policy*, 2:3, 159–73.

Österle, A. (2001) *Equity Choices and Long-term Care Policies in Europe. Allocating Resources and Burdens in Austria, Italy, the Netherlands and the United Kingdom*, Aldershot: Ashgate.

Österle, A. and Hammer, E. (2004) *Zur zukünftigen Betreuung und Pflege älterer Menschen. Rahmenbedingungen – Politikansätze – Entwicklungsperspektiven*, Wien: Kardinal König Akademie.

Rubisch, M. (1998) 'Die Umsetzung der Pflegevereinbarung zwischen Bund und Ländern' *Soziale Sicherheit*, 12, 941–45.

Statistik Austria (2004) *Statistisches Jahrbuch Österreich 2004*, Wien: Statistik Austria.

Streissler, A. (2004) 'Geriatrische Langzeitpflege. Eine Analyse aus österreichischer Sicht', *Wirtschaft und Gesellschaft*, 30(2), 247–71.

Unger, B. and Heitzmann, K. (2003) 'The Adjustment Path of the Austrian Welfare State: Back to Bismarck?' *Journal of European Social Policy*, 13(4), 371–87.

Ungerson, C. (1995) 'Gender, Cash and Informal Care: European Perspectives and Dilemmas', *Journal of Social Policy*, 24:1 31–52.

Ungerson, C. (1997) 'Social Politics and the Commodification of Care', *Social Politics*, 4(3), 362–81.

Ungerson, C. (2003) 'Commodified Care Work in European Labour Markets', *European Societies*, 5(4), 377–95.

wiiw (Vienna Institute for International Economic Studies) (2003) *wiiw Handbook of Statistics: Countries in Transition* (Vienna: wiiw).

3
Cash for Care in the French Welfare State: A Skilful Compromise?

Claude Martin[1] and Blanche Le Bihan[2]

Since 1997, in addition to medical and paramedical healthcare covered by health insurance, the main social care policy for dependent older people in France has involved the payment of an allowance: the *Prestation Spécifique Dépendance* (PSD) (implemented between January 1997 and December 2001), and subsequently (from January 2002), the *Allocation Personnalisée à l'Autonomie* (APA). The APA, allocated to older people (rather than to their carers) enables them to buy services, supplemented by a variable co-payment, depending upon their resources. The allowance can also be used to pay a member of the family (apart from a husband or wife) who provides this support. In all cases, the allowance is intended to fund the purchase of services supplied by either a professional or a relative.

These developments in the French system of payment for care confirm a trend towards the commodification of care in Europe (Martin *et al.*, 1998), but also show, as Ungerson has suggested, that 'the traditional dualism of paid and unpaid work is dissolving' (Ungerson, 1997, p. 363). Is it possible to argue that the French scheme is truly a 'routed wage', in the sense that it supplements the incomes of those in need of care so that care users can become direct employers of their 'own' caring labour (Ungerson, 1997, 2004)? However we answer that question here, it is evident that the creation of the French scheme is directly linked with French policy on unemployment, and with the desire of French policymakers to find a way both to support new jobs and to counter the threat of a 'care deficit' (Hochschild, 1995).

In the APA scheme, the most common arrangement is not direct employment of carers by care users, but an indirect one, regulated by local authorities and coordinated by local non-profit service providers, who are the employers of the formal carers. This administrative regulation of the system of payment means that, in general, the older care user does not feel like an employer, so much as a care recipient who buys his or her own services from a non-profit organization, using the allowance he or she has claimed from a local authority.

In this chapter, we begin by presenting some details about the demographic factors that lie behind this policy development, in order to assess the 'care deficit' problem that is linked to it. Next, we describe the two main stages of French social care policy for elderly dependent people, and analyse the impact of these two schemes on carers, both formal (paid) and informal (unpaid). Finally, we discuss the French scheme, using specific examples of care arrangements and situations and examining recent developments arising from the heat wave which struck France in the summer of 2003.

Demographic background and future trends

Like all European countries, France is concerned about the ageing of its population, although the situation it faces is less acute than in some other states, such as Italy, Greece, Germany or Sweden. Between 1980 and 2003, the population over 60 in France increased from 9.1 million to 12.3 million (from 17 per cent of the total population in metropolitan France in 1980 to 20.6 per cent in 2003). Over the coming 30 years, it is estimated that this growth of 'older people' will be between 60 and 70 per cent, depending on the mortality rate, with the expected increase much faster for the very aged part of the population. INSEE (the French national institute of statistics) has estimated that the population aged over 80 will almost double between 2000 and 2020 (up to 4 million), and could reach 7 million in 2040 (Kerjosse and Lebeaupin, 1993; Brutel and Omalek, 2002; Pison, 2003; Bontout *et al.*, 2002).

Three elements contribute to the ageing of a population: fertility below replacement levels; a fall in the mortality of older people; and the shift of the baby-boom generation into retirement, which affects the old age dependency ratio.[3] On the first indicator, France, like Ireland, has quite positive indicators, with a 1.9 total fertility rate in 2002, compared with its situation in the mid-nineties (1.65) and with the rest of the EU15, where the total average fertility rate is around 1.5. However, between 1980 and 2002, the mortality rate in France fell from 10.2 to 9.1, and French women still hold – with Spanish women – the record for longevity, with a life expectancy at birth of 82.7 years (75 years for men).

Last but not least, the old age dependency ratio was about 24.6 in France in 2000 (24.3 in the EU15). The estimates for 2010 are 25.5 for France and 27.3 for the EU15 (31.3 for Italy; 30.3 for Germany; 29.2 for Greece and 28.1 for Sweden).

Although the ageing of the population is less rapid than in some other European countries, France is very concerned about its impact in terms of the costs of health and social services. The number of dependent older people is in fact also increasing at the same time. At the end of the 1990s, the HID inquiry ('Handicap-incapacité-dépendance')[4] estimated that 800,000 people (6.6 per cent of the population over 60 years old) were dependent, in the sense that they needed help with standing, dressing and washing (see Table 3.1) and were eligible to claim for a specific allowance to pay for services (see below).

When we take mental health into account as well, the total estimate of dependent people over 60 is about 844,000: 333,000 (39 per cent) are physically dependent only, 295,000 (35 per cent) have both physical and mental health needs, and 216,000 (26 per cent) are mentally frail, or have mental health problems, without any physical dependency. Some mentally disabled people (about 160,000) are disbarred from claiming the APA because they have been assessed at the fifth and sixth level of the *Autonomie gérontologique – groupes iso-ressources* (AGGIR), the scale used to assess the level of dependency,[5] which excludes them from the scheme.

Turning to future projections, and depending on whether more or less optimistic scenarios are used, the number of dependent older people

Table 3.1 Number of dependent elderly people with the AGGIR grid (in thousands, 1999)

	Home	Institutions	Total
GIR 1	22	47	69
GIR 2	133	129	262
GIR 3	137	64	201
Sub-total GIR 1 to 3	*292*	*240*	*532*
GIR 4	232	32	264
Sub-total GIR 1 to 4	*524*	*272*	*796*
GIR 5	346	44	390
GIR 6	10,692	163	10,855
GIR unknown	24	21	43
All people 60 and +	*11,586*	*500*	*12,086*

Source: INSEE, HID inquiry 1998–99 (Colin and Coutton, 2000).

Table 3.2 Expected growth in the number of dependent older people (60 and over) in France, by age groups

Growth	Aged 60–79 years (%)	Aged 80 and over (%)
Between 2000 and 2020 (GIR 1 to 4)	−7	+45
Between 2020 and 2040 (GIR 1 to 4)	−4	+40
Total between 2000 and 2040	−10	+103

Source: INSEE, HID inquiry 1998 and 1999 and demographic projections 2001 – DREES calculations (Bontout *et al.*, 2002).

can be expected to grow as follows: from 850,000 people in 2000 to 1,000,000 in 2020, possibly rising to 1.3–1.5 million in 2040 (Bontout *et al.*, 2002). Once again, this increase concerns mainly those who are very old (see Table 3.2).

These projections show that demand for services and support will increase dramatically in the near future. Like other European countries, France is worried about the 'care deficit'. Three main factors lie behind the situation: the transformation of family networks, arising from marital instability and reconstituted families; the 'gender contract' or the gender division of labour, which traditionally gave the role of caretaker to women within the family; and women's increased labour force participation, which can reduce their availability for caring tasks.

In France, as in many other familialist countries, within the family network, women are the main carers for dependent older people. Informal carers are the main providers of care. Of the population over 60, 28 per cent (3,230,000 older people) receive regular help to deal with a disability or health problem (three-quarters of them at home). In 50 per cent of cases, relatives are the only care providers; 30 per cent of dependent older people receive both formal and informal help, and 20 per cent receive only professional help. The total number of these carers is about 5.9 million. Informal carers represent 60 per cent of this total (Dutheil, 2001).

Half of those who are primary informal carers are spouses (the wife in two-thirds of cases), while a third are daughters and sons (in three-quarters of the cases, daughters). The mean age of these family carers is 71 years old for spouses, and 55 for children. In fact, 80 per cent of primary carers are aged between 50 and 79 years old, and more than half of all informal carers are women between 50 and 79. Bontout *et al.*

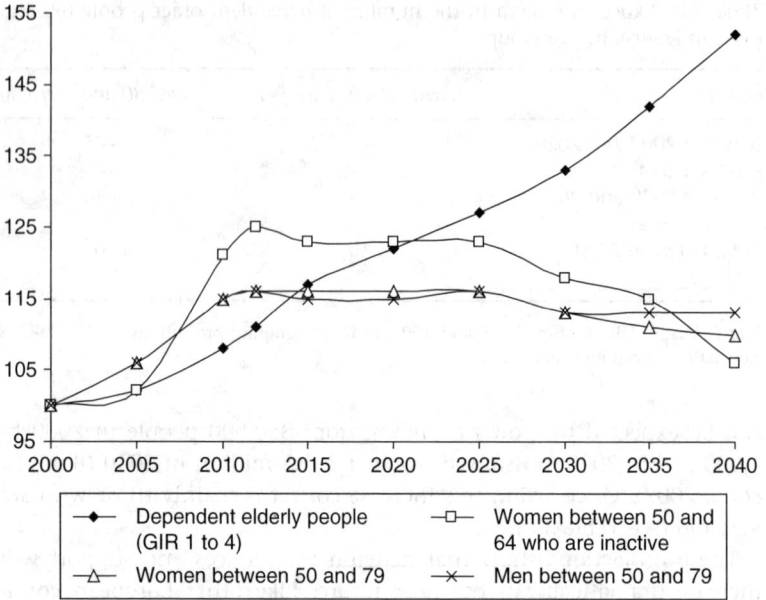

Figure 3.1 Growth in the number of dependent elderly people and potential carers (2000 = base 100)
Source: INSEE, HID and DREES calculations.

(2002) have estimated trends in the numbers of potential carers for the next 40 years (see Figure 3.1).

By 2010, the number of economically inactive women aged between 50 and 64 (the main potential carers to date) is likely to grow rapidly, faster in fact than the number of dependent older people. But after 2020, their number will decrease, while the number of dependent older people will grow rapidly, so that the gap between demand for care and its supply can be expected to be very large. 'In total, between 2000 and 2040, the number of inactive women between 50 and 64 will increase by 6 per cent, which means nine times less rapidly than the number of dependent older people, assuming a middle range scenario' (Bontout *et al.*, 2002, p. 9). These estimates do not take into account changes in women's employment patterns, which show that women are remaining in paid work for longer. This means that balancing paid work and caring responsibilities at the end of one's professional life will become more difficult. While it is hard to make estimates without taking into account potential changes in social norms and practices, this section has indicated some of the elements of the potential 'care deficit' in France.

Developing a policy relating to frail older people: A very slow process

The development of policy relating to frail older people is relatively recent in France, first coming on to the political agenda only in the mid 1980s.[6] From that time on, the care of disabled, incapacitated or dependent persons, whichever term is used, has been a major issue.[7] Until 1994, there was no specific policy towards dependency, only a political debate and many experts' reports. The main social care policy for frail older people was the one used for disabled people: the *Allocation compensatrice pour tierce personne*[8] (compensatory allowance for a third party).

The political debate was organized around a few key issues: First, should the scheme involve compulsory or optional insurance, and should it use social assistance or market principles? Second, how should the policy be funded and managed, and to what extent should the state, local authorities and social security funds be involved? Third, policy developments in this field cut across barriers between the different welfare sectors: between the social and health sectors, between family policy, old-age policy and even employment policy. Fourth, the debate raised questions about the relationship between the family, the market and the state as sources of social protection. One of the main obstacles was financial. In fact, in the context of budgetary constraints and policy of cost containment for public expenditure, it was difficult to promote a policy whose cost had not been properly estimated until a recent national inquiry (HID inquiry of INSEE 1998–99) into disabled, incapacitated and dependent people, mainly due to the difficulty of defining dependency and thus of identifying the number of people involved.

These challenges may explain the very slow process of establishing policy in this field. Even after 10 years of debate, official reports[9] and several Bills,[10] there was no clarity about the choices to be made, and no firm steer for a policy so often heralded, promised and postponed, despite a consensus on the demographic situation, criticisms of the previous system and the evident need for reform. In the face of these difficult choices, the government of Edouard Balladur first proposed a pilot scheme, implemented in 1995–96. Its aim was to test a scheme (the *Prestation expérimentale dependence* – PED), whose main parameters were to be laid down by the state, but in which the technical aspects of implementation were to be developed by local authorities, in real situations and in a few specific sites, prior to a national roll-out of the policy. (Martin *et al.*, 1996) Thus, the method selected for establishing a workable social care policy was that of experimentation and assessment. In short, a 'bottom-up' pattern of public action, in contrast to the traditional centrality and 'top-down' model used in French public policies. The government decided to use local resources, notably the goodwill of some local authorities and partners, who were anxious to promote the long-awaited reform by co-producing this public policy. The state provided the incentive, fixing the main principles, but left the political and most highly motivated local stakeholders to devise the detailed scheme. Despite this, these pilot schemes did not really live up to expectations (Martin, 1998, 2000).

The chosen system, of a cash benefit, has enabled a very flexible response to people's needs, taking their way of life and consumer behaviour into account. This type of benefit has allowed beneficiaries to make their own choices (Joël and Martin, 1997, 1998). They can either keep their need for care support within the family, by using the benefit to compensate a relative who is providing care (thus fostering informal care or the paid employment of any relative except the spouse, and leading to the remuneration of family care), or they can turn to professional care workers, either hiring them directly or through formal domiciliary care services, who employ home-helps or personal assistants.[11]

As well as responding to the need for care, which was the explicit priority, there was another more implicit objective, which is primarily the concern of locally and nationally elected representatives: that of employment and support for jobs. On a political level, the improvement of care services for frail older people also fits with the desire to support a potential source of employment, be it *relational* (family, neighbours, friends) or home-help services, which in France are called *emplois familiaux* (family jobs). In the event, however, this new scheme appears to have created more job insecurity than real jobs.

The *Prestation Spécifique Dépendance* (PSD) 1997–2001: A 'routed wage' with a very controversial impact on carers

The law passed in January 1997,[12] creating the PSD, did not follow through the early local developments, because of a lack of political continuity. The introduction of a new allowance for frail older people was one of the promises made by Jacques Chirac during his candidacy for the 1995 presidential election. It was also one of the features of Alain Juppé's declaration of general policy on 23 May 1995, on his appointment as Prime Minister. Without waiting for the evaluation of the local and national assessments of the pilot schemes, and in a move which destabilized the different actions led in the *départements*, the government introduced a parliamentary Bill (see Martin, 2003).

The implementation of this new law raised serious problems, both in terms of local cooperation and geographical equity, and of consequences for carers, both professionals and family members. With this first national policy, France remained, until the subseqent reform of 2002, on the list of countries that leave the care of frail older people mainly to the family, while the state takes care only of those who are deprived, lacking both financial resources and family support (Hennessy, 1995).

Characteristics and take-up rates of the PSD scheme

The PSD is a means-tested[13] benefit granted to frail older people, both those living in institutions and those living at home, who have been assessed using the national dependency scale (AGGIR)[14] at the first three levels of this scale (the more dependent). Beneficiaries of the PSD are all dependent people aged over 60, living in France, and can be of any nationality. There is no 'obligation to maintain' (*obligation alimentaire*),[15] but after the death of the person concerned, local authorities may recover the cost of the allowance from the estateof the PSD recipient if the net assets within the estate exceed €45,700.

The PSD is delivered by local authorities (*Conseils généraux des départements*), who have a statutory responsibility for social welfare (since the decentralization legislation of 1983). Claims for PSD have to be sent to the President of the *Conseil général du département* where the claimant lives, and are considered by a medico-social team, which assesses the level of dependency. A care package (mix of services) is identified, in consultation with the family, according to the needs assessment. The amount of the allowance depends on the care package; there is a maximum, but no minimum, in each *département*. Once allocated, the PSD must be used to pay employees to help the older person in their everyday life. The person they pay to do this can be someone chosen by the older person, a relative (although not the spouse or partner), or a home-help employed by a domiciliary care service. For a claimant in residential care, the benefit is paid directly to the institution. The benefit is paid in cash, upon receipts for expenses incurred, and its use is regularly checked by the *département*.

At the end of 2001, almost 150,000 people were receiving the PSD, at a total cost of 3.5 billions francs, compared with the 800,000 frail older people in need of care. The average benefit paid to recipients living at home was around 3,500 francs (€533) per month, and for those in residential care it was 1,900 francs (€290).

The reactions of professionals

This delaying policy was greeted with great dissatisfaction. The policy response fell far short of both promises and expectations. Professionals' first reactions were critical, to say the least. A 'black book of the PSD' was even written and signed in 1998 by the main non-profit organizations who care for older people.[16] Moreover, the risk of geographical variations,[17] already in evidence during the period of the pilot schemes, was significant. Extending the benefit to institutionalized older people accentuated these geographical inequalities, as 30 per cent of *départements* had stopped granting the compensatory allowance (ACTP) to those residents in institutions several years previously.

However, other issues were also raised: limiting this rather modest benefit (between €457 and €533 on average) to the most dependent and most needy, not only excluded many older people on the basis of their income, but also did little to help the most dependent recipients, who had to pay much larger sums of money to cover their needs; (estimates are between €1,525 and €2,290 per month for cases of severe dependency). The PSD also excluded those with average levels of dependency: the fourth group of the AGGIR scale. In the pilot schemes, those assessed at level GIR4 could claim the benefit, and in fact constituted almost 40 per cent of all recipients. By excluding average dependency a large share of the demand for assistance and welfare was put to one side. In short, there were several forms of exclusion from the PSD scheme: exclusion of those with average and low levels of dependency; exclusion of people on middle incomes; recovery from the older person's estate. The latter feature excluded *de facto* those potential beneficiaries who refused this prospect.

The impact on carers

The effects of the policy on carers were hardly positive. Instead of encouraging the development of new jobs, the chosen approach destabilized existing qualified jobs and created new, unskilled, casual labour. Professional as well as non-professional carers suffered from greater insecurity (problems of replacement, in asserting their employment status, in finding a third party with whom to discuss difficulties at work, lack of training, questions of holidays and days off, etc.). Home help professionals worried about this growing trend, and did not see it as a new source of employment. From their point of view, there was a more or less explicit recognition that no qualification was needed. Goodwill, a trusting relationship and the 'natural' domestic skills of women often seemed more important for care users than skills vouched for by a diploma or training.

It must also be stressed that the vast majority of carers, whether professional, voluntary or relatives, are women (Martin, 2001). Female relatives (wives, daughters, daughters-in-law) are the first to carry out tasks combining care and affection.[18] Some of these informal carers were paid through the PSD allowance for their informal work.[19] This feature of the scheme (which excludes spouses and partners) can be seen as way of recognizing and valuing their work. However it also has some negative effects; payment alone does not solve the question of the carer's status, nor does it do away with the obligation to maintain.[20] In our study of care agreements in the Ille et Vilaine *département* in 1999, 20 per cent of the hours of care paid via the PSD were delivered by relatives, generally daughters or daughters-in-law (Le Bihan and Martin, 2000).

The various reports on home help and care services, drawn up in the mid-1990s by different official services of statistics and experts, all underline two main points: the various measures adopted by the authorities (exemption from contributions, financial support, etc.) have been particularly effective against undeclared work, legalizing many jobs; but the jobs created, or legalized, are unskilled, subject to a lot of competition, and therefore vulnerable.[21] Although it is not always easy to distinguish the figures relating to frail older people, from those for other domiciliary work (domestic help, child minders in the home, etc.), they do give some idea of trends and numbers. They show what is referred to in France as a new sector or even a new pool of labour. Indeed, analysis of employment trends in the mid-1990s in this sector shows definite expansion. It would be more correct, however, to refer to 'legalized jobs', since most of these posts are not really new jobs, or even real jobs.

According to the DARES, the number of employers of domestic help rose from 551,000 at the end of 1991 to 771,000 at the end of 1996. At the same time, the number of employees rose from 383,000 to 475,000. The greatest increase among employers was found among those using the 'service voucher' (*chèque emploi service*).[22]

In professional care for frail older people – and this is also true for children – carers are almost exclusively women: 99 per cent of 'home helps' (who work in the home of the recipient or in institutions) are female, with an average age of 43. Furthermore, these unskilled (65 per cent of these employees have no qualification), badly paid jobs (average pay is

Table 3.3 Mean cost of services per hour in 1999–2000, by type of providing/purchasing contract (in €)

Type of intervention	Price per hour (€)
Direct recruitment	8.3
'Mandataires' services	10.0
'Prestataires' services	11.5

around 2,000 francs, i.e. €305 per month), with little esteem, were becoming increasingly insecure as a result of the choices made. The jobs which were created after the start of the pilot schemes (PED), and especially since the establishment of the PSD, offered little or no protection and very few hours, with an incentive towards direct recruitment by older people themselves, because of the difference in the hourly prices payable (see Table 3.3).

The Hespel-Thierry report (1998) points out the risk of increased job insecurity as a result of the current options in long-term care, with its incentive to recruit labour by private agreement, often without quality criteria, solely on the basis of an hourly rate and word of mouth (through neighbours and relatives). In fact, three different types of contract need to be distinguished: direct recruitment when the older person is the employer of the carer; *services mandataires*, when a non-profit organization assumes the responsibility for putting the care user and the care provider in touch (these services may also deal with the administrative papers concerning recruitment and the payment of the workers, but the care user is still the employer); and third, the *services prestataires*, when a non-profit organization is the service provider, directly employing the care workers who are sent to the homes of the beneficiaries or clients. These organizations may be entitled to exemption from social contributions and to tax reductions. The price per hour is lower in a private agreement or via *mandataires* services than the rate of a *prestataire* service (see Table 3.3).

The Institute of Statistics of the Ministry of Employment has recorded the rise in jobs within the *mandataires* services. The domiciliary care sector expanded by an average of 5.5 per cent per annum, in full time equivalents, between 1992 and 1995, according to the 'Living Conditions of Households' survey conducted by INSEE. This increase came mainly from the growth of the *services mandataires*: in 1995, the *prestataires* services employed 95,000 full time equivalents, with an annual growth rate of 0.8 per cent between 1992 and 1995; in 1995, the *services mandataires* employed 13,000 full time equivalents, with an annual growth rate of 28 per cent between 1992 and 1995, even before the introduction of the PSD scheme. So it is not surprising that the assessment of the local pilots stressed that direct employment by older people, and employment through a *service mandataire*, accounted for nearly 70 per cent of the hours paid for out of the benefit. The rest was divided as follows: 22 per cent of the hours were provided by a relative, paid out of the benefit, and only 10 per cent of the hours were provided by *prestataire* services.

If the PSD scheme has enabled a certain number of informal jobs to be legalized (including those done by family members), it has also produced job insecurity among professionals, who had previously been employed by non-profit organizations or *prestataire* services (with the corresponding advantages in terms of possible replacement, continuity of care in case of breach of contract for a stay in hospital or the death of the user, possibility of days off, further training, follow-up and access to support groups, etc.). Because of the cost of their work, such professionals have had to seek direct recruitment by the care recipients in order to provide the same services, but without the same advantages, or have otherwise had to be hired through the *mandataires* services.

Some local authorities became aware of this risk, and of the keen competition arising from these differences in cost. As a result they gave financial backing to training schemes for all new unskilled employees who are hired directly. However these initiatives were far from widespread. The move to the PSD has clearly accentuated this trend.[23]

Allocation Personnalisée à l'Autonomie (APA) from January 2002: A skilful compromise

The many criticisms of the scheme led to a new debate at the end of the 1990s, and made it necessary to reform the care system for frail older people. In December 1999, Martine Aubry, socialist Minister for Employment and Solidarity, gave this task to Jean-Pierre Sueur, a socialist former minister, who, after numerous consultations, delivered his report in May 2000 (Sueur, 2000). The aim of this development was clear: to move away from the PSD scheme, based on a cost containment objective, and to increase the number of recipients. However, these aims had to be achieved without rethinking the insurance principle, which Martine Aubry had *a priori* ruled out. Jean-Pierre Sueur, therefore, proposed the creation of the *Allocation Personnalisée à l'Autonomie* (APA), whose implementation would remain the responsibility of local authorities.

The reform was based on opening doors which had hitherto been closed: first, by allocating the APA up to the fourth level of dependency (which was excluded in the PSD scheme); second, by abolishing recovery from inheritance; and third, by guaranteeing access to the same services across the country. Thus the 'care plans', defined according to the level of GIR, give rights to a certain amount of money: a maximum of €1,067 for GIR1, €915 for GIR2, €686 for GIR3 and €457 for GIR4. The reform also introduced a 'user fee' or co-payment system. Above a fixed threshold, the recipient contributes to the funding of his or her care plan, in proportion to his or her level of income.[24] This has created, to a certain extent, a right to services (home help, alarm assistance, house improvement, etc.). The state undertakes to guarantee the same level of care package across the country, by compensating for any imbalances in the resources of *départements*.

Despite the universal nature of the new care system for frail older people, case management is still a priority, and care packages, assessed and implemented by medico-social teams, are individualized. The government expected to be able rapidly to cover 80 per cent of dependent older people (800,000 recipients according to the minister's announcement), and not 15 per cent as in the PSD scheme.

The cost of this measure was initially estimated at between 15 and 17 billion Francs (€2.3 billion and €2.6 billion) for the first two years, and 23 billion Francs thereafter (€3.5 billion). The state intended to commit one point of the CSG (*contribution sociale généralisée*)[25] to finance this, i.e. 5 billion Francs. The *départements* had to provide the remaining 11 billion Francs (i.e. 2.5 billion Francs extra, compared with the current situation). To cope with the anticipated increase in cost, the creation of a *Fonds national pour l'autonomie* (national autonomy care financing fund) was proposed, into which income from the CSG and contributions made by social security funds would be placed.

Take-up rate

The APA replaced the PSD from January 2002.[26] It has been a real success, with a very rapid increase in the number of claimants. Between January 2002 and June 2003, 1,390,000 people claimed the APA, and 723,000 people received it. This success also had a rapid impact on the political debate, both local and national, after the political change of April 2002 and the return of a conservative Government. The new Government and right-wing local authorities criticized the increased cost and the previous socialist government's failure to plan for the funding of their care system for frail older people. In April 2003, the decision was taken to reduce the threshold below which the recipient does not contribute at all to the funding of the care package, from €943 to €623 per month. This reform was supposed to increase the co-payment system, and, therefore, to contain costs.

In April 2004,[27] 827,000 frail elderly people were receiving the allowance, representing 181 beneficiaries per thousand inhabitants aged 75 or older.[28] It is thus possible to argue that needs are almost covered by this new policy. Of recipients, 58 per cent live at home and 42 per cent in residential care; 45 per cent have been assessed at the GIR4 level (the fourth level of the national scale AGGIR) (53 per cent of those who live at home and only 26 per cent of those living in residential care); 83 per cent are more than 75 years old, and 75 per cent are women. The mid level of the allowance is €489 per month (Table 3.4). Ninety-four per cent of home care packages are used to pay for home-help services. The allowance covers the cost of 91 per cent of the care package proposed by the medico-social team (leaving the beneficiary to cover 9 per cent of the cost of the care package). The April 2003 reform had a real impact: in the previous system, 67 per cent of recipients were exempt from any contribution; in the new system, only 36 per cent are exempt.

Like the PSD, the APA care system controls the use of the benefit, to ensure that services have in fact been bought. But take up has been

Table 3.4 Monthly level of APA payment for care (2004)

	Part of the local authority	Part left to the beneficiary (and % of the beneficiaries who are concerned by a co-payment)	Total
Monthly level of payment at home (in €)			
GIR1	768	93(46%)	861
GIR2	616	78(51%)	694
GIR3	497	52(50%)	549
GIR4	319	30(50%)	349
All	*442*	*47 (50%)*	*489*
Monthly level of payment in institutions (in €)			
GIR1 and 2	324	125	449
GIR3 and 4	162	118	280
All	*256*	*122*	*378*

Source: DREES, ministry of Social Affairs (Kerjosse, 2004).

so great that it has been difficult to check all situations, and only 30 per cent of recipients were asked to present the invoices relating to their spending to their local authorities.

Impact on carers

Like the PSD scheme, the allowance is used to pay for care services, delivered either by professionals or relatives.[29] The official statistics show that 89 per cent of recipients who have home help in their care package pay only professional carers, 8 per cent pay a relative, and 3 per cent pay both professional and family carers. Those recipients who use the allowance to pay a relative are often more dependent than those who pay a professional, and they receive more hours of help.

The APA scheme has had a real impact on carers. Three main elements can be identified: the type of services used; the qualifications of the carers; and the number of carers working with frail older people. With the APA care system, the distribution of hours between the different types of contract – direct employment, *mandataires* and *prestataires* services – has altered (Mette, 2004). Unlike the PSD scheme, the majority of hours are now paid through a *prestataire* organization (see Table 3.5). Of APA beneficiaries, 55 per cent receive their hours of home help via a *prestataire* service, which means that the employer is not the care user, but the organization itself. This shift clearly corresponds to policy objectives, in which a secondary aim was to enhance the level of quality and professionalization of care. It is the government's answer to the criticisms of the PSD made by the professional organizations.

However this development, assessed at the national level, may vary significantly between local authorities (Bellanger and Le Bihan, 2003).

Table 3.5 Distribution of the APA beneficiaries between the types of home-help services depending of the level of dependency

	Type of services of home-help used in November 2002 (%)				
	Prestataire service	Mandataire service	Direct employment	Different services	total
GIR1	44	13	29	14	100
GIR2	47	19	25	9	100
GIR3	53	16	23	7	100
GIR4	63	15	19	4	100
Total	*55*	*16*	*22*	*7*	*100*

Source: DREES, APA Inquiry, 2003.

Thus, in the *département* of Hérault, local authorities have decided to promote almost exclusively the *prestataire* services (more than 80% of the care users). In other departments, as in Ille-et-Vilaine, the objective is also to avoid, as far as possible, situations where care givers are only relatives. These local variations show that, in practice, the overall policy framework still leaves room for manoeuvre to local authorities and flexibility for case management.

The APA scheme has also had a significant impact on the qualification of professional carers (Bressé, 2004). We now know more about the so-called 'family jobs' (emplois de famille), whereby people work in another person's home to deliver services. Here a distinction must be made between jobs directly contracted by private households to perform housework, gardening, small repairs, etc, and services which are covered by a 'quality agreement'. The latter include services to vulnerable people, mainly frail older people and disabled people. Overall, about 700,000 people work in 'family jobs', and the 7,000 services covered by a 'quality agreement' employed 210,000 people in 1999, 194,000 of whom were home helps.

From a gender perspective, the APA has not changed anything: 99 per cent of these home helps are women, and 80 per cent work with older people. Their activities consist mainly of housework or direct personal care (getting up, washing, dressing, taking the person out, etc.). These jobs are still part-time jobs: average hours are 70 hours per month, less than half-time, and half of the home helps have hours of 62 or less per month. Only 5 per cent have full-time work providing services to one client (165 hours per month).

Until March 2002, the CAFAD (*certificat d'aptitude aux fonctions d'aide à domicile*) was the only diploma available to home helps. The training has since been improved and renamed DEAVS (*Diplôme d'Etat d'auxiliaire de vie*). This reform arises from the political desire to raise the quality and qualification of this work, alongside the implementation of the APA.

In 1999, the situation was well below the target for qualifications: only 18 per cent of home helps had a professional qualification, and only 9 per cent had the CAFAD. (A further 5 per cent had another professional qualification in the social and health sector or a qualification unrelated to health and social care.) Almost 70 per cent of home helps had no qualification at all.

Although care work is still varied and insufficiently qualified, the policy on frail older people, and in particular the APA scheme, has significantly increased the numbers of workers. Between 1994 and 2002, the number of home helps almost trebled (from 70,000 to almost

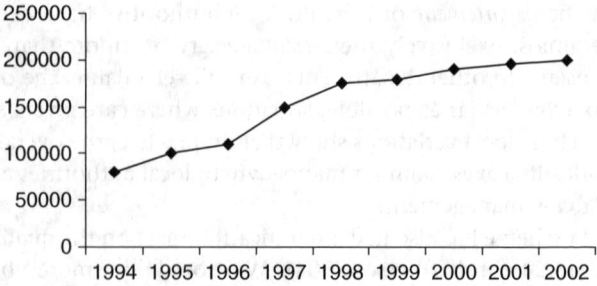

Figure 3.2 Growth in the numbers of home-helpers between 1994 and 2002
Source: INSEE.

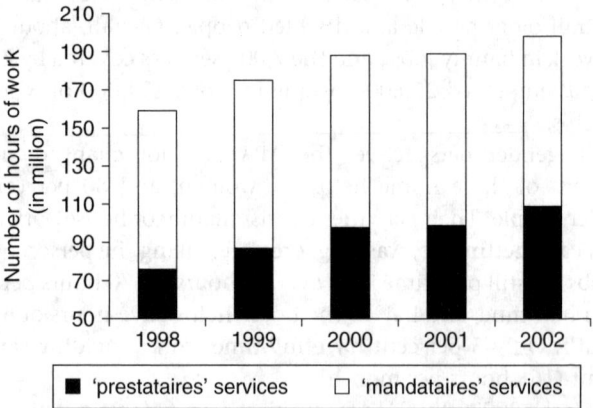

Figure 3.3 Number of hours of the certified personal services organizations
Source: DARES.

200,000) (see Figure 3.2). At the same time the total number of hours delivered through organizations covered by a quality agreement rose from 160 million in 1998 to almost 200 million in 2002 (see Figure 3.3). This increase arises mainly from hours delivered through *prestataires* services (up from 78 million to 110 million hours between 1998 and 2002).

For the moment, it remains difficult to make a precise assessment of the real impact of the APA scheme and of the new qualification implemented from March 2002 with the introduction of the *Diplôme d'Etat d'auxiliaire de vie*.

Home help: Case studies and discussion

With the creation of the APA, the routed wages and cost containment care system of the PSD, developed since the mid-1990s, changed into a more universalized, formalized and professionalized care system. The system is now more regulated, (with fixed amounts of money corresponding to the different levels of GIR, and the co-payment system), although case management is still a main principle. The aim is to encourage the employment of professionalized carers but, in practice, care arrangements are adapted to each situation. The analysis of some actual cases may help us to understand the specifics of this individualized dimension.[30]

As an example, Mr Campéon is becoming more and more dependent. He can now claim the APA in order to have more hours of home help. The social worker who assessed Mr Campéon's needs and developed the care plan has proposed 60 hours of help per month. As Mr Campéon is in GIR 3, he can receive up to €686 per month to pay for these services. By law, the *prestataire* service, which is the most qualified and regulated solution, should be encouraged. But Simone has been working at Mr Campéon's house for two years now, and he knows her very well. She does not have any qualifications, but she has been a home help for many years, and the medico-social team developing the care plan has decided to employ her. In fact, the specificity of the situation is taken into account.

The objective is to develop training of carers, to give them the competences needed to care for an older person. At this stage, the process is at its beginning, and the market in care services is varied. On the one hand, there are care workers who have the traditional profile of a home help, that is, unqualified employees, women who wished to work again after having brought up their children, and who found work as a housekeeper in different families and in the homes of older people long before the development of a care system for frail older people. Monique is one of them. She is now 58 years old, and has been working as a 'home help' for 15 years. She has no diploma, but a lot of experience. Her initial status is that of housekeeper, but in practice, she does much more than domestic tasks. Nevertheless she considers herself to be too old to undertake a training course:

> I have been working for Mrs Martin for 15 years. Before the APA and even before the PSD, I used to come twice a week. At the beginning it was only for domestic tasks . . . And then of course, I came more and more . . . now I come every day! The APA is a very good thing

> of course, because Mrs Martin can stay at home! (...) I come in the morning, I come to get her up and help her to get dressed. Twice a week, I come back in the afternoon to do the cleaning up, the washing up, or whatever has to be done! But I have no qualification... I am too old now to go back to school and receive training!! I don't want any training!

On the other hand, there are professional care workers, who present their activity as a 'real profession', for which qualifications and specific competences are needed. Marie-France is 50 years old. When she started working, she had no qualification. Like Monique, she had brought up her children and wanted to work again. She became a home-help and decided to pass the CAFAD. Now she works with the most dependent frail older people, and she regularly gets training to specialize in Alzheimer's disease cases.

> Here, at Mr Barbier's house, I do not do any cleaning or house work. My job is to be with him, to help him to eat, to get him up, to go in the garden with him... And when I am here, Mrs Barbier can go out and have time for herself... He is very very dependent. He cannot do anything alone. He is in a medical bed and must be helped for everything.... The nurse comes every morning to wash him and dress him. I help her to do that... and when she is in a hurry, I dress him alone once he is washed.

In practice, these care workers undertake a wide variety of tasks, both domestic tasks and caring tasks such as washing, getting the older person up, dressing him or her, putting him or her to bed, doing the shopping, completing forms, etc. Qualification is not the only problem. Working conditions are neither stable nor regularized, and caring work remains a very unattractive sector. The care workers we have met pointed out the different problems of their work, mainly the fact that it is not recognized as a profession: 'The profession is not recognized. You are really a cleaner, a housekeeper. Of course, we do all that! But when you allow yourself to wash somebody, do the shopping, fill in the forms... you are a long way from the job of a cleaner... Nobody understands.'

In fact, working conditions vary a great deal from one situation to another. In some cases, when the home help is employed by an organization and works in *prestataire*, a monthly salary is now specified in the contract of employment, but in other cases, each month the care worker has as many pay slips as employers, and her wage varies according to the numbers of hours of work she has done. As the cost per hour of work is still low, some home helps care for many older people, usually four or five, but sometimes eight and up to thirteen.

Because of these difficult conditions of work, the stability of the care services market is a real problem. Once they have taken a training course and obtained their diploma, some care workers, particularly young ones, prefer to find other work in residential homes, where the conditions of work are stable. And when the employment market is good, unqualified employees prefer to work in other sectors where they receive a regular salary and work the same number of hours every day.

Another element of instability in the care services market must also be stressed: the possibility of employing one's relative. As with the PSD, the APA can also be used to pay a relative. Of course, when this happens, the situation is controlled by the medico-social team. But for the carers, this solution is ambiguous. On the one hand, they emphasize that they now have a status, a recognition of their work and a clear position as a carer. But this positive view of the payment of relatives has another side. It is far from an ideal response to the issues raised by dependency among older people. Some family carers may choose not to assume the role of paid carer for their dependent parent.

Clare is 40 years old. She lives with her mother, who is very dependent and needs help in every aspect of daily life. Because she was unemployed, the allowance at first seemed a good solution for her, offering her a job and to be paid for the caring tasks which she would do anyway. But Clare rejected that solution, and on the contrary wanted her mother to employ professional carers. Several reasons lie behind this choice, mainly concerning the notion of 'risk'. The first risk is that of finding oneself in a relationship of subordination to the parent; the second risk is that of being, by virtue of being paid, the only one to bear the burden of family solidarity; another is the risk of enclosing the older person within their family circle, cutting them off from the social world outside; the main risk, however, is certainly the reverse – that of locking the carer into the relationship of care. How can one raise the issue of working conditions or insist on one's rights as an employee in a relationship which is not that of employment? How can one assert the need for replacement or respite care without conveying a sort of abandonment? This confusion of roles is a real trap for the carer–recipient couple.

As we can see, although the APA has introduced more regulation and developed professionalization, the care services market remains unstable. In fact, informal care provided by the family is still the pivot of care arrangements, and within the family, women are most affected.

Since more and more women are employed full time, sometimes developing a career, the dependency of elderly parents and the need to find time to care for them is becoming a real problem. Caring requires time, time previously devoted to paid work, to their children or to their personal life. The issue here is how to reconcile professional and family life? How can women combine working, having children and coping with the dependency of their parent(s)? Among the possible solutions, especially in view of current childcare policy, is the leave formula (parental-type leave), of offering paid or unpaid leave to free up time to care for one's elderly parents. But qualitative interviews with women between the ages of 42 and 55, working in different employment sectors, and who have frail elderly parents and in some cases young children, show that professional life is considered a necessity, and that above all, daughters and daughters-in-law involved in caring for their elderly dependent parent(s) want to hold on to their jobs.

> Well, fortunately I work. That really has been my safety mechanism. Because the next day I had a different perspective...

> I didn't take a single day off! Even when I had doctor's appointments, I arranged them for outside working hours, or I asked for time off, and as I sometimes stay later, that compensates for it... However, I could have had other problems in other departments, but I stopped here. My doctor would have stopped me anyway. I never stopped for a day! But as far as my morale is concerned, it was better for me to work, it helped me. Work helps too! But it was hard going!

Professional activity is both a resource for them, through the salary they earn, and also a source of identity and of social relationships, whatever their level of qualification. As a result, when the time comes to agree on a care arrangement, the first area of their life which is reduced to accommodate this new responsibility is personal life. If this is not enough, the women we have met prefer to cope by compromising their time available for other close relatives – their children and husband. In short, caring for a frail elderly parent is becoming a major problem for women, who have to find the means of coping with such care needs and of being a good carer, even when their mental resources are exhausted. Access to services is, therefore, crucial when the family needs to organize a professional care arrangement. This applies even when delegating the caring tasks to professionals, which is a slow process, with interim arrangements needed that combine formal and informal resources.

Recent developments and conclusions

In summer 2003, France was confronted with a major tragedy, the 'heat wave epidemic'. Between 4 August and 10 August, 6,500 people died in the heat wave. Between 10 August and 13 August, the temperature remained extremely high, with a minimum of 25.5 °C during the night, and the number of dead rose to 10,000. On 25 September, INSERM (and more recently INSEE) confirmed that over 15,000 people had died because of the heat wave: 42 per cent in hospitals, 35 per cent at home, 19 per cent in retirement homes, and 3 per cent in private hospitals. In September, some newspapers and politicians commented on the lack of responsibility of those families who had left their elderly parents alone, without any support, while they took their normal summer holidays. This argument received considerable coverage, despite the experts' analysis which (on the contrary) insisted that the family is the main source of help and care towards frail elderly.

The different official reports and inquiries published subsequently show clearly that the lack of responsibility and reaction lay on the side of the government and the administrative authorities. The heat wave demonstrated the need to combine formal and informal sources of support, and to connect health and social services. It revealed the importance of local responses to such a crisis, and the need for the administrative authorities to prepare for such events. The political impact of the heat wave was important: the Minister of Health was not re-elected, and some newspapers even considered that the strong decline in popularity of the conservative right-wing government was a direct consequence of the event.

This tragedy led the government to adopt new measures. Whereas in April 2003, the Raffarin government had reduced access to the APA, criticizing the financing measures adopted by the Jospin government, in September, Prime Minister Raffarin and the Ministers of Health, Social Affairs and Aged people, announced a new plan to guarantee the financing of APA and to increase responsiveness. The 'Grand Plan for frail older people' was organized around three main dimensions: first a development programme to prepare for any new heat wave (air-conditioning in retirement homes and hospitals, recruitment of professionals); second an improvement of the epidemiological warning system; and third, a new scheme to guarantee funding for the policy for frail older people and the creation of a new fund. The latter is provided by two main sources: an employers' contribution (0.3% of total wages) in return for the abolition of one day of public holiday and 0.1 point of CSG (*Contribution sociale généralisée*). This contribution, by both employers and wage-earners – who will in future work one more day per year – has been assimilated into a new insurance fund. However, because there is no social partnership with the trade unions and other professional organizations for its management (as in the other branches of the French social security system, which is a Bismarckian system, based on compulsory social insurance) it is possible that in future this agreement will break down.

These recent developments show that the French system of social care for frail older people is still likely to change and be reformed. The political agenda still has a strong influence on the development of the system.

The lessons from the different schemes implemented to date show the complexity of the French situation. On the one hand, it seems relatively clear that this scheme conforms to the 'routed wage' principle, in the sense that it supplements the incomes of those in need of care so that care users can become direct employers of their 'own' caring labour. Nevertheless, this 'routed wage' is also strongly regulated by the local authorities. Even if the recipient is allowed to pay for part or all of the services needed, local authorities are in charge of both the definition of these needs and the assessment of the implementation of the care package. Some *départements* even pay directly the organization organizing the care services when the care recipient uses the *prestataire* option. Thus care users are less and less the direct employers of their caring labour, because one of the policy objectives is to develop a more professionalized service sector and better quality of care. Even if the qualifications level of home helps is still very low, improvement in the quality of care and the professionalization of carer is nevertheless occurring.

On the other hand, this scheme is defining a middle way between assistance and insurance. With APA, the French cash-for-care system is no longer an assistance policy, reserved for the poorer and more dependent, but a more universal scheme, open to all people in need of support because of their dependency. A fifth risk or an insurance scheme is still rejected at the moment, but could be the next step in this process of defining policy for dependent older people.

Notes

1. PhD sociology, senior researcher at CNRS and Director of LAPSS, National School of Public Health and University of Rennes 1.
2. Researcher in political science, LAPSS, National School of Public Health, Rennes.

3. This indicator represents the population aged 65 and over as a percentage of the working age population (15–64) on 1st January of a year.
4. This HID inquiry is the first and only representative investigation to have assessed the number of dependent and disabled people in France.
5. All professionals (in the social and health care sector) use the AGGIR scale to assess the level of dependency of frail elderly people. The scale has 6 levels of GIR (Groupe iso-ressource), from 1 (the highest, in which people who are totally dependent require close and constant care) to 6 (the lowest), knowing that only the first four levels give access to the benefit. The scale tends to underestimate mental illness related to ageing, and is, therefore, sometimes used alongside another indicator, EPHA ('enquête auprès des établissements d'hébergement pour personnes âgées').
6. Dependency became a specific issue in 1986, at the time of the preparation of the report by Theo Braun of the National Commission on the study of frail older people, which aimed to analyse the exact causes of the phenomenon and to identify inadequacies in policy responses (Kessler, 1994).
7. For a development, and some international comparisons, see Martin (2003).
8. As this allowance was freely used by older people without control or regulation, it clealy corresponded to the 'symbolic payments', as defined by Clare Ungerson: 'symbolic payments are paid by care users using their own money, or money coming in the form of benefits, in an effort to lubricate a reciprocal system within kin and neighbourhood networks (may be contractual, but in a diluted form, with care user as "quasi-employer")' (Ungerson, 1997, p. 365).
9. In particular, the Boulard report of the National Assembly's Social Affairs Commission (1991); the Schopflin report submitted to the government by a group of experts as part of the preparation of the tenth plan (1991) (see also Joël and Bungener, 1991).
10. Francis Kessler (1995) synthesized the main orientations of the proposals put forward between 1986 and 1993. In his view, they follow two axes: improving the solvency of the elderly, and fostering a better organization of the supply of services.
11. In this chapter, we use the expression 'home-help', which is the exact translation of the French name: 'aide à domicile'.
12. Official Journal of the French Republic, 25 January 1997, pp. 1280–4.
13. The PSD is granted according to the level of income: less than €11,000 for a single person, less than €18,000 for a single.
14. See note 5. The French definition of 'dependency' is as follows: the condition of a person who requires help for the essential acts of daily life or regular supervision.
15. The *obligation alimentaire* means that the payment of local authorities is subsidiary to family solidarity.
16. In this document, a list of case studies were presented to show how the shift from domestic help to the PSD or from the ACTP to the PSD can cause significant financial loss (1,400 F–2,000 F per month, i.e. €213 to €305) and also drastically reduce the in-kind assistance provided to the frail older person by the local authorities (Comité de vigilance de la PSD, 1998).
17. We have assessed these local variations in comparative work on 6 *départements* (Le Bihan and Martin, 2000).

18. Men are also included in the care of elderly dependent relatives. They play a part in 10–20 per cent of family arrangements, especially when there is no daughter among the siblings or when they are single or married and childless (see Bouget and Tartarin, 1990; Lesemann and Martin, 1993).
19. This had already been, unofficially, the case in the previous ACTP scheme, but there had been no formal agreement as to this type of payment for care. The change here is to give a formal wage to the carer-relative.
20. In other words, when an older person pays his or her daughter out of the PSD for all or part of her work, part of the sum paid may have to be refunded in the action to recover from their estate.
21. Regarding France, see Causse *et al.* (1998). For international comparisons, see the work of Susan Christopher for the OECD (1997).
22. The *chèque emploi service* or voucher is a cheque that allows care recipients to pay for the services they receive, without requiring any other administrative procedures. The latter in France are very burdensome (and involve declaring the employer's social security contribution, or delivering a payslip).
23. As the 'Black book of the PSD' pointed out, 'direct employment or employment through "services mandataires" means that the more dependent people may be cared for by poorly trained and poorly supervised staff . . . The professionals thus have to abandon people previously cared for and, above all, are stripped of the occupation they trained for and invested in' (Comité de vigilance de la PSD, 1998, p. 15).
24. No user fee is required for a €914 income per month or less.
25. The CSG is a new tax implemented for the first time in 1991, whose objective from 1994 is mainly to compensate the deficit of the French social security system: a ring fenced system.
26. Law of 20 July 2001.
27. On 1 April 2004, the maximum amount of APA depending of the level of dependence has slightly increased: €1,125.58 for GIR 1; €964.79 for GIR2; €723.59 for GIR3 and €482.39 for GIR4.
28. From January to April 2004, 7 per cent of the recipients stopped receiving the allowance, in 8 cases in 10 because of the death of the beneficiary.
29. Except partners, mainly children of the elderly – in 60 per cent of the cases where a relative is a main carer – or a partner of one of the children (20 per cent) or other members of the family, like brother and sister, friends or neighbours (19 per cent).
30. These interviews have been conducted in two different studies: a national study of home-care services in four *départements* (Le Bihan *et al.*, 2004) and a survey of the impact of caring for elderly parents for women who work (Le Bihan and Martin, 2002 and 2006a). The latter has been presented at the ESPAnet 2003 Conference, (Le Bihan and Martin, 2003 and published Le Bihan and Martin, 2006b).

References

Bellanger, M. and Le Bihan, B. (2003) 'La mise en œuvre de l'Allocation personnalisée à l'autonomie dans six départements', *Etudes et résultats*, no. 264, Paris: Direction de la recherche, de l'évaluation, des études et des statistiques (DREES).

Bontout, O., Colin, C. and Kerjosse, R. (2002) 'Personnes âgées dépendantes et aidants potentiels: une projection à l'horizon 2040', *Etudes et résultats*, no. 160, Paris: DREES.

Bouget, D. and Tartarin, R. (eds) (1990) *Le prix de la dépendance*, Paris ; La Documentation Française.

Boulard, J. C. (1991) *Vivre ensemble. Rapport d'information déposé par la Commission des Affaires culturelles, familiales et sociales sur les personnes âgées dépendantes,* Assemblée Nationale no. 2135, Paris.

Bressé, S. (2004) 'Le personnel des services d'aide à domicile en 1999,' *Etudes et résultats,* no. 297, Paris: DREES.

Brutel, C. and Omalek, L. (2002) 'Projections démographiques pour la France, ses régions et ses départements à l'horizon 2030,' *Données sociales. La société française,* Paris: INSEE.

Causse, L., Fournier, C. and Labruyère, C. (1998) *Les aides à domicile: des emplois en plein remue-ménage*, Paris: Syros.

Christopher, S. (1997) 'Childcare and Elderly Care: What Occupational Opportunities for Women?' *Labour Market and Social Policy Occasional Papers*, no. 27.

Colin, C., Coutton, V. (2000) 'Le nombre de personnes âgées dépendantes d'après lèuquête Handicap – incapacités – dépendance; *Etudes et Résultats*, no. 94, Paris: DREES.

Comité de vigilance de la PSD (1998) *Le livre noir de la prestation spécifique dépendance.*

Dutheil, N. (2001) 'Les aides et les aidants des personnes âgées,' *Etudes et résultats,* no. 142, Paris: DREES.

Hennessy, P. (1995) 'Social Protection for Dependent Elderly People: Perspectives from a Review of OECD Countries,' *Labour Market and Social Policy Occasional Paper*, no. 16.

Hespel, V. and Thierry, M. (1998) *Synthèse des constats et propositions de la mission sur les services d'aide aux personnes*. Inspection générale des affaires sociales et Inspection générale des finances, Rapport no. 1998–132, IGAS.

Hochschild, A. (1995) 'The Culture of Politics: Traditional, Post-modern, Cold-modern, and Warm-model Ideals of Care', *Social Politics*, 2(3), 331–45.

Joël, M. E. and Bungener, M. (1991) *Le financement de la prise en charge de la dépendance des personnes âgées*, Rapport MIRE, Paris, ministère des Affaires Sociales.

Joël, M. E. and Martin, C. (1997) 'La part des arbitrages économiques et familiaux dans l'organisation du soutien à domicile des personnes âgées dépendantes,' *Revue française des affaires sociales*, no. hors série, octobre, Paris: *La documentation française.*

Joël M. E. and Martin, C. (1998) *Aider les personnes âgées dépendantes. Arbitrages économiques et familiaux*, Rennes, éditions de l'ENSP.

Kerjosse, R. (2004) 'L'allocation personnalisée d'autonomie au 31 mars 2004,' *Etudes et résultats*, no. 321, Paris: DREES.

Kerjosse, R. and Lebeaupin, A. (1993) 'Un million et demi de personnes âgées dépendantes,' *La Société française, Données sociales 1993*, Paris: INSEE.

Kessler, F. (ed.) (1994) *La dépendance des personnes âgées: un défi pour le droit de la protection sociale*, Strasbourg: Presses universitaires de Strasbourg.

Kessler, F. (1995) 'Quelles prestations pour les personnes âgées dépendantes? Panorama des propositions de réforme,' *Droit social*, 1, 85–94.

Laroque, G. *et al.* (1993) *Rapport sur la dépendance des personnes âgées*, Paris: Inspection générale des Affaires sociales.

Le Bihan, B. and Martin, C. (eds) (2000) *La mise en œuvre de la prestation spécifique dépendance dans six départements*, Working paper no.8, Paris: DREES.

Le Bihan, B. and Martin, C. (2002) *Aider un parent âgé dépendant. Impact sur la vie professionnelle et sociale des femmes*, Rapport de recherche pour le service.

Le Bihan, B. and Martin, C. (2003) 'Working and Caring: Active Daughters in Law Caring for a Dependent Elderly Parent in France', communication at the ESPAnet Conference 'Changing European Societies – the role for Social Policy', 13–15 November 2003, Copenhagen.

Le Bihan, B., Martin, C. and Schweyer, F.-X. (2000) 'La prestation spécifique dépendance à domicile en pratiques dans six départements', *Etudes et résultats* no. 64, Paris: DREES.

Le Bihan, B. and Martin, C. (2006a) 'Travailler et prendre soin d'un parent dependant', *Travail, genre et sociétés*, no. 16 (in press).

Le Bihan, B. and Martin, C. (forthcoming 2006b) *Travailler* et prendre soin: Des femmes face à la dependance d'un parent âgé, Rennes éditions ENSP (avec B. Le Bihan). A paraître en 2006.

Le Bihan, B., Campéon, A., Rivard, T. and Martin, C. (2004) *Recherche auprès des associations d'aide à domicile et des bénéficiaires de l'Allocation personnalisée d'autonomie*, Working paper, Paris: DREES.

Lesemann, F. and Martin, C. (eds) (1993) *Home-based Care, the Elderly, the Family and the Welfare State: An International Comparison*, Ottawa: University of Ottawa Press.

Martin, C. (1998) 'L'expérimentation territoriale de la prestation dépendance: fenêtre d'opportunité ou rendez-vous manqué?' *Politiques et management publics*, 16(3), 69–91.

Martin, C. (2000) 'Atouts et limites de l'expérimentation: l'exemple de la prestation dépendance', *Revue française des affaires sociales*, no.1, 47–58.

Martin, C. (2001) 'Le politiques de prise en charge des personnes âgées dépendantes', *Travail, genre et sociétés*, 6, Paris: L'Harmattan, pp. 83–103.

Martin, C. (ed.) (2003) *La dépendance des personnes âgées. Quelles politiques en Europe?*, Rennes: Presses universitaires de Rennes.

Martin, C., Jourdain, A., Mohaer, F. and Schweyer, F.-X. (1996) *La prestation expérimentale dépendance en Ille et Vilaine. Leçons d'un apprentissage*, Rennes: éditions ENSP.

Martin, C., Math, A. and Renaudat, E. (1998) 'Caring for Very Young Children and Dependent Elderly People in France: Towards a Commodification of Social Care', in Lewis, J. (ed.), *Gender, Social Care and Welfare State Restructuring in Europe*, Aldershot: Ashgate Publishers, pp. 139–74.

Mette, C. (2004) 'Allocation personnalisée d'autonomie à domicile: une analyse des plans d'aide', *Etudes et résultats*, no. 293, Paris: DREES.

Pison, G. (2003) 'La population de la France en 2002', *Population et sociétés*, 388.

Schopflin, P. (1991) *Dépendance et solidarité. Mieux aider les personnes âgées*, Rapport de la Commission du Commissariat Général du Plan, Paris: La Documentation française.

Sueur, J.-P. (2000) *Làide personnalisée à làutonomie: Un nouveau droit foncé sur le principe d'égalité*. Rapport remis à Martine Aubry, Ministre de l'Emploi et de la Solidarité, Paris: La documentation française.

Ungerson, C. (1997) 'Social Politics and the Commodification of Care', *Social Politics*, 4(3), 362–82.

Ungerson, C. (2004) 'Whose empowerment and independence? A cross-national perspective on "cash-for-care" schemes', *Ageing & Society*, 24(2), 189–212.

4
The Commodification of Care – The Italian Way

Cristiano Gori and Barbara Da Roit

The context

In recent decades, a marked ageing process has led to Italy becoming one of the European countries with the highest percentage of older people. In 2000, people aged 65 or over represented 18 per cent of the overall population, consistently above the European average (EU15), a trend which is not likely to reverse in the near future. Forecasts show that the pace of this trend will be faster in Italy than elsewhere: in 2010 the population aged 65 years or more is predicted to be 20.4 per cent and in 2030 27.0 per cent (Eurostat, 2003) of the whole. The age structure of the elderly population is of great importance from a policy perspective. The link between age and disability is well known: the older a person, the higher the probability of being disabled. In Italy, the population aged 80 or above will increase at a faster pace than the overall elderly population, and is expected to rise from 3.8 per cent of the population in 2000 to 5.9 per cent in 2010 and to 9.7 per cent in 2030 (Eurostat, 2003).[1]

Alongside this rapid ageing process, and the concomitant increase in care needs, the availability of family support – the traditional source of care for older people – has weakened. This has happened for different reasons. As a result of demographic developments, the number of children per older person has diminished over the years and will decrease further in the future. Women's increasing participation in the labour market has reduced the availability of informal care resources within families, and continues to do so. Relatives have traditionally provided most of the care for older people and Italy has been characterized by an attitude which places great importance on the family's role in the care of older people, and considers care to be a private matter. Now, with the family under strain and unable to support older people as much as in the past, clear challenges arise for public policy.

Against this background, public policies towards frail older people remain underdeveloped by both quantitative and qualitative standards. The provision of residential and community care, for which health and social services are responsible,[2] is limited, as in other Mediterranean countries. There is a high degree of both regional and local variation, with respect to the supply of services and to the eligibility criteria. Not only is there greater provision of services in the Centre-North compared with the South, but within each region provision of care facilities differs substantially between municipalities and between local health authorities (Gori, 2003). Nevertheless, even in those regions and areas where the provision of public services is higher, it is quite low in comparison with the countries of central and northern Europe (Saraceno, 2003). At the beginning of the millennium, the overall percentage of people aged 65+ receiving long-term care in institutions in Italy was around 2.1 per cent (ISTAT, 2003a).[3] Where older people receiving community care are concerned, Italy again has very low percentages of users: they amount to nearly 3.3 per cent of people aged 65+ (Pesaresi and Gori, 2003).[4]

In this context, the most important policy measure, both in terms of expenditure and of the number of older people affected is a national scheme, named the *indennità di accompagnamento* ('companion payment'). This is a payment available to severely disabled people, regardless of their age, based on an assessment of needs and paid irrespective of the claimant's financial situation: some 7.3 per cent of people aged 65 or more receive it (2003) (Da Roit, 2004). Alongside this national measure, several regional authorities and municipalities introduced local payments for care in the 1990s: generally means-tested measures, these were available mostly to highly dependent older people, aiming to prevent their institutionalization (see below).

Access to privately paid care has become an important issue in recent years in Italy. The total amount of paid care delivered is much greater than the public supply of personal services. Italy lacks definitive data on this but, according to a national estimate, 5.2 per cent of people aged 60–69, 12.4 per cent of those aged 70–79 and 20 per cent of those aged 80 or more receive some kind of private assistance at home (for either personal care and/or home help), a much higher percentage than for older people receiving public personal services (Census-ASSR, 2004).[5] Furthermore, privately paid carers deliver a huge number of hours per week (often they live with the elderly person), whereas public domiciliary care delivers only a few.

The private care supply system has some specific characteristics. Individual workers dominate this market, while organizations (both private and non-profit) mainly work under contract to the public sector and tend not to offer services directly to families (Gori, 2002). In fact, the 1990s saw a considerable increase in the number of private organizations supplying home care to frail older people, as services previously undertaken by the public sector were contracted out. These organizations, however, did not contribute to the development of a private market in paid care for older people, which remains strongly linked to individual suppliers. This key feature of the supply of private care is consistent with the low qualification of workers, the limited social recognition of these jobs, and the weak position of employees in this market. In most cases, carers of older people are untrained assistants – often coming from countries outside the European Union – paid directly by older people and their families in a 'grey market'.

According to estimates based on the national accounting system, in 2001 around one million people were working in 'domestic services for families and communities',[6] less than a quarter of whom regularly registered for contributions and tax purposes (ISTAT, 2003b).[7]

'Routed wages'

There are two different types of 'routed wage'in Italy. The *indennità di accompagnamento* ('companion payment') is a national benefit introduced in the 1980s. In the 1990s, several regional authorities and municipalities also introduced their own local payments for care. The former are much more widespread than the latter.

The *indennità di accompagnamento* is the only care allowance for disabled people provided at national level (see Table 4.1). It was first introduced in 1980 and took its current shape in 1988, as a national measure intended to support the care needs of non self-sufficient people, irrespective of their age. It is a needs-tested benefit provided by local health authorities. The *indennità* is not means-tested or linked to a system of contributions, but is financed by the national government through taxation. It is delivered on the sole basis of the disability, regardless of financial circumstances. It is available to people who are wholly (100 per cent) disabled because of their physical or mental ill health, and who cannot walk without the help of a companion or who need constant assistance due to their inability to carry out everyday tasks.

Table 4.1 The indennità di accompagnamento

Area	Definition
Funding	Financed by the national government through taxation. It is a national benefit
Target	People who are wholly (100%) disabled because of physical or mental diseases and cannot walk without the help of a companion or need constant assistance due to their inability to carry out the tasks of daily life. Payments are needs-tested but not means-tested.
Admittance	Claimants apply to their local health authority which decides whether the degree of disability and care needs meet the eligibility criteria set by national legislation.
Purpose	The payment goes to the disabled person for the purchase of commercial services or to pass on to care-giving relatives. There is no control over the use made of the allowance: no care plan is made and it is not necessary to prove that the money has been spent on care.
Amount	The level of payment is quite high: €437 a month.

Claimants apply to their local health authority, which decides whether the degree of disability and care need meet the eligibility criteria set by national legislation. The *indennità* is provided to enable the disabled person to buy commercial services or can be passed on to care-giving relatives. There is no control over its actual use: no care plan is made, and it is not necessary to prove that money has actually been spent on meeting care needs (it can be used for any purpose). The delivery of the *indennità* is completely detached from the local system of public welfare: there is no link between the *indennità* and the provision of (social and health) services in kind.

The level of the payment is €437 per month (2004); this is enough to purchase an appropriate number of private home care hours per month. Given its total cost and the number of users, the *indennità* has become a cornerstone of Italian public policy for frail older people. In 2003 there were 1,148,000 recipients of this payment; of these 797,000 were aged 65 or above (some 7.3 per cent of the older population) (Da Roit, 2004). The percentage of older people receiving the *indennità* far outweighs the numbers receiving local payments for care (see below).

In the 1990s, several regional councils and municipalities introduced local care allowances (see Table 4.2). Although these allowances were designed at local level, some common features can be highlighted. Payments are financed by regions and municipalities through their

Table 4.2   Local care allowances – common features of the Italian arrangements

Area	Definition
Funding	The payments are financed by regions and municipalities through health and/or social funds. It is a local benefit.
Target	The allowances are both needs-tested and means-tested; made available to highly dependent elderly with low economic resources, they are mainly designed to prevent institutionalization.
Admittance	Claimants apply to the local health authority/municipality providing the benefit. Admittance is usually decided after an evaluation of the health, social and economic conditions of the elderly person and his/her family.
Purpose	Payment generally goes to the disabled person for the purchase of commercial services or to pass on to care-giving relatives, as in the majority of cases; in a few circumstances it goes directly to the caregiver.
	The allowance is usually provided along with a care plan set by welfare professionals who should then monitor the conditions of the older person and the allowance's impact over time. In practice, control and monitoring seem to be very difficult.
Amount	This varies greatly between areas. Usually it is graded according to the economic resources and dependency of the older person and whether she/he also gets the *indennità di accompagnamento*.

health and/or social funds. They are both needs-tested and means-tested, made available to highly dependent older people with limited economic resources; and, in most cases, they are designed to avoid institutionalization. Claimants apply to the health authority/municipality providing the allowance. Procedures differ between areas, depending on local rules, and admittance is usually decided after an assessment has been made of the health, social and economic conditions of the older person and his/her family.

The allowance is usually provided along with a care plan set by (social and/or health) welfare professionals, who should, subsequently, monitor the conditions of the older person and the impact of the benefit over time; however, controlling and monitoring over time seem very difficult to undertake. Payment generally goes to the disabled person for the purchase of commercial services, or to pass on to care-giving relatives; in a few circumstances it goes directly to the care-giving relative. The amount varies considerably between areas. In most areas, they are graded according to both the economic situation and dependency of the older person and to whether she/he receives the *indennità di accompagnamento* as well. Finally, it is important to emphasize that the profile of the local allowances – for example, the extent of take up – varies a great deal between different areas.

Despite a lack of definitive data on the spread of local payments for care in Italy, the trends are quite clear.[8] Until the mid 1990s, they were available in only a few areas. Since then, payments have become increasingly widespread; this development affects mainly the North and Centre of the country. The latest national survey (2001) showed that in the North and the Centre a payment was delivered in some 60 per cent of the areas,[9] while in the South the figure was only 10 per cent (Gori and Torri, 2001). Other evidence shows that, more recently, local payments have, in the North and the Centre of the country, spread further (Formez, 2003; Monitor, 2003). It is widely expected that they will continue to spread in coming years, for the same reasons that underpin their growth to date (see below). It is reasonable to state that local payments for care are now delivered in more than two-thirds of the areas in the North and the Centre, while they are still scarce in the South.

The data given above concern the percentage of health author-ities/municipalities providing local payments for care. Another issue concerns the number of older people receiving them. Despite local vari-ations, a trend emerges: where local payments are available, they are (in most cases) a minority of all community care users,[10] but they are increasing. The experience of the past decade shows that usually the number of recipients has increased each year since their introduction.

The introduction and spread of routed wages

The development of routed wages arises for a range of reasons, related to traditional features of the Italian welfare regime, as well as to more recent changes. Although the histories of the *indennità di accompagnamento* and of the local care allowances are quite different, common reasons which, to various degrees, prompted their introduction and growth can be pinpointed.

Consistency with the profile of the Italian welfare regime

A first observation must be that the growth of 'routed wages' is consistent with well-established features of the Italian welfare regime. In Italy, public provision of care services has always been limited and state inter-vention has focused on the provision of cash benefits (mostly pensions). The care of older people has traditionally been deemed a private issue, to be kept completely within the family domain.

Routed wages fit very well with this scenario, being primarily a measure to support the family in its established role of sole care provider for older people and a measure that can support the family without interfering in its daily life. Furthermore, as public provision of care is extremely scarce, the introduction of this measure is seen by many people as an acknowledgement of the hard work carried out each day by carers, who are otherwise left alone by public services.

Squaring the circle between growing needs and scarce resources

The elderly population has grown very significantly in Italy and is expected to increase further. This growth, in a context of the declining availability of informal care, has increased demand for public long-term care. Demand outstrips the supply, and the economic resources devoted to it – although increased – are scarce. The Italian long-term care system is thus squeezed between growing demand and inadequate public funds.

Against this background, routed wages have been identified as a key tool to square the circle between growing needs and scarce resources. For the public budget, they are usually cheaper than services in kind as a response to increasing needs. Many feel that it is only by providing allowances that it is possible to increase the number of recipients of public care at costs which are affordable for the public purse. The majority of the allowances, furthermore, are targeted on older people at high risk of institutionalization. Routed wages are designed as an alternative to residential care, in comparison to which they are usually cheaper in economic terms for the public sector.

Maintaining frail older people at home

In the Italian debate, as abroad, there is a wide consensus about the importance of maintaining frail older people at home as long as possible, giving domiciliary care priority over residential care. The international literature agrees on the benefits older people gain from living longer at home (e.g., OECD, 2005). Evidence for Italy shows that older people want to stay at home as long as possible, and that their relatives share this view (Facchini, 1997). In Italy, routed wages have been designed mostly as an alternative to residential care. Many policy-makers, academics and practitioners have supported routed wages as a tool for maintaining frail older people at home, and this goal has been an important rationale for their development.

Appreciating freedom of choice and flexibility

Routed wages are more flexible to use than services in kind and guarantee high freedom of choice to users and families, who can arrange their own care as they prefer. Their particular design is the key to their success, as older people and their families greatly appreciate these features (Gori and Torri, 2001). Evidence from abroad shows that in other European countries users also appreciate the flexibility and freedom of choice that routed wages assure (Weekers and Pjil, 1998).

Ease of delivery

The growth of routed wages is also linked to the problems of delivering welfare services in Italy. Difficulties arise at local level, when attempts are made to increase the supply of care services (which often takes longer than expected); this is consistent with long-term weaknesses in Italian public administration and the limited tradition of providing care services in kind (see above). The growth of routed wages instead of services in kind is a way of overcoming these difficulties. Delivering cash is, for the public bureaucracy, obviously not only cheaper but also easier and quicker than providing services in kind (either domiciliary or residential).

Who receives routed wages: A profile

Characteristics of the care market

It is widely recognized that social policy has a direct impact on developments in the service sector labour market (Esping-Andersen, 1999; Reyneri 2003). Limited provision of care services is related to occupational structures characterized by low employment rates in the care service sector, both in private and public services. Key features of the Italian case are the high fragmentation of a rather underdeveloped care labour market, and the parallel development of a significant grey labour market, particularly in care services for older people.

In both the regular and the grey market, individual workers represent the overwhelming majority; they are directly employed by families and do not belong to care organizations. This is especially true in services provided directly to families, whereas organizations tend to provide services funded by the public sector. Care and home help can be depicted as a virtually unstructured economic sector, with increasing numbers of migrant workers, both in the official and grey economy. In 2002, more than half of all individual workers regularly operating in this sector were foreigners – almost all from non-European countries. Although the overwhelming majority of these workers were women, where male workers exist it is usually among the non-Italian employees.[11]

The regular care market is quite fragmented, as working conditions, social rights, minimum wages and the labour costs of professional carers differ greatly, depending upon how the job is arranged and what type of contract is operated. Individual workers employed directly by older people or their families are paid different wages, and benefit from different social rights, compared with workers employed by – for profit and non-profit – organizations, such as cooperatives, institutions owned by public authorities, and private companies.

The national collective agreement[12] which, normally, applies to individual workers employed directly by families, establishes minimum wages lower than those established for similar activities covered by other types of contract in the service sector. Even pay, usually set higher than the minimum wage, tends to be lower than pay in service sector jobs which have less emotional involvement and personal responsibility, such as supermarket cashiers. Furthermore, the social rights granted to individual care workers seem to be weaker as well. Dismissal is possible at any time, and for any reason, when an individual worker is involved,[13] whereas any company with at least 14 employees has to meet more rigid rules and has the right to sack workers only for 'a just cause or a justified reason'. Finally, while the working week is usually a 38–40 hour schedule, this rises to 44 and even 55 hours where individual domestic workers are concerned.

In sum, the economic and social conditions of professional carers are clearly worse than those of low-skilled workers in other sectors. Low pay, job insecurity and the stresses of the job are likely to make people unwilling to undertake this work if they have other options. We can, therefore, expect that many professional carers are workers who are not able, do not have the opportunity, or do not have any interest in entering another occupation. In fact, it was the labour shortage in the care sector among Italian workers which led to the growth of foreign women working as carers in private homes, as mentioned above. In recent years, migration from non-EU countries and paid care have been two closely linked phenomena. Despite limited national data, it is widely recognized by both researchers and policy makers that, when informal carers are not available, or cannot meet all the needs of frail older people, care rests mainly on migrants (Andolfi Foundation, 2003; Ismu Foundation, 2003). Domestic work represents a suitable job opportunity for foreigners, especially women. According to an OECD study conducted in six countries – including Italy – household services are one of the core economic sectors for both authorized and unauthorized migrant labour, along with agriculture, construction, tourism and family services. A desire for flexibility and to minimize costs seem to be the most important reasons for the link between immigrants and work in this sector. Female-dominated migration flows have arisen in only a few countries of migrant origin, such as the Philippines, Peru and Romania. These countries exactly match the country of origin of most regular non-Italian domestic workers. In fact, the most important national group of foreigner domestic workers is the Philippines, followed by Eastern Europeans and Latin Americans.

Activity in the grey market is a major feature of the Italian labour market, as in other Mediterranean countries (Schneider, 2001). The care market is dominated by irregular work even more strongly than the wider economy. Care workers are found in the grey market both in part time jobs (carried out by migrants but also by Italian workers such as pensioners and middle aged 'housewives') and in full time live-in jobs (particularly carried out by foreigners).

For both employers and employees there are strong incentives to enter or to stay within the grey market. First, overall labour costs are higher in the regular market, because of taxation and social contributions. Second, the illegal labour market escapes regulation and, therefore, reduces the costs of services: working hours, weekly and daily rest, leave entitlements, night shifts and work outside scheduled hours, are all regulated aspects that in an informal relationship can be managed in a more flexible (and less costly) way. In many care arrangements where 24-hour assistance is requested, live-in foreign workers accept quite difficult and under-paid working conditions, which are counterbalanced (to a certain extent) by the advantage of safe and cheap housing.

Third, in some cases it is difficult to find workers who are available for a regular job. Especially when few hours of care per day or per week are needed, workers may not be interested in a regular position, and the post is treated as a secondary activity, and a way of supplementing personal or family income.

Finally, the grey market may not even be the choice of the employer or employees, as foreign non-EU citizens without permission to stay are not allowed to undertake regular work. This situation emerged as a very common one during the last mass regularization of undocumented foreign domestic workers.[14] In fact, this was just the latest in a series of mass regularizations that have periodically taken place in Italy since the 1980s. It has been shown that, after a short period in which undocumented migrants emerge as regularized workers, there has always been a tendency towards new developments of grey market activities (Reyneri, 2003).

Routed wages – between family caregiving and paid work

Interpreting Italian cash allowances as routed wages presents several problems, as shown by the evidence collected. First, cash allowances are generally regarded by older people and their relatives as more of a supplement to the family income for expenses related to disability than as a specific allowance enabling them to purchase care. The money from this benefit is often considered 'just like the money from my pension', as one of the older people we interviewed put it, since it is used by the household to cover general expenses such as shopping, medicines, rent, telephone, gas and power bills. The design of the Italian care allowance has clearly played a role in shaping this image, and the consequent relations within the (extended) family. Money received through public schemes usually becomes part of the general family budget, where it is almost impossible to track its use. The benefit received goes into a 'common purse' together with pension income, which might or might not be used for buying private care. In fact the allowance, which when first received is often used for daily household necessities, is sometimes spent on paying a private carer when the older person's health deteriorates and the informal caregivers are no longer able to carry out all the care tasks on their own. In such changed situations the allowance 'is not enough to pay the woman' and has to be supplemented with additional resources taken from pensions.

Second, in many cases, carers and older people themselves claim that care is provided out of family responsibility and solidarity. This is particularly true when the caregiver is a spouse: taking care of a disabled partner is not seen as a job at all, especially when the caregiver is old and already out of the labour market. According to a 65 year old wife we interviewed, looking after her husband is her duty: 'I'm his wife, and when we married, I promised to stand by him in both good and bad times . . . '

Moreover, as the allowance belongs to both spouses and forms part of a single family budget, no transfer of money is detectable. Similar circumstances can be observed when the caregiver is a co-resident child. On the other hand, when someone from another, informal, network assumes the role of main caregiver (as in the case of a child living in a different household) there may be some exchange of money. Nevertheless, there is normally no explicit link between the delivery of a service and a payment. More often, children and relatives receive income support and/or small gifts, as part of a reciprocal exchange, rather than of a 'contract' between the older person and the caregiver.

Among the interviewees, a few non co-resident children received financial support from their mothers either in the form of small gifts, in recognition of the care they provide, or due to their difficult financial circumstances: nevertheless these were not regarded as payments for care work. Only in one case was a transfer of money from the older person to a relative – a daughter – meant as a compensation for care. This occurs when the caregiver gives up paid employment in order to take care of the dependent older person. In that situation, part of the older person's income, normally equivalent to the allowance, is passed on to the caregiver.

Such care arrangements represent the traditional response to the care needs of older people in the framework of the Italian welfare system. Nevertheless, in recent years, a trend towards the externalization of care tasks has been observed in relation to the growth of a market dominated by individual migrant women. This trend is often associated with the diminution of family care resources arising from two processes: the declining number of children per older person, and the increasing participation of women in the labour market. Without denying the importance of such elements, it is worth noting that even where significant family care resources exist, an externalization of care tasks often occurs, as a result of a change in the role of the main caregiver, shifting from the direct provision of care to the assumption of overall supervision and management of the care (Da Roit and Castegnaro, 2004). Access to paid care is clearly extended by care allowances, as an increase in the older person's income makes paid care more affordable, even for less affluent households. In general, access to paid care is not limited to the upper classes, but has become a mass phenomenon, again through relatively cheap foreign labour.

Sometimes the allowance is saved for future more extensive needs. A daughter providing unpaid care explains that she prefers to save the money from her father's *indennità di accompagnamento* to spend it 'when my father needs more help, because his disease will surely get worse in the future'.

These features of the allowance have a clear impact on the amount of money paid for care and on the types of contract made between employer and employee. Here, there is a double link between care allowances and access to the irregular labour market. On the one hand, since use made of the allowance does not have to be documented, grey labour does not represent a major obstacle. On the other hand, if care needs are particularly demanding, and a full time employee has to be paid, the grey market allows for optimization of the resources from the point of view of the older person and their family (see above).

When a paid worker is present, the picture changes significantly. Suddenly, care becomes a job, whereas it was not when carried out by spouses, children and relatives. Care arrangements may vary significantly. At one extreme the employee's activity can be seen as a supplement to the informal care provided by the family network: here the job is usually limited to a clearly defined number of hours per day or per week, and remunerated accordingly. Usually the tasks carried out by these workers are limited to household activities, such as cleaning, ironing or keeping the house tidy, while the main informal carers continue to provide personal care. Sometimes a person is paid to stay with the older person while the main caregiver goes out shopping or takes care of administrative matters. In such situations workers are paid on an hourly basis in the grey market.

At the other extreme, paid workers tend to assume all tasks normally carried out by unpaid carers: not only personal care and housework, but also contact with the outside world. In these cases, workers normally live in and provide a full-time service, with a very blurred definition of the daily and weekly schedule. A Romanian woman caring for a 92 year old lady tells us that she works night and day, from Monday to Sunday, and has only an hour a day of 'freedom', when she has to go out shopping. Similarly a Peruvian woman working for a 90 year old lady 'night and day', from Monday to Sunday, has only 5 hours of freedom per week, and says: 'every night I must help her go to the bathroom, because she's afraid of falling'.

Intermediate solutions are also possible. As the first type of worker may be either an Italian housewife, or a pensioner – perhaps a neighbour – or a foreign worker, the second type of worker is more likely to be a migrant. The latter are well aware of the demand for labour in the sector of elder care sector before leaving their home country, and are available for full-time and living-in jobs which are not an option for Italian workers (Da Roit and Castegnaro, 2004).

At the beginning of their stay, most care workers tend to have short to medium migration plans, to have 'self exploiting' attitudes, and to accept very hard working conditions in order to accumulate as many resources as possible and go back to their home country. As some of them change their plans and lengthen their stay in Italy, they tend to express needs and goals more similar to those of Italian workers: moving from the living-in to an independent living arrangement; shifting from full-time to hourly jobs; leaving home care to work in residential care; specializing in nursing activities or moving out of the care sector.

Issues at stake

Routed wages in the Italian welfare regime: Back to the past?

The rise in routed wages needs to be seen in the broader context of the Italian welfare regime, which is built upon the family's responsibility for caring for dependent relatives. The public sector provides mostly cash benefits, while the provision of services in kind is low.

The introduction of the *indennità di accompagnamento* was consistent with this profile: the response to the increasing demand for care was a cash payment, delivered without any control or monitoring of how it is actually spent. Local payments for care are also rooted in the traditional welfare regime. They mark a shift for local health authorities and municipalities, which usually deliver services in kind to meet care needs, towards increasingly providing cash. Paradoxically, in the current debate, local allowances are considered by many to be a key innovation in the care system. On the contrary, delivering cash instead of care is a return to the past, which strengthens the traditional features of the Italian welfare regime.

Furthermore, over the past three decades, routed wages have spread more than community and long-term care services. From the 1970s onwards, there have been requests and pressures – from many commentators, activists and social workers – to increase the provision of services in kind. These have grown, nevertheless, but at a lower rate than expected, and remain extremely scarce: the goal of developing services in kind has not been accomplished. The call to increase the delivery of services in kind is actually at the centre of the current debate. In short, the growth of routed wages from the 1980s onwards has not been accompanied by a strong development of long-term care services in kind.

In search of a well-designed policy?

Two issues lie at the centre of the debate about the design of routed wages: control and quality. The *indennità di accompagnamento* lacks any kind of control over its use, a particularly troublesome aspect because of the profile of the Italian welfare state. Italy offers weak protection against unemployment and poverty (it lacks a safety net income for all citizens). The *indennità* has – inappropriately – been used by many as a benefit to combat poverty. The greater density of beneficiaries in depressed areas – particularly in southern Italy – can only partially be explained by the higher level of disability there, and suggests that it has often been used merely to raise poor families' income; in the late

1990s tighter controls were put in place to address this, with some success. The lack of control also allows older people and their families to spend the *indennità* on hiring private assistants in the grey market, without any regulation. In such a scenario, it is unrealistic even to think of promoting the quality of care provided through the *indennità* (Glendinning and McLaughlin, 1993).

Local payments for care have sought to overcome some of the *indennità*'s shortcomings. They are mostly delivered through a process involving several steps: assessment, care planning and monitoring over time. This process is a positive development and seems consistent with suggestions in the international literature (Jenson and Jacobzone, 2000). By setting up a care plan and monitoring over time it should be possible to control what the cash provided is actually used for, that is, whether it is used to meet the care needs of the older person or for other purposes, and whether it is used to hire personal assistants on a regular basis. Proper management of planning and monitoring would also be the best way of guaranteeing the appropriateness and effectiveness of the care provided.

Such a process is, nevertheless, complex to manage, and requires significant financial and human resources. The evidence indicates that difficulties in this arise in all areas of Italy, and that only a minority seem able to address them adequately. Assessment, for example, is very difficult, and professionals often find it difficult to decide in which cases providing the allowance is appropriate (Gori and Torri, 2001). Also, devising a care plan, arranging proper use of the allowance, and setting adequate goals with the agreement of all parties involved is a task professionals find difficult when they approach it systematically. This is true also of monitoring, as here professionals need to understand the impact of the allowance on both users and carers.

The difficulties that arise in the process of assessment, planning and monitoring have several causes. A key problem is the scarcity of human resources committed to it. Since a main reason for the extension of the care allowance – mentioned above – was the need to contain public expenditure, it is not surprising that the human resources (social workers and others professionals) committed to the assessment, planning and monitoring functions are usually quite limited. Scarcity of human resources nevertheless has a strong negative impact on the ability to operate these functions properly. In effect, properly managed local payments for care require the time of professionals: but thereby lose the cost-containment features that make them so attractive to policy-makers.

Gender issues

Routed wages can be spent on hiring paid assistants or can be passed on to informal carers; the latter are mostly women (daughters or wives of the older people concerned). Informal carers are usually satisfied with the allowances, appreciating the opportunity to use them in a flexible way. Payments are perceived as an acknowledgement by the state of their significant caring effort, and a support in enabling dependent older people to remain at home. There are contrasting views on routed wages: many experts criticize them, but they are strongly supported by most informal carers. Any proposal to modify the allowances should not underestimate the huge support they receive from the latter.

Informal carers uphold routed wages despite the negative consequences on their lives. The international debate has for some time stressed the damaging impact on their occupational prospects (Ungerson, 1995). The allowances encourage them to extend the time spent taking care of the older person, thus lengthening their period out of the labour market. When they cease caring for their elderly relative (because she/he dies, is institutionalized or for other reasons) it is then more difficult to enter or re-enter the labour market. The longer one is outside the labour market, in fact, the more difficult it becomes to enter or re-enter it. Some commentators stress the relevance of this process for Italy, particularly when the allowance is passed to women on low incomes (Saraceno, 1995). This is very often the case with local payments for care (which are means-tested) and with the *indennità di accompagnamento* when it is provided to older people in low-income families. The allowance is attractive to them because it is often not much lower than the wage they could earn in the labour market. These women usually face difficulties in finding a good job, especially if they have little education and few professional skills. For such women, the allowance can be particularly attractive in the short term, but creates real difficulties in the medium and longer term, as it decreases their chances of finding a job in the future, raising their risk of poverty. Another feature which tends towards this outcome is that, contrary to arrangements in countries such as Germany, no pension contribution is paid for the carers of older people receiving the allowances.

Strengthening the link between public services and private care

Routed wages are often used to hire private assistants, some employed in the grey market and some working officially. Recently, increasing attention has been paid to the quality of the care provided by the latter and to their safety, including to the safety of older people and the families employing them. A number of programmes have been set up, at local level, to promote better quality of care and the safety of all the stakeholders involved. They are run either by municipalities, local health authorities or other welfare agencies (such as labour offices) and, in most cases, are not part of the routine delivery of services, but are pilot schemes. Voluntary sector personnel usually run these programmes (often with public funds).

One kind of programme offers training to personal assistants, whose care skills are often inadequate. The training courses are usually quite short and provide a range of general skills (concerning Italian culture and language, care and household tasks). For some, training is needed just to complete their knowledge, whereas others have bigger gaps to fill. Sometimes it is necessary to teach care skills, while often what privately paid carers need first – as they are foreigners – is to learn the Italian language.

Some municipalities, local health authorities and other local public agencies provide elderly citizens and their families with information about private workers available in the area. They supply a list of private care workers whose skills they can guarantee. In order to join the list, care workers have to meet criteria concerning, for example, previous working experience and care skills. Once the list is set up, the agency responsible develops a communication strategy, to ensure older people who may be interested become aware of it.

Agencies are also set up to overcome the unstructured nature of the care labour market, to foster demand and to locate supply to match. When families need a private worker to assist an elderly relative, they usually rely upon their informal networks, friends, neighbours, the local church, trade unions and so on. Often, older people and/or their families have to cope with all the risks and problems of finding a private worker and of checking her/his reliability. Workers, however, are not protected from possible exploitation by older people and their families, or by other workers who arrange their recruitment by the family, in return for an arrangement fee. These public agencies can help workers and families to meet, and can provide assurances on both sides (Piva, 2002; Rossi, 2004).

These are a few examples of the many programmes arranged at local level to promote quality of private care, and safety for the different stakeholders involved. They are arranged both by private (mostly third-sector) personnel and by public services. With respect to the latter, they share a common aim: not only to support older people and their families in paying for private assistants (through routed wages) but also to provide policy instruments which promote quality. Delivering local payments for care using a care plan, and monitoring its implementation over time, is a step in this direction; the problems with this approach have been indicated above. The organization and management of the programmes described is also very complex and so far has occurred only through experimental schemes, which cover very small parts of the country. It is not clear to what degree these will be able to spread in the future.

A crossroads between labour, migration and care

As shown above, the Italian care market is highly dominated by workers directly employed by families. Such arrangements make both users and suppliers of paid care vulnerable to discontinuity and low qualification. On the one hand, caring for a dependent older person is, by definition, a temporary job: a direct and exclusive working relationship makes the worker dependent on the employment and vulnerable in case of loss of the job. On the other hand, a similar dependence on the single worker is observable from the point of view of the family. In addition, replacement care in the case of sick leave, holidays or training may be quite problematic both for the employer and the employee. A different organization of the market, for example through workers' associations or through their affiliation to care organizations, would give more flexibility and the opportunity to qualify care. However, this would substantially change the nature of the contract between carers and families. Informality and low costs – the main characteristics and 'pillars' of such a market – would give way to more formal and necessarily more costly care arrangements.

Two elements have played a major role in developing a care market in Italy: the recourse to grey labour and the availability of relatively cheap migrant labour. Recent debate among public authorities often centres on the need to increase the regulation of both work relations and migrant flows. Those involved must face the fact that these very characteristics of the care market are what permitted its development and made possible the externalization of tasks traditionally carried out by informal carers. On the one hand, irregular work and irregular immigration – which are both consistent with the tradition of Italian economic regulation (Reyneri 2003; Sciortino 2001) – are crucial ingredients for the success of this particular care market, as they help contain costs and, at the same time, respond to the expectations of short- to medium-term migration plans that have the accumulation of resources as their aim.

The most recent regularization of foreign workers revealed, even more clearly than previous ones, the importance of domestic work and care for the elderly as a job opportunity for migrants and the degree to which the grey market in this sector has developed (Barbagli *et al.*, 2004). Nevertheless, as underlined by all commentators, the employment relation has only partially emerged from the grey market. In most cases, employment relations between families and foreign workers are still informally regulated in terms of working hours and pay: an actual regularization of the working contract would render access to paid care unaffordable, as costs would more than double, not so much in relation to payment of social contributions and taxation but in relation to the number of hours worked and their actual value (Da Roit and Castegnaro, 2004). Regulating and qualifying paid care would require a huge injection of public resources to fill the gap between the costs of grey and regular labour, not only because of the relationship between fiscal and social contributions, but also from the organizational changes that would follow the emergence of care work from informal regulation.

The issue of the total amount of resources needed to finance long-term care is thus a central one in defining not only the degree of socialization of the risk of dependency in old age and the distribution of responsibilities between the public and private spheres, but also the nature of developments in the care sector and the type of social integration granted to paid carers.

Notes

1. All the forecasts presented here refer to Eurostat central hypothesis (Eurostat, 2003).
2. In Italy, the 20 Regional Authorities are in charge of the health services, which are managed by the 197 Local Health Authorities (each Regional Authority is composed of several Local Health Authorities). Over 8,000 Municipalities, recently associated in inter-municipal boards, are in charge of personal social services.
3. Great variations are detectable throughout the country. The institutionalization rate is around 3.2 per cent in northern regions, 1.5 per cent in central regions and lower than 1 per cent in southern regions and the islands (Istat, 2003a)
4. This datum comprises also older people receiving local payments for care (see below). Both the data regarding residential care and community care refer to 2001.
5. Data on private care must be considered with care. As much private care is delivered in the grey market (see below) it is difficult to monitor properly.
6. This definition includes childcare, elderly and disabled care, home help and various activities provided in private households and residential structures

7. Due to the regularization of migrant domestic workers in 2003 (see below) the rate of unregulated jobs has temporarily declined. Nevertheless – based on previous amnesties – it is likely to grow again in the medium term.
8. Italy has limited national data on local payments for care, and on many features of the long-term care system.
9. This survey investigated whether in any area at least one of either the Local Health Authority or the Municipality provides payments for care.
10. 3.3 per cent of Italians aged 65 or above receive community care funded by the public sector (see above).
11. Domestic workers registered for social security purposes numbered 224,400 in 2002. Of these, 126,400 were foreigners. Among Italians, 97 per cent were women, while among the foreigners, women represented 81 per cent (www.inps.it)
12. The so-called *'colf'* contract (*collaboratori familiari*, domestic workers)
13. Except for a few special cases, such as pregnancy and sickness
14. Between 2002 and 2003 an amnesty for undocumented migrants working both in domestic services and in industry was passed by law. There were some 340,000 applications for regularization of a foreign domestic worker (Ministry of the Interior). Although such a procedure is not new in recent Italian history, this most recent regularization process was the most important numerically.

References

Andolfi Foundation (2003) *Il lavoro dipendente dei cittadini extracomunitari: occupazioni e retribuzioni in Italia e in Lombardia*, unpublished, Milan.
Barbagli, M., Colombo, A. and Sciortino, G. (2004) *I sommersi e i sanati. Le regolarizzazioni degli immigrati in Italia*, Bologna: Il Mulino.
Censis-ASSR (2004) *L'assistenza agli anziani in Italia*, Rome.
Da Roit B. (2004) 'Il riordino delle erogazioni monetari per gli invalidi civili', in Gori, C. (ed.), *La riforma dei servizi sociali*, Rome: Carocci, pp. 84–96.
Da Roit, B. and Castegnaro, C. (2004) *Chi cura gli anziani non autosufficienti?*, Milan: Franco Angeli.
Esping-Andersen, G. (1999) *Social Foundations of Postindustrial Economies*, Oxford: Oxford University Press.
Eurostat (2003) http://epp.eurostat.ec.europa.eu/portal/page?_pageid=0, 1136184,0_45572595&_dad=portal&_schema=PORTAL
Facchini, C. (1997) 'Gli anziani e la solidarietà tra generazioni', in Barbagli, M. and Saraceno, C. (eds), *Lo stato delle famiglie in Italia*, Bologna: Mulino, pp. 281–9.
Formez (2003) *L'attuazione della riforma del welfare locale*, Roma: Formez.
Glendinning, C. and McLaughin, E. (1993) *Paying for Care: Lessons from Europe*, London: HMSO.
Gori, C. (ed.) (2002) *Il welfare nascosto*, Rome: Carocci.
Gori, C. and Torri, F. (2001) *Gli assegni di cura in Italia*, in Ranci, C. (ed.), *L'assistenza agli anziani in Italia ed in Europa. Verso la costruzione di un mercato sociale dei servizi*, Milan: Franco Angeli, pp. 233–75.
Inps (2001) *Statistiche nazionali su previdenza e mercato del lavoro*, Rome: Inps.
Ismu Foundation (2003) *Nono rapporto sulle migrazioni*, Milian: Franco Angeli, 2003.

ISTAT (2003a) *L'assistenza residenziale in Italia: regioni a confronto: anno 2000*, Rome: ISTAT.

ISTAT (2003b) 'La cura e il ricorso ai servizi sociosanitari. Indagine multiscopo sulle famiglie', *Condizioni di salute e ricorso ai servizi sanitari*, Anni 1999–2000, Roma.

Jenson, J. and Jacobzone, S. (2000) 'Care Allowances for the Frail Elderly and their Impact on Women Caregivers', Paris: OECD, Labour Market and Social Policy – Occasional Papers, 41.

Monitor (2003) *Nelle regioni intanto*, 4, pp. 63–73.

OECD (2005) *Long-term Care Policies for Older People*, Parigi: OCSE.

Pesaresi, F. and Gori, C. (2003) 'Servizi domiciliari e residenziali per gli anziani non autosufficienti in Europa', *Tendenze nuove*, 4/5, 433–70.

Piva, P. (2002) *Buone pratiche per la qualità sociale, Roma: Ediesse.*

Reyneri, E. (2003) *Migrants in Irregular Employment in the Mediterranean Countries of the European Union*, Geneva: ILO: International Migration Papers, 41.

Rossi, A. (2004) *Anziani e assistenti immigrate*, Roma: Ediesse.

Saraceno, C. (1995) 'Le politiche sociali alla luce delle nuove richieste di prestazione e di inclusione', in Mariani, G. and Tognetti Bordogna, M. (eds), *Politiche sociali tra mutamenti futuri e scenari normativi*, Milan: Angeli, pp. 23–38.

Saraceno, C. (2003) *Trasformazioni della famiglie e politiche sociali in Italia*, Bologna: Il Mulino.

Schneider, F. (2001) 'The Value Added of Underground Activities: Size and Measurement of the Shadow Economies and Shadow Labour Force all over the World', Revised version of a paper presented at the Worldbank Summer Research Workshop on Market Institutions, Worldbank, Washington DC, 17–19 July.

Ungerson, C. (1995) *'Gender, Cash and Informal Care: European Perspectives and Dilemmas', Journal of social policy*, 24, 1, pp. 31–52.

Weekers, S. and Pijl, M. (1998) *Home Care and Care Allowances in the European Union*, Utrecht: NIZW.

5
Contracting One's Family Members: The Dutch Care Allowance

Marja Pijl and Clarie Ramakers

Introduction

The PGB (Dutch Care Allowance or personal budget) was first introduced in 1991 and was gradually extended until, in 1995, it became
a regular element of the Dutch long-term care insurance system (the
AWBZ). Heavily regulated, to prevent misuse of the money (despite its
inevitable bureaucratic aspects), the PGB became a very popular scheme,
giving recipients (budget holders) the opportunity to receive care closely
tailored to their needs and preferences. Within a few years of its widespread implementation, however, the costs of the scheme became a
problem. This forced the Dutch government to acknowledge that long
waiting lists for care were unacceptable under an insurance scheme, and
that more money had to be found for long-term care. As a result, costs to
the long-term care insurance increased dramatically, as did the number
of people opting for PGB.

Coming into office in 2003, the new neo-liberal government acted
immediately to contain the costs of long-term care. This directly affected
the PGB scheme, and led to public debate about the desirability of
paying family members to care. As we will show in this chapter, which
draws on our research in 2000/2001, all parties concerned had reasons
to be satisfied with the PGB as it was at that time. Budget holders could
choose their carers, and had a considerable say in the way their care was
organized. The paid carers received reasonable wages and had a stronger
legal position than workers recruited on the grey market. The scheme
was also cheaper than care provided using formal services.

Despite its popularity and efficiency, the Dutch government is
committed to reducing the scheme's scope and costs, and is expected
drastically to reduce AWBZ entitlements. Ahead of its amendments to

(and the possible abolition of) the *Long Term Care Act*, the government has limited access to long-term care, imposing both more rigorous eligibility criteria and higher co-payments. This chapter discusses the PGB as it was in the year the research was done, the consequences of the changes that were introduced subsequently and the uncertain future of the PGB.

The context: Some facts and figures

In 2004, The Netherlands had a population of 16.2m people, of whom about 10 per cent were first or second generation migrants. By comparison with other European countries, the proportion of older persons was still relatively low: 10.4 per cent were aged 65–79 years, and 3.4 per cent were aged 80 or older (CBS).

In 2003, 65 per cent of Dutch persons aged 15–64 participated in the labour market; 75 per cent of men and 55 per cent of women were engaged in paid work. (These figures exclude those working less than 12 hours per week.) More than 70 per cent of all employed women worked part-time, compared with only 19 per cent of men. In the same year, 190,000 women and 206,000 men were unemployed, while 3.5m people of working age were unavailable for work because they were studying, disabled, had retired early, or were unavailable for employment because of their household or caring responsibilities. Two-thirds of this category were women.

Although a male breadwinner model had been dominant in the Netherlands for a long time, by 2003 it had lost ground: the most common pattern (36 per cent) among married or cohabiting couples was that one partner worked full-time and the other part-time. In couples in which there was just one full-time worker (28 per cent) the latter was almost always the man, while in 14 per cent of cases both partners worked full-time. In 5 per cent of cases both partners worked part-time, in 10 per cent neither partner participated in the labour market, and in 6 per cent one partner worked part-time while the other had no paid employment (Portegijs *et al.*, 2004).

Despite this situation, part-time work remains a positive choice for many women in the Netherlands, as shown in Table 5.1. However the government has set a target that, by 2010, 60 per cent of women of working age should be economically independent, defined as earning at least 70 per cent of the net minimum wage. On this measure, just 41 per cent of Dutch women of working age were economically independent in 2001.

Table 5.1 Preferred number of working hours per week, women with a partner (2003)

Hours	Percentage
0	20
1–11	7
12–32	65
33 or more	8

Source: Portegijs *et al., Emancipatie Monitor*, 2004.

In 2001, 3.7m Dutch people aged 18 or older were unpaid carers (Timmermans, 2003). Of these, 2.4m had been caring for either longer than 3 months or for 8 hours a week or more, and 750,000 fell into both these categories of carers. Women formed the majority of carers (58 per cent), and had an average age of 49 years. Eight per cent of carers felt they were very heavily burdened, or overburdened, while among those who had been caring both for over 3 months and for more than 8 hours per week, 15 per cent felt overburdened. One-third of carers indicated that they would like more help from formal care organizations, but about half of these had not applied for it. They were deterred by the length of waiting lists and by a reluctance to admit a stranger to the house. Nineteen per cent of those under 65 years old lost income through caring, either because they could not start a job or were unable to work longer hours when offered them, or because they had to reduce their working hours or give up their job altogether (de Boer *et al.*, 2003).

A Social and Cultural Planning (SCP) Bureau report in 2004 demonstrated that formal services were reaching about half of those aged 55 or older who were heavily impaired, and much lower proportions of those with less serious disabilities. This needs to be set in the context of official estimates of future demand for care.[1] By 2020 the 'potential' demand for home care is estimated to increase by 40 per cent, 'met' demand for care by 18 per cent, and 'recognized' demand by 20 per cent. Even in 2003, the gap between those potentially entitled to care and nursing (including care in residential and nursing homes) and those who actually received care was around 600,000 persons (Timmermans and Woittiez, 2004). It is this latent demand for care, and its cost implications that worries policymakers.

For a number of years, the government, trade unions and employers have cooperated in pursuing an active personnel policy in the care sector. They have tried to safeguard jobs in the healthcare sector at times of recession, and to retain workers by offering good working conditions and reasonable salaries in times of labour market shortages. Women in the care sector earned on average 3.5 per cent more than those in other sectors (OSA, 2003). The majority of care workers state that they like their work and feel their job is meaningful. However, about half feel pressed for time, 40 per cent fear there are no prospects of a career, and 75 per cent consider their wages too low compared with their responsibilities.

Considerable efforts have been made to attract legal migrants as workers in the care sector. These have been successful among women from Surinam and the Antilles, who speak Dutch and come from a culture where women are expected to earn their own living. Recruitment among women from Turkey and Morocco has proved more difficult. These women have language barriers to overcome, often lack information and education, and feel they have to prioritize their obligations to care for their own children and older relatives (de Graaff and Devillé, 2003). Similar problems have been encountered with refugees, although many of these have higher educational qualifications (not always recognized in the Netherlands) (Pen and Tissing, 2000).

Data on illegal migrants working in the care sector do not exist. Illegal migrants cannot work in agencies financed with public money, because there all employees must have a social security and taxation number, obtainable only by legal migrants. This also means that illegal migrants cannot work for recipients of the PGB.

Policy on income, health, care and well being for older people

In principle, Dutch older people need not be dependent on their children. Their income is guaranteed by the State Old Age Pension (AOW), they are covered by mandatory health care insurance (ZFW), and their long-term care is provided on the basis of the AWBZ. Adapted housing, wheelchairs and special transportation are provided by local authorities, who have responsibility for supporting the well-being of older people.

All citizens under 65 pay, along with their taxes, a premium for the AOW, and anyone who has lived in the Netherlands from age 15 to 65 is entitled to the full AOW pension.[2] Only a minority of people living in the Netherlands do not receive the full AOW, most of them first generation migrants. Those who have an income lower than the state pension can apply to the Municipal Social Office for income support. The state pension is individualized, payable not per household but per person.

Each partner in a married or cohabiting couple receives €631.76 gross per month. A single person receives €921.28 gross a month (2004 figures). These amounts are supposed to be enough to live on, but for many older people who have no additional sources of income it is quite hard to make ends meet. To make the system sustainable as the population ages, several options are under discussion. These include: breaking the link between pensions and the cost of living; raising the pensionable age to 67; and making pensioners pay an AOW premium.

At present there is mandatory public health care insurance in the Netherlands, covering the medical costs of two-thirds of the population. Those with an annual income above €32,600 must take out private insurance. From 2006, all citizens will be covered by the same mandatory insurance scheme, which is a private scheme, run by insurance companies and regulated by the government.

A separate long-term care insurance scheme, the AWBZ, was created in the late 1960s to pay for uninsurable health care costs, such as a stay in a nursing home or residential care for persons with mental illness or disabilities. All Dutch citizens are insured, and they pay their premiums alongside their income tax. The PGB is operated as part of the AWBZ scheme. Over time, more and more services have been brought under the AWBZ, including home help and residential homes for older persons. As coverage and demand for care increased, expenditure on the AWBZ rose, and, in an attempt to contain expenditure, the budget of the AWBZ was capped. This created waiting lists which grew rapidly.

Following legal actions in 1999, a ruling confirmed that the government was responsible for providing sufficient funds to purchase insured care. These legal cases had an enormous impact, in effect making the AWBZ an open-ended financial scheme, with the government obliged to provide funds enabling all those assessed to be given care. The ruling could not be implemented immediately, because care providers, even with enough money, could not increase their production overnight as the additional recruitment and training of personnel took some time. Here the PGB brought some relief. While previously only a small amount of money was set aside each year for the PGB, from 2001 this restriction was lifted, and anyone who wanted a care allowance instead of care in kind could get it.

Because the AWBZ became an open-ended system both the costs and the premiums of the AWBZ rose enormously. In 2001, total AWBZ expenditure was €15.9bn, while for 2004 it is expected to reach €21.4bn (CVZ, 2004). In 2001, the premium was 10.25 per cent on taxable income up to a threshold of €27,050 per annum, while in July 2004 the premium was raised to 13.55 per cent on taxable income up to €29,543. Thus those with an income of €29,543 or more per annum paid €333 each month into the AWBZ scheme. Interestingly, there has been no public protest at these changes, perhaps reflecting a lack of awareness on the part of taxpayers, since long-term care premiums and taxes are deducted together. However the Dutch like to live in a welfare state, and they know it is costly.

When rationing care using waiting lists was no longer possible, the new neo-liberal coalition government which came to power in 2003 adopted other strategies to contain costs. One was raising co-payments. Means-tested co-payments remained low for the lowest income groups (under €16 per 4 weeks), but middle and higher income groups had to pay €11.80 for each hour of home care until the maximum amount for their income level was reached. This meant the maximum co-payment for home care was €528 per 4 weeks (*Kleine gids*, 2004). Another strategy was to tighten the criteria used by the Regional Needs Assessment Boards in making their decisions about AWBZ financed long-term care.

The most dramatic changes are still to come. The AWBZ will be drastically cut back; some provisions will be transferred to medical care insurance, and others will be taken out of the AWBZ and brought under the new *Social Support Act* (WMO). Local authorities will be responsible for the WMO. Provisions under the *Provisions for the Handicapped Act* (WVG) and the *Well-Being Act* (Welzijnswet) will be brought into the WMO, and local authorities will be responsible for a very broad range of support. Citizens will lose their legal entitlement to support which is no longer part of the AWBZ. When this will happen, and its precise impact, is not yet certain, but it is most likely that in 2006 responsibility for domestic care will be transferred to the municipalities (Ministerie van VWS, 2004a).

The origins of the PGB (Dutch care allowance)

The Dutch allowance for nursing and care (the PGB) started in 1991 as a carefully evaluated experiment with very positive results. Recipients of the PGB were as satisfied as, or more satisfied than, users of regular home care services, and managed to arrange care that suited their needs. The PGB strengthened their position *vis à vis* their care workers, and gave them more control over their use of time, while relations with their family carers became less stressful than before. In the experiment, 45 per cent of those who were given a choice opted for the PGB (Miltenburg *et al.*, 1993).

Although the scheme was considered successful, there were also some objections. Would recipients of the PBG use the money properly? Would they buy goods or services other than care covered by the AWBZ?. Would they be good employers, providing their employees with satisfactory working conditions? Would workers declare their earnings? Would the care provided be of high enough quality? Despite these concerns, the PGB became a recognized provision within the AWBZ in 1991, enabling those entitled to AWBZ financed care to opt for a care allowance instead of care in kind. However, only a limited amount of money was set aside for the PGB (3–4 per cent of the total home care budget); once that figure had been reached, other applicants had to accept services in kind, or join the PGB waiting list (Weekers and Pijl, 1998).[3]

In 1996, the PGB became much more strongly regulated. The government, and especially the Ministries of Finance and Social Affairs, were willing to agree to its continuation only under strict conditions, fearing that without regulation the money might not be used properly, care workers might be hired on the grey market, and that they might not be given proper working conditions. The new regulatory arrangements laid down that budget holders could receive a maximum of €1,090 per annum on their own account, available to be used as they pleased. The rest of their budget was to be administered by the Social Insurance Bank (SVB) and used only for paying workers contracted by the budget holder. Budget holders had to make legally valid contracts, checked by the SVB, with their workers. On this contractual basis the SVB paid the workers and deducted taxes and social security premiums.

Workers who were self-employed, or who worked for the same employer for no more than 12 hours on a maximum of 2 days per week, received their wages without deductions, and were responsible for declaring their own earnings. Nevertheless, the SVB had to pass their social security details to the tax office, so that their earnings were known. These rules made it impossible to pay workers undeclared wages, other than with the unregulated €1,090 per year. Budget holders could be helped to make valid contracts both by the SVB and by Per Saldo, the Association of Budget Holders, and over time, model contracts were developed, to suit different situations. Budget holders were free to decide how much they wanted to pay their helpers, so long as it was not below the national minimum wage. The budget was available to pay for six different kinds of work, each valued at a specified rate, as shown in Table 5.2.

The Regional Needs Assessment Boards (RIOs) assess how many hours, of which type of care, a person needs. Thus the PGB was calculated as the

Table 5.2   Rates of pay for different types of care work

Type of care	Remuneration per hour (€)
Specialized nursing	44.05
Nursing	39.55
Specialized personal care	28.77
Personal care	22.90
Domestic care	17.95
Simple household tasks	9.40

Note: Figures are for 2001.

number of assessed hours, multiplied by the corresponding hourly rates, less the means-tested co-payment, which all users of AWBZ services have to pay. Thus budget holders have to spend an additional amount of their own money, equal to their means-tested co-payment for AWBZ financed care.

The procedure for PGB budget holders was as follows. Applicants approached the RIO for assessment, and after this body had decided what kinds of care, and how much of it, they needed, they were given the choice between care services and a personal budget (PGB). If they opted for the PGB, the Care Insurance Office allocated the money. It paid €1,090 into the budget holder's account and the remaining amount to the SVB (Social Insurance Bank). Budget holders could then recruit their helpers, make a contract and employ them, with the SVB paying their wages.

The amounts paid to budget holders were about 75 per cent of the costs of care delivered as services. Here the rationale was that formal agencies have overhead costs which budget holders do not incur. Nevertheless, the net saving to the AWBZ was less than 25 per cent, because of the SVB's administrative costs in providing other facilities to budget holders: payments to budget holders when their contracted carer was ill, enabling them to hire someone else; advice about employment law; liability insurance; and legal assistance (CVZ, 2004b). Over time, Per Saldo developed into a helpful agency for its members, and became a strong and influential voice on policy relating to the PGB.

By 2000, the PGB had become a popular scheme, with demand outstripping resources (van den Wijngaart and Ramakers, 2004). Once the AWBZ became an open-ended scheme and all those entitled to AWBZ financial support could opt for cash and get it, the number of budget holders increased rapidly.

The *Shifting Boundaries* study in the Netherlands

In 2001, as part of the original project of which this study was a constituent part, interviews with budget holders and their carers were conducted in two rural areas not far from a fairly large city: Groningen in the north and Nijmegen in the east of the country. We obtained the names and addresses of budget holders, who met the requirements of the study, from the regional care insurance offices in these areas. In our sample there were 15 budget holders: 11 women, two couples and two men.

Even within this small sample, very large variations occurred in the amounts that people received in their budgets, related to their degree of incapacity. For example, one man who was totally dependent as a result of a major accident thirty years earlier received the largest budget of €34,090 a year. His wife was his principal carer and the SVB paid her wages into the household account. Another PGB user received €22,900 a year which she used to contract her daughter to deliver her care. In contrast there were also some budget holders with a small PGB. A woman aged 70 who had a back problem and could not walk well enough to do her own shopping received €400 a year for 3 hours of domestic help over a period of 3 weeks. Another couple where the wife had multiple physical problems received €1,090 a year which they used to pay someone who did 3 hours of housework for them. They also used care services (not paid for from the budget): a nurse came twice a day to give an insulin injection. Thus the budget arrangement allowed for very considerable flexibility in the type and source of care received.

All of the 14 helpers who were interviewed were women. The youngest was 35, nine were aged between 40 and 60, three between 61 and 70 and one helper was 79. Six of the 14 were relatives of the person they cared for: one spouse and five daughters and daughters in law. Five helpers had been recruited by word of mouth, one was a friend, one an acquaintance and one was recruited through formal advertisement. Among these helpers were two professional nurses, one person with a secondary education, but the remainder had only elementary education and a few years of vocational training, mostly in the domestic sector. A fairly typical life course pattern was that they had worked in the household or the conventional labour market before they married and stopped working either at marriage or at the birth of their first child. They had recommenced paid work when they considered they could reconcile it with their family responsibilities.

Helpers and their satisfaction with the work

Among our interviewees there was nobody who complained or seemed dissatisfied with the work or the working conditions. On the contrary, we received positive to very positive responses. People who had previously been strangers to each other developed strong attachments to the person they cared for. Several helpers who were not a relative of the budget holder said that they felt as if they were part of the family, that it was like being friends or that it was *'gezellig'* a Dutch expression meaning companionable. Only a few helpers fully realized that the budget holder was their employer.

Relatives contracted to deliver care also reported strong satisfaction. A number of daughters said that they liked to take care of their mother and/or father and that they knew their parent/s preferred to have a carer with whom they were familiar. Several helpers who were relatives mentioned explicitly that the payment had not affected their relationship at all. One daughter had noticed that her mother seemed to become a little bossier when she obtained the budget, but that did not last long. When her mother said she 'must' do certain things, the daughter replied she 'might' do them. She also let her mother know that all her demands could not be met immediately, she must wait until the daughter had time. Over the years this relationship had developed into an equable understanding of each other's needs.

Another daughter, one of the trained nurses in the sample, was her mother's paid carer but she also worked for some other budget holders, which she enjoyed. This contrast enabled her to understand the particular affective elements of the care relationship with her mother:

> With your mother it is different. It is in itself harder to give that care. When she is sad, it is also a bit your sadness. That is much closer. It is quite hard to care for your own relatives. I have only found out now. You only know that when you do it. But it is enrichment. You get to know many things about your parents that you might not understand otherwise.

Wages and working conditions of the carers

None of the helpers complained about the level of payment, but several (among them the two trained nurses) mentioned that they did much more than they were paid for. Most of them also said they did not mind or that they were happy to give that extra amount of care. For some helpers the payment meant a nice extra, a possibility to buy presents for grandchildren or to buy some nice clothes. But in other cases the wages constituted an important part of the income of the carer. An exceptional case was the man who broke his back when he was young and whose wife had taken care of him, unpaid, for almost 30 years. They considered their large budget as compensation for the hardship of the years before. Others felt similarly that the payment for their care was 'justice'. A carer daughter said:

> I find it a perfect scheme. I have somehow the feeling for myself of finally justice. I sacrifice days and nights and the community always speaks about care here and residential homes there. Then I think justice because I take care of her and it saves society a lot of money. For if she were in a residential home that would be much more expensive. I have had to give up a lot for it.

A majority of the helpers were rather poorly informed about their social rights. Best informed were those who had another job in the care sector beside their work for the budget holder. Most of them did not seem to mind very much. This can probably be explained by the fact that they relied on their husbands for income, occupational pension and medical insurance.

The issue of being unable to go away on a holiday occurred in several interviews. Some carers thought it was impossible to take a vacation because of the circumstances of the budget holder and regretted it. Others simply had not yet thought about it or said they did not find it important.

The situation of the carers

Our sample is by no means representative of the Dutch population, but it clearly illustrates the existence of a category of women who want to work and earn some money but who are not intent on having a career or maximizing their income. They want to be able to reconcile their work with their family life and the caring job is for them both convenient and satisfying. For a number of the helpers their paid job had formerly been an unpaid job. They considered the new situation as a continuation of the existing relationship and, therefore, they hardly considered themselves as employees on the formal labour market, which, in fact they were. The relatively informal character of the work also stimulated many helpers, including those who were not relatives, to do rather more than they were contracted for.

Even though the contracts of the helpers give them some security, their position is weak in more than one respect. Nothing has been regulated about time off and several helpers did not think they could or would want to take holidays or even a weekend off. Officially the helpers have paid holidays, but their practice shows it is difficult to realize that right. It also entails extra costs because during the absence of the helper substitute care is needed. Carers, as much as anybody else, need time for themselves. The financial position of the helpers is weak, because for most of them the PGB represents only a part-time job. They depend to a large extent on their husband's income and pension. Should they get divorced or if their husbands die, they may be faced with poverty. If the personal budget is continued we think that two improvements should be envisaged. Paid helpers should have guaranteed time off, and they ought to be able to build up an occupational pension.

Budget holders and their satisfaction with the scheme

It was striking that none of the budget holders considered themselves to be 'employers' in the fullest sense, although they were all positive about their helpers being paid to care for them. This was considered as a matter of course when the helper was someone from outside the family whom they did not know before. But the budget holders also felt very satisfied about payments to members of their family. For some it ameliorated problems of reciprocity and fairness: an elderly widow cared for by her daughter said: 'I am pleased to be able to give her something for the work she is doing. I have always taken care of my parents and I never got anything.'

Others liked the fact that the payment guaranteed that their relative would care for them: 'I like it [the payment] very much. In good and bad weather, in winter when it snows she comes' and yet others felt that the payment allowed them to have precisely the carer they most preferred. In this case their daughter was their carer: 'As long as she gets her money I think it is splendid. My husband and I get cared for and that is the most important thing. I would not know how we could manage otherwise. He does not want anyone else. He does not want a nurse, so she does it.' None of the budget holders were unhappy with the quality of care they received, and some respondents emphasized that they were very happy with the quality of the care. Where they were cared for by relatives, this often reflected the fact that the individuals involved had shared a very long biography. The husband who broke his back 30 years ago said: 'I think nobody can do it better or more easily than my wife, because she has done it for so long. The district nurse was here one day and said: "we could never do this, you don't have to say a word, if you two look at each other that is enough." '

An elderly woman who did not want to be washed by a male nurse said about her daughter's help: 'Nice, really fantastic'. She also thought it was cosier (more *gezellig*) than being washed by a nurse. The daughter had had some problems at first with the intimacy of washing her mother, but both mother and daughter had overcome this and were very satisfied with the situation.

Relations with helpers who were not members of the family were friendly. Some budget holders explicitly called the helper a friend. One respondent called her helper 'such a dear'. Several budget holders stressed the importance of being able to trust the helper and rely on her. The interviews also showed that, even if they did not understand the scheme, the budget holders knew they could tell their helpers how they wanted to be cared for. Those who were capable of managing the relationship told their carers what they wanted and their carers listened. In one or two cases the budget holder mentioned that she talked with the helper when an argument came up, but resolving problems was certainly not an important issue.

Thus the presence of the budget in the care relationship had only positive effects. The one difficulty that the budget holders reported was the bureaucracy pertaining to the scheme itself. They were rather confused about the details of the various arrangements that make up the PGB scheme and were unable to say how high their budget was, what the entitlements of their helpers were in terms of wages, paid holidays or social security. On the other hand, several budget holders were aware of the fact that there were problems with the payment of the workers, because the SVB was quite often late with its payments. In one case the family of the budget holder paid the helpers when the SVB was several months late. A number of budget holders were unable to deal with all the paperwork so the administration was in the hands of somebody else, one of the children, a son-in-law or the helper herself.

Budget holders' experiences with the PGB

From the point of view of the budget holders, the PGB was a much valued scheme. They could arrange their care the way they wanted it: it was real user-directed care. They liked their helpers, and where the helpers were relatives the budget holders were happy to be able to reciprocate by paying for the care they received. They did not have to say 'please' and 'thank you' all the time. This contributed to their quality of life. The only drawback was the enormous and often incomprehensible bureaucracy of the scheme.

Clearly the PGB is a very good innovation that should be made available to those who opt for it and who can handle it. We have one reservation, however: we consider that the PGB should only be given to those who can handle it by themselves or to those who have a network whose members understand finance. There are reasons to be cautious about situations where budget holders lose grip on their life, become confused or are otherwise unable to successfully negotiate with carers and do not have such a network whose members can keep an eye on them.

Equity and cost effectiveness of the PGB

It surprised our colleagues from other countries that rather high amounts were allocated and they wondered how this was justified. The question of equity was also raised because similar cases received different amounts of money.

Let us look at the most striking case in our sample, that of the elderly lady who had taken care of her husband with a broken back for almost 30 years. Her husband's budget amounted to €34,000, which was given for 19 hours of nursing and 3 hours of domestic care a week. The wife did the nursing and she paid for someone to undertake the domestic work with the PGB. After deductions for tax and social premiums payable on the PGB (which reduced her gross income by over one-third), and payment for the domestic help, the wife's net earnings were considerably less than €34,000 but still quite a high amount. This arose because most of the help was defined as nursing, and the rate of pay for nursing was relatively high. However, the wife had no nursing qualification. According to the PGB rules, the budget holder has the responsibility to hire help of sufficient quality. In this case the budget holder was more than satisfied and even the district nurse had to admit that the wife was doing a splendid job. Quality in this case was not based on diplomas. Although the wife was paid for 19 hours she had to be available 24/7 to do a heavy caring job. We think it is not unreasonable to pay good wages to someone who is responsible for such demanding work. However, this case seems, even in the Dutch context, a bit exceptional. We had in our small sample an almost identical case, in the other region where we did our fieldwork. Again a male paraplegic had broken his back many years ago, was only a few years younger than the case discussed above and his wife had also taken care of him. But in this case, the gross budget was €17,000 a year, about half the amount received in the other case. This budget consisted of 7 hours of domestic help and 8.5 hours of nursing bought from the home care agency. The total number of hours was lower and contained less nursing time and more domestic care time, paid at a much cheaper rate. Having paid for the nursing care, delivered by the formal services the wife of the budget holder had less than half this amount left for herself.

The difference between the two cases is mainly caused by differences in the assessment: one assessor has been a lot more generous than the other. Additionally, we must bear in mind that some people are much better than others in presenting their case. The second largest budget (€22,900) was allocated to a widow who lived with her daughter who was a professional nurse. She was paid with the budget for 18 hours of work. She also worked for some other patients, but the care of her mother was her main occupation. In this case the budget could be considered a realistic remuneration for 18 hours of work by a self-employed nurse. If the mother had not lived with her daughter she probably would have been in a nursing home.

In these three cases the carers all did a lot more than they were paid for. We found similar results for other family members who were paid carers. Even some of the non-family paid carers did more work than they were paid for. Although some improvements could be made, we judge that the PGB mostly works out fairly equitably, with helpers receiving reasonable wages for their work. If they have to give up other paid work, the PGB offers them fair financial compensation.

From a financial point of view the PGB is an effective scheme. It is cheap in comparison with care in kind. Budget holders receive 75 per cent of the price of home care provided by the formal home care services. In addition it turns out that, over the years, budget holders spend on average not more than 85 per cent of their allowance (CVZ, 2004b). Taking the costs made by the SVB into account one could conclude that personal budgets cost on average only two-thirds of care delivered by formal organizations. But there is one more reason why the PGB is cost saving: it encourages family members to keep persons in need of care at home even if they qualify for a nursing home. There were quite a few examples of this effect in our sample. One would think there would be every reason for Dutch policymakers to continue the PGB scheme, both because of its financial merits and because of user satisfaction. The future of the PGB, however, is as yet uncertain.

Current policy change and debates concerning the Dutch care allowance

Since the fieldwork was undertaken in 2001, there have been considerable changes in the AWBZ in general and in the PGB in particular. In April 2003, AWBZ entitlements were redefined more globally as 'functions'. The seven functions are: domestic care, personal care, nursing, supporting supervision, activating supervision, treatment and permanent or temporary stay. For all these functions (except for treatment and long-term stay), a personal budget was obtainable. The personal budgets for people with different needs were drawn together, so that only one personal budget remained for the different categories of users.

The amount of money that budget holders could use without having to account for it was changed from €1,090 a year to 1.5 per cent of the total budget with a minimum of €250 and a maximum of €1,250 a year. Budget holders were no longer obliged to use the services of the SVB to pay their care workers, but these remained available for those who wanted them. Budget holders could receive the money directly into their bank account to pay their care workers, but they had to account for their expenses afterwards (Per Saldo, 2002).

At the end of 2004 the Junior Minister of Health, Well-being and Sports (VWS) published a policy document on the personal budget. This estimated that by the end of 2004 the total number of budget holders would reach almost 70,000. The growth of the number of budget holders slowed down in 2004.[4] 52 per cent of the budget holders were assessed as needing one single function, while 48 per cent needed two or more functions. Sixty-seven per cent of budget holders needed domestic care, 28 per cent personal care and 16 per cent nursing. Over the years it appeared that budget holders underspent: on average they did not use 15 per cent of the budget, which they had to pay back. It was estimated that in 2004 the total costs of all personal budgets would amount to €889 million. This was 4.5 per cent of the total AWBZ expenditure, but served 10 per cent of all AWBZ users (Ministerie VWS, 2004b).

At the same time, the Regional Needs Assessment Boards (RIOs) tried to determine more precisely how much care family members could be expected to give each other for free. A paper on 'customary care', offered some provisional guidelines. At the end of 2004 the concept 'customary care' was applied only to people who needed care and shared their household with others. People living alone were not considered to have others who could be expected to take care of them. If, however, a neighbour or friend had been providing care prior to the assessment, the RIO would consider this as 'customary care' and allocate only as much AWBZ care as was needed *in addition to* the care provided by the neighbour. Within a household consisting of several adults, the healthy adults were expected to do all the housework, so the assessment could not include domestic care.[5] The partner of the sick or disabled person was also expected to provide personal care during the first three months of the sickness or disability. After that period a new assessment could include personal care, depending on the situation of the healthy partner (e.g., which other obligations s/he had in terms of work, social participation etc.). Carers were not required to give up a paid job (LVIO, 2003). The care individuals had to give each other according to these RIO norms was referred to not only as 'customary care' but also as 'enforceable care'.

The application of these guidelines on 'customary care' led to reduced entitlements. Some care users who did not agree with the decision of the RIO presented their cases to the CVZ.[6] The CVZ concluded that family carers had become less willing than they used to be to provide care without pay. The CVZ called this: monetarization of informal care, a trend which it considered highly undesirable, and advised the Junior Minister:

- to extend the concept of 'customary care' so that partners should be expected to provide personal care for longer than 3 months; and
- to forbid budget holders to hire as their paid carers co-resident family members (CVZ, 2004a).

In response, the Junior Minister requested more data about the effects of the guidelines on customary care prior to making a decision. She also presented another proposal, based on suggestions made by Per Saldo. A person in need of care who applies for a PGB on the basis that his/her carer is overburdened should not be allowed to pay this carer unless s/he gives up other activities, notably paid work, in order to become a paid carer. The Junior Minister also proposed to reintroduce the system of capping the total amount of money for PGBs. In 2005, a maximum of €942 million was available nationally for PGBs (Ministerie van VWS, 2004b). If the *Social Support Act* comes into effect in 2006, this too will have considerable consequences for the PGB, because domestic care (and in time possibly other functions as well), will be taken out of the AWBZ.

The uncertain future of the personal budget: An appraisal

The state of affairs at the end of 2004

The cost containment policy for long-term care has already had its impact on the personal budget in two ways:

1. due to higher co-payments for AWBZ financed care, persons who formerly had a low budget (lower than the new means-tested maximum co-payment) have lost it, others have received smaller sums; and
2. access to AWBZ financed care is no longer based exclusively on the need for care. A new criterion, the absence of informal care, has been added. According to the new guidelines, informal care is to a certain extent *enforceable* among members of the same household.

As far as we know, the Netherlands is unique in trying to enforce family care. We have serious doubts about this course of action. The study by the SCP has once more confirmed that most Dutch people consider it only natural to take care of their family members. Why should they then be forced to do it? Caring puts a heavy burden on many carers, but this burden produces even more stress when it is enforced.

The Junior Minister expressed in her recent policy paper concerns about the quality of care delivered by family members who were paid out of a PGB. She feared that some family members might care primarily for financial reasons. We believe there is even more reason to be concerned about the quality of *enforced, unpaid* care by family members. What will this do to the relationship between carer and cared-for? It is also the case that the Assessment Boards are entitled to probe quite deeply into family affairs. They base their decisions concerning the allocation of care on their judgement of family relationships and circumstances of the persons involved and they prescribe how much care family members should give each other. Here ethical issues arise concerning the extent and type of public intervention in private life which need to be further addressed.

The uncertain future

It is difficult to predict what will happen to the PGB. Developments will depend on:

- which functions are kept in the new AWBZ (if any) and whether they are suitable for personal budgets;
- what tasks will be given to the municipalities and under what conditions; and
- how personal budgets will be regulated if their allocation is transferred to local authorities. It is likely that eligibility criteria will become even stricter than at present, perhaps becoming means tested.

Commentary

Dutch policies are at the moment mainly inspired by the so-called Lisbon strategy, which aims at making Europe the most competitively driven economy in the world. As a consequence, productivity must be increased and public expenditure reduced. To enhance labour market participation, early retirement is discouraged and will be phased out, to be replaced by a scheme which allows individual workers to save up earnings in order to leave the labour market maximally 2.5 years before the formal retirement age. The efforts to increase labour market participation concentrate on older workers, but scarcely focus on women of working age who are outside the labour market or working part-time. The earlier policy goal to increase the economic independence of women seems to have been forgotten.

Large reforms are under way in the social sector in an attempt to reduce expenditure. The reforms in health and long-term care can be seen in the same perspective. The ageing of the population has made the issue of cost containment in the care sector yet more urgent. Other ideological considerations, which have driven the agenda, include:

- the existence of a latent demand for care, which should be prevented from becoming manifest;
- disapproval of the monetarization of informal care; and
- the value system of the Christian Democratic Party which wants to enhance the role of the family.

In the design of care policy important facts and research results have been ignored. The SCP study on family carers has shown that Dutch citizens do not shun their responsibilities. Not only do 13 per cent of the adult population invest time and energy in the care of relatives or friends, many carers also invest in it financially. In 2001, 8 per cent of carers felt very heavily burdened or overburdened. This was before the criteria for admission to AWBZ care had been tightened. The figures on the use of care services by the population of 55 and over demonstrate, that in 1999,

73 per cent of this age group did not use any help at all and that more or less equal percentages (±10) used formal, informal or private care. Only 50.5 per cent of those who were heavily impaired used formal home care services. This certainly does not confirm the hypothesis that the Dutch turn too readily to the formal services.

Another relevant study, which looks at proposed policy changes and their effect on the demand of care, indicates that income plays a decisive role in enabling dependent people to stay at home (RIVM and SCP, 2004). If the AOW pension does not keep up with inflation it is to be expected that the demand for intra-mural care by older people with lower incomes will increase. No decisions have been taken yet about the future of the AOW, but policy makers ought to be aware that such decisions will have undesired consequences in the care sector. The same study also calculates the effects of the removal of domestic care from the AWBZ. Almost half of those who receive nothing but domestic care from the AWBZ are also entitled to other AWBZ functions, but do not claim these because they have access to informal or private care. If domestic care were taken out of the AWBZ the estimated demand for personal care would increase by the year 2020 with ±50 per cent in addition to the increase on the basis of demographic factors, while the demand for intra-mural care is estimated to increase by 40 per cent.

Keeping these facts in mind, we believe the government has over-looked the unintended consequences of its policies. Not only will these policies reduce the labour market participation of women, the effects on the costs of care may also be other than predicted. In the short term, care expenditure will fall, but over time there will be increased demand for more costly care provision. When this demand becomes manifest, how are the needs to be met?

We think it would be more effective to stimulate the use of personal budgets than to remove domestic care from the long-term care insurance because:

- the personal budget is cheaper than care in kind;
- those who are paid with a PGB, especially family members, give a lot more care than they are paid for, in other words paid care does not drive out but helps to retain unpaid care;
- carers who feel appreciated because they are being paid for their work and/or who know there is money to buy help when it is needed most, will be able to continue their work as carers longer;
- the personal budgets together with unpaid family care can keep heavily dependent people out of institutions;
- from a psychological point of view it is better to reward those who do their best to keep a dependent relative or friend at home than to

create an atmosphere of distrust by pretending that family carers are only calculating and should be kept under sharp control lest they give too little care. The latter has a negative effect on the social climate as well; and

- it creates opportunities for women to participate in the labour market.

It seems unlikely, however, that the Dutch government will change its course of action.

Effects of the proposed policies on the cared-for and their carers

We have studied the effects of the PGB on the cared-for, their carers and on their mutual relationship. Our findings were very positive, in spite of a few weaknesses of the scheme. Budget holders were very pleased with the scheme and their carers were satisfied as well, even though the budget did not give them the full range of social security. We found no negative effects at all of the payments on the personal relationships between carers and cared-for.

The new policies will provide those in need of care with less help unless they pay for it privately. Those who cannot afford it will become dependent again on their informal network, and even if they receive a personal budget their informal network will be expected to provide an amount of care for free to be determined by the Assessment Board. We noticed how pleased some of our respondents were about being able to pay for their help. It is doubtful how much of this facility will be retained. We fear that the relationship between carer and cared-for will become much more stressful when family care is felt to be enforced. Less formal care and more informal care will lead to a reduction of jobs in the formal care sector as well as with budget holders. The jobs, which disappear, are primarily those which consist mainly of domestic care. What will the women do who lose their jobs? Some might decide not to return to the labour market at all. Considering their age and education the labour market opportunities of a considerable number of the helpers in our study are slight. They will become fully dependent on their partner again. Others may leave the care sector and find a formal job elsewhere.

Others again may decide to look for employment on the grey market. Some care users will prefer to hire someone on the grey market instead of paying €11.80 per hour for home care by the formal services. Those who end up employed in this way will lose their formal contracts and what social security they had (such as sick pay), but their net income will remain about the same, if they don't declare their wages. Growing competition on the grey market may emerge once women in the new EU member states discover that they can earn relatively high wages on the Dutch grey care market.

The implication of the policy changes described is that formal work will be changed back into informal paid or unpaid work. Those who pay the price of these policy changes will be mostly women, especially those with limited opportunities in the labour market. The PGB helped them to enter the labour market or to stay in paid employment, by becoming the carer of a budget holder. One of the helpers in our sample said about the PGB: 'finally justice'. She had given up a lot to be able to take care of her mother and thought it was only right to be paid. Along with many other paid helpers of budget holders, she must feel very disappointed by recent policy developments.

Notes

1. The SCP made a distinction between:

   - *The 'potential' demand for care*: This covers the care needs of all those who would be entitled to care on the basis of an assessment of a Regional Needs Assessment Board (RIO) if they ask only for an assessment;
   - *The 'met' demand for care*: This is the expected use of care extrapolated on the basis of actual use in 2002; and
   - *The 'recognized' demand for care*: This is the care that would be needed if all those who were assessed would receive the care they were entitled to. In other words, if there were no waiting lists.

2. For those who have lived abroad between ages 15 and 65, 2 per cent of the state pension is withheld for every year abroad.
3. three more allowances for persons with specific problems were introduced:

   1. an allowance for persons with learning disabilities (1996);
   2. an allowance for persons with mental health problems (2001); and
   3. an allowance for persons with physical handicaps (2001) (van den Wijngaart and Ramakers, 2004).

   In this chapter we exclusively focus on the allowance for nursing and care (referred to as personal budget or PGB).
4. These figures comprise all budget recipients, not only those who used to get the budget for care and nursing. Therefore, they are not comparable with figures for the period before 2003.
5. There were a few exceptions, e.g., for persons older than 75.
6. The Care Insurance Board, an independent administrative Board which coordinates and implements the mandatory medical care insurance and the AWBZC.

Bibliography

Boer, A. H. de, Schellingerhout, R. and Timmermans, J. M. (2003) *Mantelzorg in getallen*, Den Haag: Social and Cultural Planning Bureau.

Centraal Bureau voor de Statistiek (CBS) online at: www.cbs.nl/cijfers/kerncijfers

College voor zorgverzekeringen (CVZ) (2004a) *Signalement PGB en mantelzor*, Diemen.

College voor zorgverzekeringen (CVZ) (2004b) *Kernmonitor PGB nieuwe stijl*, Diemen.

College voor zorgverzekeringen (CVZ) (2004c) *Financiële positie Algemeen Fonds Bijzondere Ziektekosten*. Diemen.

FNV loonwijzer, online at: www.loonwijzer.nl

Graaff, Fuusje de, and Devillé, W. L. J. M. (2003) *Kansen en belemmeringen voor allochtonen op de arbeidsmarkt in de zorg-en welzijnssector. Een literatuurstudie*, Tilburg: OSA-publicatie, ZW 43.

Keuzenkamp, S. and Oudhof, K. (2000) *Emancipatiemonitor*, Den Haag: Social and Cultural Planning Bureau.

Kleine Gids voor de Nederlandse sociale Zekerheid (2004) 2, Kluwer, Deventer.

Klerk, M.M.Y. de (ed.) (2004) *Zorg en wonen voor kwetsbare ouderen: Rapportage Ouderen*, Den Haag: Social and Cultural Planning Bureau and LASA.

LVIO (Association of Assessment Boards) (2003) *Werkdocument Gebruikelijke Zorg*, Den Haag.

Miltenburg, T., Mensink J. and Ramakers C. (1993) *Experimenten Cliëntgebonden Budget Verzorging en Verpleging. Beleidsgerichte evaluatie*, Nijmegen: Institute for Applied Social Sciences.

Ministerie van Volksgezondheid, Welzijn en Sport (2004a) *Op weg naar een bestendig stelsel voor langdurige zorg en maatschappelijke ondersteuning*, Den Haag.

Ministerie van Volksgezondheid, Welzijn en Sport (2004b) *Beleidsbrief 'Het PGB Gewogen'. Evaluatie en Vooruitblik*, Den Haag.

OSA (2003) *Rapportage Arbeidsmarkt in Zorg en Welzij*, Tilburg: OSA, publicatie ZW 48.

Pen, M. and Tissing, H. A. (2000) *Vluchtelingen op de arbeidsmarkt in de sector Zorg en Welzijn*, Tilburg: OSA, publicatie ZW 10.

Per Saldo (2002) *PGB Actueel*, Utrecht.

Portegijs, W., Boelens, A. and Olsthoorn, L. (2004) *Emancipatiemonitor*, Den Haag: Social and Cultural Planning Bureau and CBS.

RIVM and SCP (2004) *Ouderen nu en in de toekomst*, Bilthoven.

Timmermans, J. and Woittiez, I. (2004) *Advies ramingen verpleging en verzorging*, Den Haag: Social and Cultural Planning Bureau.

Timmermans, J. M. (ed.) (2003) *Mantelzorg: Over hulp van en aan mantelzorger*, Den Haag: Social and Cultural Planning Bureau.

Weekers, S. and Pijl, M. (1998) *Home Care and Care Allowances in the European Union*, Utrecht: NIZW.

Windt, W van der, Kalsbeek, H. and Hingstman, L. (2000) *Verpleging en verzorging in kaart gebracht*, Utrecht: LCVV.

Wijngaart, M. van den and Ramakers, C. (2004) 'Het persoonsgebonden budget in Nederland van 1990–2003. Een overzicht van ontwikkelingen, beleid en onderzoek', in *Handboek Zorg Thuis 3/45–3/60*, Maarssen: Elsevier Gezondheidszorg.

6

Issues in the Development of the Direct Payments Scheme for Older People in England

Sue Yeandle and Bernadette Stiell

Introduction

This chapter examines the Direct Payments Scheme as it applies to older people in England. The scheme for older people was introduced through parliamentary regulations in February 2000, and at the time the *Shifting Boundaries* project was undertaken in 2002, was being used by only a comparatively small number of older users. Between 2000 and 2004 the UK government emphasized its intention to extend and develop the scheme on a number of occasions, urging local authorities, through their Social Services Departments and in cooperation with other agencies, to encourage older people to consider this option. That official emphasis remains today, although, as we show below, take-up of Direct Payments among older people has been slow. Almost all English local authorities now operate a version of the Scheme, which, as already indicated in the opening chapter, differs in a number of important respects from the cash-for-care schemes in place in the other countries studied in this book.

Compared with some of these other cash-for-care schemes, the UK's Direct Payments scheme is a relatively regulated policy development which has sought, from the outset, to enable care users to employ their care workers or personal assistants in ways which are consistent with UK employment law. Arrangements have been in place to ensure that the Direct Payment received is spent on purchasing caring labour and related services, and does not disappear into the receiving household's finances. A stated aim of the policy has been to enable care users to make their own choices about when, how and from whom they receive care services. One particularly important feature has been the rule that members of the care user's family or household are not eligible to be paid to provide care to the person receiving Direct Payments, although this strict veto on payment of relatives has, since 2003, been relaxed a little in a very small number of special circumstances.

The Direct Payments scheme is the result of extensive lobbying by campaigners for the rights of disabled people, particularly with regard to independent living, and has been heralded by government as an important development in the delivery of personal social services, which it wishes to see extended, developed and promoted by all local authorities as an option which older care users can choose. It arises, as this chapter will demonstrate, in the context of very extensive demand for domiciliary care services in support of older people, a group which, in the UK as elsewhere in Europe, is projected to grow rapidly in the first half of the 21st century.

This increased demand for services to people living in their own homes, and for services which are more flexible, more tailored to individual needs and preferences and over which care recipients can exercise considerable personal control, needs to be met from a supply of caring labour which is under pressure from several fronts. The care needs of dependent older people living at home can be met through either the paid work of care assistants, 'home helps' and social work or health service staff, or through the unpaid work of 'informal' (usually family) carers. The latter are usually co-resident with, or live within daily proximity of, the elderly care recipient. Traditionally, the main sources of both these types of caring labour have been middle-aged women (Yeandle *et al.*, 1999). Those who took on the roles of 'home help' or care assistant were typically unqualified women who had taken a long break from paid employment, or who had not been able to enter qualified jobs in their thirties and early forties, often because of the responsibilities of motherhood. 'Informal' carers of older people were often their middle aged daughters, with the daughter who had weakest attachment to paid employment traditionally accepting this role (Lewis and Meredith, 1988). For a variety of reasons, indicated below, this source of caring labour is shrinking. More men are now in caring roles, often supporting frail elderly wives – but spouses caring for their very aged partners are frequently unable to meet all of their needs, especially if these are physically demanding or complex. Recent policy in this area has thus been developing in the context of an increasing demand for caring labour and a shrinking supply of those who have traditionally provided it. It is important that the introduction and development of Direct Payments for older people is explored in this context.

A key question concerns not only how much more flexible and responsive caring services can be when delivered through Direct Payments, but also whether the employment arrangements facilitated by the Direct Payments scheme are, or can become, positive for care workers, and capable of attracting new sources of labour into this type of work. Most previous work on Direct Payments has explored what the policy is like for those requiring and using care services. The study reported here explores this aspect, but has also asked, 'What is it like to provide caring labour through the Direct Payments scheme?'; 'Does the scheme and its regulations offer protection from employment risks to care workers, and is it capable of assuring high quality in both service provision and job quality?'

This chapter will suggest that despite being heavily regulated in some respects, the UK's Direct Payments scheme, as exemplified in the cases we studied, does not protect and support care workers in relation to requirements to work beyond contract, issues of health and safety, or protection from unreasonable or inappropriate behaviour on the part of employers. There is, despite a regulatory framework, considerable variability in the type of labour that comes forward, and the quality of the relationship that emerges.

As part of the wider ESRC funded study described in Chapter 1, the UK study explored the context for, and policy background to, the development of Direct Payments as a cash-for-care scheme. The study looked at how the policy was extended to the 65 plus age group, and, in one large northern city, examined the operation of the scheme in considerable detail. The research methods used included documentary analysis of relevant literature and policy statements, policy-focused interviews with key individuals involved in the development and opera-tion of the policy, and in-depth face-to-face exploratory interviews. The latter were conducted both with older people using the scheme, and with the paid care workers/personal assistants they employed using the cash they received as a Direct Payment. The older care users were accessed via the city's Scheme for Direct Payment Users (SDPU, described below), and their care workers were contacted following the care user interview, with the agreement and permission of the older people concerned. Most of the interviews with care workers and care users were conducted in the older person's home. Care users were not present at the care worker inter-views, and vice versa, although some care users were in the presence of a spouse or other family member during their interview. In total 10 inter-views with care users and 15 interviews with care workers were undertaken. The research enabled us to gain a clear picture of some of the practical issues facing users, workers and supporting agencies, and to explore how the scheme was experienced by both care users and care workers.

The chapter begins with a review of factors affecting the demand for domiciliary care among persons aged 65 years old and over, giving also a brief outline of some of the issues affecting the supply of caring labour in the UK. We then describe the introduction of the Direct Payments scheme, and discuss how the scheme was extended to older care users, using the northern city where we carried out our research as our example. The final section of the chapter explores the experiences of the older people and care workers who were using the scheme, focusing on both the benefits of the scheme as they saw them, and giving voice to some of their concerns about its operation.

Supply and demand in the care of older people living at home

In 2003 there were an estimated 11 million people of pensionable age[1] resident in the UK, representing 18.5 per cent of the total population. Their distribution, by sex and age group, is shown in Table 6.1. Rising life expectancy for both sexes has resulted in a marked growth in the number of people over 85 years, now numbering almost 1.2 million – an increase of about 30 per cent over the previous decade (*Population Trends*, 2003).

Recent changes among the older population in the UK include substantial growth in the number of older people living in single

Table 6.1 Older people in the UK: Mid-2003 estimates of the resident population (thousands)

		All persons	*Men*	*Women*
All of pensionable age				
	65/60+	11,014	4,038	6,976
In age bands:				
	65–69	2,657	1,279	1,378
	70–74	2,348	1,075	1,273
	75–79	1,933	820	1,112
	80–84	1,468	551	918
	85–89	706	219	486
	90+	399	94	305

Note: Figures may not add to totals due to rounding.
Source: Office for National Statistics. Crown Copyright 2004.

person households. In 2001, among those aged 85 and over, more than 70 per cent of women and about 42 per cent of men lived alone. By contrast, only a small minority of older people lived in residential care. In the same year, just 4 per cent of people aged 65 and over (compared with 5 per cent in 1991) resided in communal establishments, and even among the very aged (those aged 85 or older) only 18 per cent (compared with 21 per cent a decade before) were living in a residential care environment.

Level of care need among the older population

Many older people are independent and active, particularly among those who are under 85. Nevertheless, about a third of people aged 65 or over report that they need some help with routine domestic tasks, self-care and mobility within the home. A recent assessment of the proportion of older people living in private households who are unable to manage some aspects of daily living alone is shown in Table 6.2.

Most of those who need help report that their usual source of support is their spouse or partner or another household member, a source of help by definition not available to those older people who live alone.[2] As Table 6.2 shows, women report higher levels of disability than men

Table 6.2   Older people who are unable to manage certain tasks without help, by gender and age, 1998–1999 (percentages)

Age group		Domestic	Self-care	Mobility
65–69	Men	17	13	7
	Women	26	24	9
70–74	Men	17	16	5
	Women	35	33	15
75–59	Men	28	28	11
	Women	45	40	21
80–84	Men	46	47	22
	Women	58	54	28
85+	Men	56	51	24
	Women	80	67	52
All aged 65+	Men	25	23	10
	Women	42	38	20

Source: General Household Survey, Office for National Statistics; *Continuous Household Survey*, Northern Ireland Statistics and Research Agency (Table 5.22) from Social Focus on Men, © Crown copyright 2001. Published with the permission of the Controller of Her Majesty's Stationery Office (HMSO).

Table 6.3 Usual sources of help for those aged 65 and over able to do various tasks only with help, UK 1998–1999 (percentages)

Usual source of help	Mobility*	Getting in/out of bed	Walking down the road	Using public transport
Spouse/partner	57	54	46	48
Other household member	19	14	10	7
Non-household relative	11	9	25	24
Friend/neighbour	3	0	12	9
Paid help	3	2	1	1
NHS or personal social services	2	20	4	3
Other	5	1	2	7
All	100	100	100	100

Note: *Getting around the house, getting to the toilet, using stairs.
Source: *General Household Survey*, Office for National Statistics; *Continuous Household Survey*, Northern Ireland Statistics and Research Agency.

in all older age groups. In addition, because of differential longevity between the sexes, older women are less likely than older men to have a spouse available to care for them. About a fifth of those who need help in getting in and out of bed usually rely on support provided by health and social services (see Table 6.3), but otherwise reliance on providers of care who are paid to deliver the service they give is limited.

Future projections of the demand for care

In England, the numbers of very old people (aged 85 and over) are projected to rise by 88 per cent, from 0.9 million in 1996 to 1.7 million in 2031 (Government Actuary's Department; Office for National Statistics 2000). The financial implications of providing long-term care for this growing number of older people prompted the *Royal Commission on Long Term Care 1997–9* and led to renewed interest in the future demand for, cost of and affordability of care provision. It is clear that domiciliary services for older people will need to expand substantially to keep pace with these demographic pressures. The number of home care hours will need to rise by about 48 per cent from the 1996 figure (about 2m hours per week) to nearly 3m per week in 2031 (Wittenberg *et al.*, 2001). To deliver this volume of home care will require at least 40,000 additional home care workers, assuming each can provide 25 hours of direct care each week.

The financial circumstances of older people

Older people's average incomes vary, with disparities relating to age, sex and ethnicity, and with the oldest among the poorest. However, the average net incomes of UK pensioners grew by 64 per cent in real terms between 1979 and 1996/7 (compared with 36 per cent for the whole population). This trend has continued in recent years, with average incomes rising faster for pensioners than for the rest of the population, and with a widening gap between the richest and poorest pensioners (Age Concern, 2001b).

Much growth in pensioners' incomes arose from increases in occupational pensions, investments and benefits. State benefits account for about half of pensioners' income, occupational pensions about 26 per cent, investments and private pensions 14 per cent, and earnings 8 per cent (DSS, 2000). Although the majority of older people have occupational pensions, recent calculations show their median value was just £55 a week in 1999/2000, with 30 per cent of pensioners receiving less than this (Age Concern, 2001b). Almost three-quarters of pensioners have investment income (DSS, 2000), but, again, the median amount received is small. Of pensioner households, 43 per cent have less than £1,500 in savings, while only about one in five has over £20,000 (Age Concern, 2001b).

State benefits available to older people include the state retirement pension (in 2004–05 it was £82.05 per week for a single pensioner), and income-related benefits such as the Minimum Income Guarantee, Housing Benefit and Council Tax Benefit.[3] About a third of older people receive these income support benefits (DSS, 2000). Disability benefits[4] – Attendance Allowance, Carer's Allowance,[5] Disability Living Allowance[6] – are received by about one in five pensioners.

These trends and projections suggest a likely future scenario of sharp growth in demand for domiciliary care among older people, with the richest pensioners increasingly able to resource their own needs, even when living alone. This affluent group will undoubtedly seek to exercise choice, and is more likely than the less well-off to have earlier life or work experience, such as managing employees and financial affairs and making strategic plans, which will enable them to do so effectively. This affluent group is likely to welcome the introduction of Direct Payments, with its flexibility to add in their own resources, and the greater control and choice the system offers. At the same time, most older people, and especially those who are poorest (and who typically have the more severe health and disability needs) are likely to remain in need of support which is almost entirely publicly funded. All evidence suggests that the preference for remaining as long as possible in one's own home is widespread across all groups of older people. The Direct Payments scheme has been heralded by some as offering flexibility and choice for care users alongside cost-effective and manageable delivery for both statutory agencies and care providers. Its success, however, will also be dependent upon the continuing availability of sufficient caring labour, and it is, therefore, to labour supply that this chapter now turns.

The demographics and economics of care supply

The evidence presented above suggests strong growth in the potential demand for caring labour on the part of older people, and great variation in older people's capacity to cover the costs of their care from their own resources. Likely increased demand for caring labour has been highlighted, and the continuing debate about how far this demand should be met from public funds has been alluded to. This section considers supply issues in all forms of caring labour, paid and unpaid, and outlines some of the demographic and economic factors that are currently shaping labour supply.

In previous work, the editors of this volume have identified a range of categories of people providing care to older people (Ungerson, 2004), and it is relevant to return to this here. It includes:

1. *Carers* (sometimes 'informal carers') – unpaid, usually friends or relatives;
2. *'Supported carers'* (carers who receive an income replacement payment, e.g., Carer's Allowance, from the state in recognition of their caring labour and responsibilities, again usually kin);
3. *Employed care workers* (variously employed by statutory, voluntary or private organizations, including some with professional or vocational qualifications to care);
4. *Agency workers* (for whom providing caring labour may be only one part of their job description, and who may be technically 'self-employed');
5. *Personal assistants* who are directly employed by older care users with their own resources or with resources made available to them by the state in lieu of services (e.g., via Direct Payments).

Categories 1 and 2 above have historically been co-resident or locally resident kin, most often daughters or daughters-in-law. They have typically included women with weak attachment to the formal labour market (often those who have left employment for long spells to raise families), with short or broken employment histories and relatively low levels of formal qualification. They also include co-resident spouses, usually themselves over retirement age. The growing numbers of older people living alone, increased intergenerational geographical mobility, and the rising educational attainments and labour force participation of women will all affect the future availability of these types of unpaid care. Rising living standards for many younger people, and many families' dependency on two incomes from employment to meet living and housing costs, also contribute to a marked drop in the numbers of people available to fulfil unpaid caring roles, whether as wholly unpaid carers, or as 'supported' carers in receipt of income replacement benefits (which in the UK have never been large enough genuinely to replace possible alternative earned income). However, recent evidence confirms that many people now combine paid employment and unpaid caring.

For the first time in 2001, the Census of Population in the UK, conducted every ten years, asked everyone to indicate whether or not they provided unpaid care for another person. This revealed that 82 per cent of households containing a person with a limiting long-term illness aged 65–74, and 86 per cent of households containing a person with such an illness aged 75 or older, did not contain a co-resident carer. About 3 per cent of these needy older people were cared for by an unpaid carer who lived in a separate household, while most of the remainder (about 10 per cent and 7 per cent respectively for the two age groups) were cared for by a person living with them who was 'economically inactive', a status which includes retired and permanently sick or disabled people (Office for National Statistics, 2003).

In the Census, among people of working age, more than 10 per cent of men and over 14 per cent of women were carers, i.e., they had unpaid care responsibilities towards an older, sick or disabled person. The likelihood of providing unpaid care varied by ethnicity, and men and women residents of Pakistani and Bangladeshi origin were more likely to be carers than White British people or those from other ethnic minority groups. Overall, 2.3 per cent of men and 3.9 per cent of women reported that they were providing 20 or more hours of unpaid care each week. About 60 per cent of male carers, and about 36 per cent of female carers, also had full-time paid employment. Even among those with the most onerous unpaid caring responsibilities (50 hours or more per week), over a third of men and one in eight women also had full-time paid work.

However, in this group of people who care for 50 or more hours per week, 45 per cent of women and 21 per cent of men said that they were fully occupied with family and caring responsibilities, and gave this as their employment status (Office for National Statistics, 2004).

In recent decades, the employment of care workers and of agency care workers (categories 3 and 4 above) has been profoundly affected by developments in community care policy and by the government's modernization agenda for social services. The development of a mixed economy of care, and the shift (for statutory providers of care services) away from delivering care through their own workforces, towards procuring caring labour via private and voluntary sector organizations, have had a major impact. Among other things, this has affected job security, wage levels, and terms and conditions of employment. Meanwhile, the UK government's modernization agenda for social services has introduced new thinking about client choice and quality assurance in care delivery, and a much greater emphasis on training and accreditation for care workers.

The overall workforce in health and social care in the UK was estimated to include over 2.5m people in 2001, almost 10 per cent of all employees. Care assistants and home carers were the largest single occupational category within this group. In 2002 (March–May), the Labour Force Survey estimated that there were 554,000 people employed as care assistants and home carers in the UK. Of these, 501,000 (90 per cent) were women and just 53,000 were men (almost 10 per cent). Among the women working in this occupational category, 46 per cent were employed full-time and 54 per cent part-time. Among the men, however, only about 24 per cent were employed part-time, while about 76 per cent worked full-time (Office for National Statistics, Labour Force Survey March–May 2002). The UK New Earnings Survey has repeatedly listed care workers as one of the lowest paid occupational groups (Low Pay Commission, 2005) and the 2003 analysis of the state of the social care workforce (Eborall, 2003) confirmed very low hourly pay rates for both domiciliary care workers and care workers in care homes.

Paid care work is thus strongly feminized, low paid by comparison with other occupations, and often performed on a part-time or irregular hours basis. Many care workers have no formal qualifications directly applicable to their employment. In the most recent review, Eborall (2003, p. 241) found that 21 per cent of workers in adult and elder care had no qualifications at all, although almost one-third were qualified to GCE Advanced level or above. It is now widely recognized that work of good quality in this area requires great sensitivity, good interpersonal skills, and considerable flexibility on the part of the worker, and as such should not be considered unskilled labour. Domiciliary care workers are being required to perform increasingly complex tasks, and a wider range of personal care and medical procedures, and there is a current public policy agenda in the UK to extend accreditation of the skills needed in delivering care, and to ensure minimum standards are met (Department of Health, 2001b).

Official data on the personal social services shows that between 1999 and 2003, the number of home care contact hours delivered in England rose by 16 per cent (to 3.1 million hours), although at the same time the number of households receiving home care services declined by 11 per cent (to 362,800). A quarter of these households were receiving 'intensive' home care – defined as more than 10 contact hours or 6 or more visits each week. By 2003, two-thirds of all home care (66 per cent) was being delivered by the independent sector, a strong continuation of the trend seen since 1993 (see Figure 6.1). This strong shift towards delivery by independent providers resulted in 226,500 households receiving care from the independent sector by September 2003 (Department of Health, 2004).

A key problem faced by suppliers of domiciliary care is that alternative sources of demand for the labour supplied by employed/agency-based care workers have developed rapidly over this same period. Many localities have seen large increases in demand for part-time work at lower levels of employment. Between 1991 and 2002 there was a net increase of 2.1 million part-time jobs in England. These were taken up by 1.2m women and almost 900,000 men. Of these additional part-time jobs, over 880,000 are calculated to have been in the distribution, hotels and

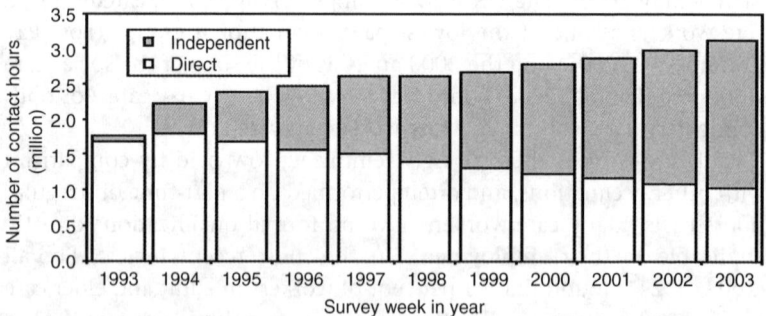

Figure 6.1   Number of contact hours of home care, by sector
Source: HH1 form, Table 1. (Department of Health 2004).

restaurants sector (ABI, 2002; Census of Employment/AES, 1991; ONS, 2004). This growth of part-time employment arises from big changes in retail distribution, including extensions to opening hours, from rapid expansion of employment in leisure and sport-related businesses, and from the wider availability of part-time and flexible jobs in clerical and secretarial employment, which continue to be major employers of women (over 400,000 additional part-time jobs were created in the banking, finance and insurance sector between 1991 and 2002). Employers in these fields often compete for labour from a similar labour pool, and offer better terms and conditions of employment than are available in care work.

When the study reported here began, very little was known about care work delivered by personal assistants employed through cash-for-care arrangements (category 5 above), such as through the Direct Payments scheme. As we shall see below, by late 2002 local authorities in England were making Direct Payments to just under 8,000 individuals (all categories), well over double the number recorded two years before, suggesting quite rapid growth in the number of personal assistants. Our exploratory study thus offered an initial opportunity to consider the work and working conditions of care workers employed as personal assistants. While the study does not provide a basis for generalization, it did reveal that some recipients of Direct Payments recruit their personal assistants through agencies supplying care (as in category 4), while others, including some older people, have also become the direct employers of their caring labour, taking on the full legal responsibilities of an employer, but also acquiring an employer's powers – to hire and fire, to control how and when tasks are performed, and to influence the quality of the job as experienced by the employee. The implications of this development are considered below in the final section of this chapter.

Direct Payments schemes in the UK

Two key developments lie behind the introduction of the Direct Payments cash-for-care scheme in the UK. The 1990 *NHS and Community Care Act*, and its impetus to increase choice and diversity in service provision through the development of local 'mixed care markets', represented a fundamental policy shift. Even before this, the disability movement's active promotion of social justice and empowerment had sought to transform disabled people from 'passive' care recipients to individuals able to exercise choice and control over when and how they received services and what services they need (Kestenbaum, 1996; Morris, 1993; Pearson, 2000). The broader European *Independent Living Movement* has also campaigned for cash-based solutions for independent living, enabling disabled people to become employers of 'assistants' whom they can choose and hire themselves.

The introduction of Direct Payments for older people thus owes much to the 'independent living' movement started by mainly younger disabled people over two decades before Direct Payments finally became available for people over 65 in England. The early 1980s saw a growing number of disabled people voicing their dissatisfaction with the care offered by, or through, local authorities and who wanted to exercise more personal choice and control over the support they received. At this time, it was illegal for local authorities in England to offer cash payments direct to their clients in lieu of services, so a small number of local authorities responded by setting up 'third party' schemes,[7] usually run by local voluntary organizations and used to facilitate the financial aspects of the relationship (Means and Smith, 1998, p. 60).

Many such schemes still operate, receiving local authority funding through the organization's payroll system before passing it on as cash payments to individual care users. The schemes' most fundamental role remains in providing advice, information and support services to scheme users who employ their own personal assistant or PA.[8] PAs assist the user in a range of daily activities, including personal care, domestic support, assistance with transportation, employment, education and social support. Some offer a full recruitment agency service for personal assistants, and a formalized system of on-call support (Hasler *et al.*, 1999).

Early political concerns about adopting a direct payments policy centred on concerns about its 'cost efficiency' and the 'accountability' of public expenditure (Pearson, 2000). However, research commissioned by the BCODP[9] (Zarb and Nadash, 1994) comparing the experiences, cost effectiveness and relative benefits of Direct Payments, showed Direct Payment users had higher levels of satisfaction through their increased choice and control over their care, compared with a higher incidence of unmet need reported by mainstream service users. This research also found that Direct Payment services were, on average, 30–40 per cent cheaper than comparable social service provision. Shortly after the report's publication, the Conservative government announced its plans for introducing Direct Payments in the next parliamentary session.

The *Community Care (Direct Payments) Act 1996* came into effect from 1 April 1997 and gave local authorities discretionary powers to offer cash payments to some people instead of arranging the community care services they had been assessed as needing. As this was 'enabling legislation', local authorities were not under a duty to provide Direct Payments, nor were people forced to accept them if they preferred their authority to arrange and provide their care services. However, local authorities were required by this legislation to consider all requests for direct payment and to assess each individual application on its own merits.

The 1997 Regulations specified that to be eligible for Direct Payments, claimants must be:

- a disabled person, as defined by section 29 of the *National Assistance Act 1948*;
- aged between 18 and under 65 on application;
- assessed as being eligible for community care services; and
- willing and able to manage their Direct Payments, either alone or with assistance.

Exclusions included:

- people who were subject to certain mental health or criminal justice measures; and
- direct payments to a close relative, partner, or someone living in the same household as the user.

Third-party schemes were able to continue operating their own criteria and eligibility rules,[10] and local authorities remained free to use their discretion on a wide range of implementation issues. Official policy and practice guidance urged local authorities to 'consider how to include people with different kinds of impairment, people from different ethnic backgrounds and people of different ages' within the limitations of the scheme. The guidance recommended that care managers adopt their usual community care criteria in assessing Direct Payments, while encouraging authorities to explore 'innovative and creative options . . . to identify alternatives which both cost less and meet the user's needs more effectively' (Department of Health, 2000b). An important protection has been that the user has the option of withdrawing from Direct Payments at any time, and returning to other forms of community care.

Another feature of Direct Payments has been that the legislation does not set any maximum or minimum amount of care or amount of money to be given as a Direct Payment.[11] Authorities are merely urged to ensure fair and equitable treatment of all home care recipients, by using the same charging policy for Direct Payment users as are used for other equivalent services.[12] This has been highlighted as an area of concern for some authorities (Zarb *et al.*, 1998). Until late 2001, local authorities had total discretion on whether or not (and how much) to charge for home care (and, therefore, also for Direct Payments), resulting in considerable variation in charging policies across the country.[13] In November 2001 the Department of Health announced new statutory guidance on charging, setting clearer objectives to enable local councils to implement fairer and more consistent charging systems (DoH press release, 23/11/01), and to reduce some of the disparities in charging for community care and Direct Payment services.

Local authorities are obliged to ensure that Direct Payments are at least as cost-effective as the *equivalent* community care services. In assessing this, consideration can be given to the quality of the service provided, the 'added-value' of enhanced flexibility, choice and control, and the lower administrative costs. In the longer-term, Direct Payments are also promoted as offering greater cost-effectiveness, by enabling people to remain in their own homes for longer. Direct Payments have been shown to be less costly (by 30–40 per cent) than the provision of in-house local authority home care and private agency provision (Zarb and Nadash, 1994). Kennard (1999) also showed that in one large city, Leeds, Direct Payments cost £5 per hour for home care, compared with £11 for local authority provision, although here the Direct Payment hourly figure did not include administrative and other costs.

Once a Direct Payment is in place, the contractual responsibility for employing workers and arranging care falls to the user. If there is a break-down in the arrangement, however, the local authority has the same responsibility to the care user as it would have if no Direct Payment existed. Local authority social services departments are thus expected to make alternative or emergency arrangements where needed, to monitor and review the package and arrangements regularly, and to re-adjust the support offered if necessary. Most local authorities insist on users having separate bank accounts for their Direct Payments, with payments made by cheque, and attention given to accurate record keeping for auditing purposes, although scheme managers try to ensure that monit-oring is not excessively onerous or bureaucratic for the users (Zarb *et al.*, 1998).

Financing Direct Payments

The UK government did not provide any additional funding to local authorities for the provision of Direct Payments, seeing them as in lieu of care services that the authorities already had a statutory duty to provide.

Some local authorities have used charitable funding to enhance provision (Hasler *et al.*, 1999) or accessed their *Promoting Independence* grant from the Social Services Modernization Fund, (Department of Health, personal communication, December 2001).

Early implementation of Direct Payments was tracked in a survey carried out by the Policy Studies Institute (PSI) in 1997. This found that just under half of local authorities were operating some form of direct payment scheme – mostly third party schemes – and that many planned to extend their scheme in line with the 1996 Act. Provision was very low in the north of England, Wales and Northern Ireland, and much higher in London, the South West and Scotland.[14] A later survey, conducted in 2000, surveyed all local authorities in England and Wales and revealed that 80 per cent of local authorities had used their discretionary powers and introduced Direct Payment schemes (Jones, 2000).

Establishing and implementing a Direct Payment scheme is a complex process for social services departments, requiring significant adjustment in the authority's approach to providing community care, and a major change to concepts of control and risk. The evidence to date suggests that successful direct payment systems have been established where local authorities, disability groups and users have worked in partnership. This underlines the importance of responsiveness, flexibility and transparency, of acknowledging the unequal power relation between disabled people and the local authority, and of involving disabled people in the planning and implementation of the scheme (Dawson, 2000).

Extension of Direct Payments to people over 65

Following the introduction of the 1996 Act, many felt that the exclusion of people over 65 was discriminatory and unfair. Lobbying by NCIL[15] and Age Concern, among others, strongly urged the government to extend Direct Payments to older people. In 1998, the incoming Labour government signalled its intention to extend Direct Payments to people over 65. Although implementation remained discretionary, the government made its support clear, and a review of how Direct Payments were supporting independent living was commissioned (Hasler *et al.*, 1999). The report of the Royal Commission on Long-Term Care (1997–99) fully endorsed the government's plans.

The Community Care (Direct Payments) Amendment Regulations 2000 came into force on 1 February 2000, making Direct Payments available to people over 65. Eligibility criteria were otherwise as for Direct Payments under the 1996 Act. Although new guidance for local authorities placed Direct Payments for older people squarely in the context of independent living (Hasler and Zarb, 2000), it was recognized that older people might need more structured support, information and time to decide whether Direct Payments were suitable for them. Key issues include:

- The basis on which the older person is assessed as being 'willing and able' to manage their care package, payments and the responsibilities of being an employer.
- Evidence that many older people would consider Direct Payment unsuitable for their needs (Barnes, 1997, cited in Hasler *et al.*, 1999).
- Older people's probable preference for a more structured package of support, to relieve them of some of the burden of managing their care arrangements.
- Traditionally, older people have generally had fewer options for independent living compared with younger, disabled people. Hence, far fewer older people will have considered the possibility of managing their own care.

Take-up of Direct Payments by older people

By September 2004, official figures published by the Department of Health showed 17,300 adults aged 18 plus in England receiving Direct Payments. In 2002, when the research for the *Shifting Boundaries* project was undertaken, seventeen (of 354) English local authorities had schemes covering over 100 care users, including two large county authorities with over 500 care users. Within these totals, the numbers of older people receiving Direct Payments remained low, at 1,032 in all. Only two authorities had schemes covering more than 40 older people. Twenty local authorities had no older users, and 98 had between 1 and 9 older users. The northern city where our exploratory study was conducted was in a group of ten local authorities which had between 20 and 39 older users of Direct Payments.

Direct Payments in a northern English city

Our selected city is a large metropolitan district in England, where – at the time of our study – the local authority served a population of more than half a million people, spending over £100 million on social services, of which some £66.5 million was used for the care of older people. Of this, nearly £18 million was spent on home support, including home care and 'meals on wheels'. Over 5 per cent of residents over 65 received community-based care services, and the authority provided 4,300 clients with home care. The city's *Modernizing Social Services* plans included an older people's strategy, and the 'older people helped to live at home' indicator (relating to the authority's performance) gained the maximum possible score in 2000, placing it among the top English local authorities for this category (Department of Health, 2000c).

The city had an early and large third party Direct Payments scheme, initially established as a one year pilot project in 1993. A well established, local independent voluntary organization (hereafter referred to as the IVO) was recruited to set up a third party 'Scheme for Direct Payment Users' (SDPU), with legal, payroll and administrative support from the IVO, under contract to the city's Social Services Department (SSD). Growing demand for information and advice regarding the disabled person's responsibilities as an employer led to the appointment of a coordinator in 1994, with a remit to develop guidance and support mechanisms for scheme users. A key aim here was to ensure the fully legal employment of personal assistants. Shortly after, Direct Payments were made available to anyone in the locality in receipt of community care, including older people. At the time of our research, SDPU had a coordinator, two advisers, and a development worker, to support 123 Direct Payment users of all ages.

Demand for Direct Payments continued to increase steadily, but because of the scheme's cap on numbers imposed by the SSD's funding arrangements, access had to be carefully managed. Indeed in 1999, the SDPU had to close to new users for a while when its maximum limit was reached. In 2000, the scheme received £45,981 grant aid from the city's SSD (accounting for 87 per cent of total SDPU income) to cover staff, payroll and administrative costs, excluding the Direct Payments made to users. In 2001 this funding associated with older people was increased, to £58,306, using additional resources from the budget for social work with older people. This was intended to increase the number of 'people over 65 independently managing their own care packages by employing their own staff... from 10 to 100... [to provide] more flexibility and control for users; [and to] reduce [the] cost of care packages by approximately £2.00 per hour' (local authority report, 2000). The SDPU coordinator estimated that this increased budget (and subsequent initiatives) doubled the number of older people on the scheme in that year, to 23, out of a total of 105 users (all ages), in March 2001.

The fundamental rationale of the SDPU was to increase the care users' choice, control and power over the care they receive. This was done by furthering users' independence and self-determination (rather than merely providing a more individualized, flexible care package) and ensuring that users (rather than their informal carers or other professionals) had control of the payments and the care package. As a result, SDPU was more easily accessed by people willing and able to take charge of their care decisions and lifestyle. These tended to be articulate people with the confidence, experience and skills to obtain the care they need in order to be as independent as possible, rather than those with mental disabilities or with more fundamental physical care needs (Speyer, 1998).

Figure 6.2 illustrates the payments and support structures in place in our chosen city. The funding for the administration of the SDPU (shaded boxes in Figure 6.2) is provided through two separate social services budgets – for disabled people and for older people – at a rate agreed by the social services department.[16] The rate is based on the number of users who can be supported per hour of SDPU staff time, within a fixed overall budget. Annually, the scheme coordinator negotiated this budget with social services, with an agreed maximum caseload. Figure 6.2 also shows the different ways in which care users deployed their Direct Payment to recruit care workers. Here both the complexity and flexibility of the scheme is immediately visible, since care users, even in our small study, may employ one or several care workers directly, contract with an employment agency, or use a person with power of attorney to manage their use of the Direct Payment.

Operation of the scheme

The detailed operation of the Direct Payments scheme in our chosen city, and the arrangements in place to support it, are important features which may affect take-up and user satisfaction, and which can potentially offer protection to both the care user and the care worker who becomes their personal assistant. They are, therefore, discussed in some detail in this section. As Figure 6.2 shows, the scheme involves a range of agencies and a variety of funding arrangements. Even within this regulated system, a variety of outcomes is possible: in Figure 6.2 five possible arrangements are shown and all five of these actually occurred in our small sample of older people receiving Direct Payments.

The SDPU service provides users with advice, support and information on issues such as advertising for and recruiting workers, drawing up employment contracts and record keeping. The SDPU also provides a payroll service to ensure all tax and National Insurance liabilities are met and a users' group, where Direct Payment recipients can meet to discuss any concerns about the scheme or about the direct employment of care workers.

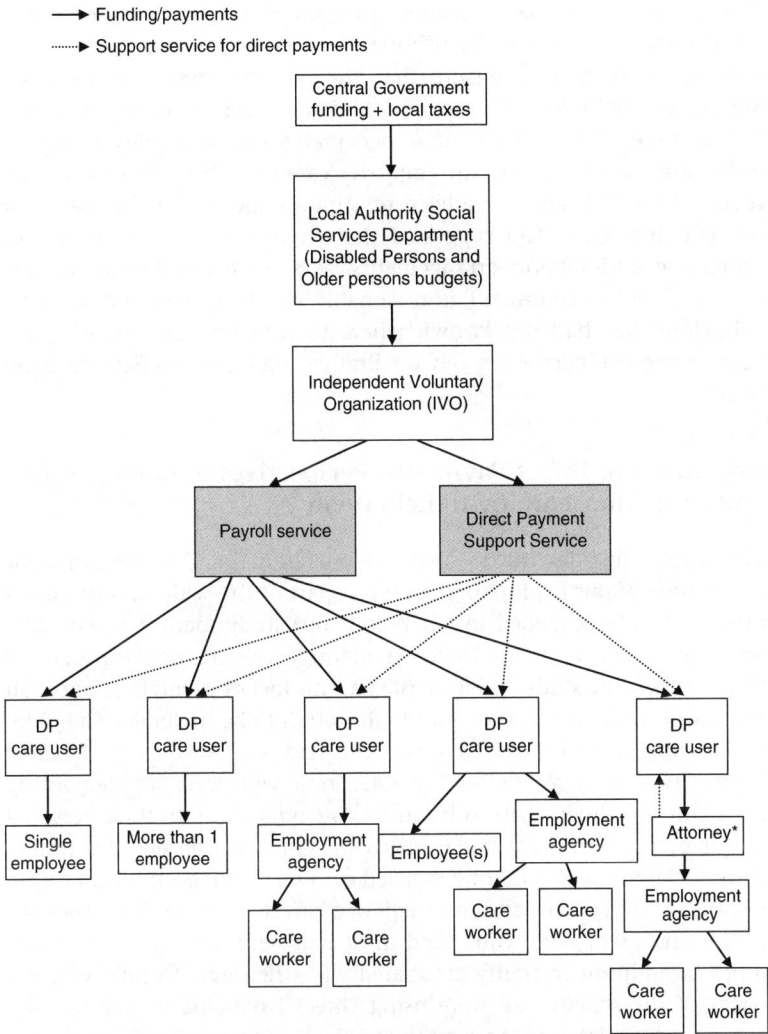

Figure 6.2   SDPU payment and support structures
Note: * Person with legally approved 'power of attorney' to manage an individual's financial and business affairs. In the case here, the person with these powers was a solicitor.

The SDPU sees these formalized payment, contractual and support systems as a way of protecting the wishes of the user, rather than of promoting an equitable working relationship. The system described is highly regulated, with detailed attention to features designed to support the care user in acting according to employment law. Some elements are designed to prevent unauthorized use of the Direct Payment, to prevent fraud, and to ensure that the personal assistants recruited are remunerated in a transparent and auditable manner. However, at the time of our study, if a personal assistant/employee experienced any problems with an employer/care user, they had no formal redress to SDPU, and no advice or support mechanism to fall back on. Our interview data suggested that there was a need for worker protection and support arrangements, as a small number of workers felt they had encountered unreasonable employer expectations and behaviour, but had not known where to turn for support. We now turn to the evidence from our qualitative interviews to explore these issues.

Experiencing Direct Payments: Perspectives of older people and those they employ to help them

The scheme just described was newly operational and in development at the time of our exploratory study. As part of the wider international project already described in Chapter 1, our study identified ten older people who were receiving Direct Payments, accessing them through the SDPU. When the study was undertaken, this meant involving almost all those who were not considered too ill or frail to be included. The older people interviewed included some who had been recipients of Direct Payments as younger disabled people, some who were supplementing their Direct Payment with substantial co-payments from their personal resources, some who also had unpaid carers in their household or immediate social network, and one married couple, where both spouses were eligible for the scheme and in receipt of a Direct Payment. Most (not all) of the care users were white, and most had significant physical disabilities in addition to frailty associated with their age. In line with the terms of the scheme, all were using Direct Payments to pay for care assistants (unrelated to them by ties of kinship) to care for them in their own homes, or to assist them in participating in their communities. The group we studied were mostly using Direct Payments for personal, domiciliary care, enabling them to maintain both their bodies and an independent household, and to exercise some choice about how and when they received care. Few were buying support to empower them to lead the kind of active lives many had previously led.

Other research has already shown that when Direct Payments are set up effectively and work well for older people, they report 'feeling happier, more motivated and having an improved quality of life' (Clark *et al.*, 2004) than before. There is also evidence that the scheme is a good way of enabling older people to receive culturally appropriate support, for example someone speaking their own language and skilled in preparing meals or providing health care that is culturally acceptable to them. Such evidence also emerged in our study, although older people's experiences as recounted to us were not straightforwardly or exclusively positive. Among the topics discussed with us were: joining the scheme and recruiting a suitable care worker; managing the financial and employment responsibilities; negotiating an employment relationship with the person/persons appointed, and terminating this in relevant cases; negotiating the content of the job; and living in a situation where one's home had become another person's workplace.

As little research has so far been done in England to explore the experiences and perspectives of those who are employed by older people using the Direct Payments scheme, our study offers an important window on this group of workers. We interviewed all the care workers who were employed by our group of older recipients of Direct Payments who could be accessed and who agreed to be interviewed. Because of the scheme rules, all were unrelated to the older person receiving care. Some had other current jobs, sometimes in other types of care work; some had entered care work following quite different previous careers; some were previously known to the older person they cared for, and had been personally recommended to them. Some had first provided care for the older person in question in another capacity, and had been directly recruited to their current role because of a previous successful caring relationship. Others were comparatively casually recruited, using the kinds of advertising often used to recruit home cleaners or newspaper deliverers, while others had been introduced to their current employer quite formally, through the local Job Centre. Most, but not all, were female, and all met formal British residency requirements. The bureaucracy associated with the SDPU in our northern city seemed to have deterred any 'grey labour', so that all those we interviewed were legally employed and covered, through their and their employers' national insurance contributions, regarding the basic employment rights which are minimally provided for in British law.

An important group of our care worker interviewees were not paid directly by the older care user, but via employment agencies. In these cases, the Direct Payment was being used by the care user to contract directly with the agency, agreeing the detailed hours of work at the individual level and usually negotiating with the agency about who they would send. This is an important variant of the scheme, and one which we anticipate will become more common in the UK as Direct Payments for older people are extended. Since agencies providing caring labour normally aim to have a pool of additional care workers on whom they can draw as needs arise, this arrangement has the potential advantage of immediate 'back-up' for the care user, in the event of a care worker's illness or absence, without recourse to the Social Services Department. The SSD nevertheless, as explained earlier, still retains a statutory responsibility to provide emergency care and to step in if things go wrong. Agency arrangements also have a benefit for the care worker, since alternative employment is more likely to be quickly available through an agency if a regular client dies, or is hospitalized.

When we interviewed the care workers, we discussed many of the same issues as were covered in the interviews with the older people: the employment relationship, the nature of the work, how they were recruited and how they handled financial matters and any disputes over work, time or other matters. These interviews also explored the care workers' pay and working conditions, their experiences of employer requirements and control, and how they fitted their work into other aspects of their lives, including the other paid jobs which some of them held.

Issues for older people receiving Direct Payments

Though small, our study has highlighted a number of issues for older people in receipt of Direct Payments. Only further research could identify how far these issues relate to the wider population of all older people in this situation, but our interviews gave detailed insight into the matters raised by those taking part in the study. Some of the most important aspects involved choice and control, trust and dependability, and attitudes to bureaucracy.

Being able to choose the person providing their care, rather than having simply to accept that whoever was sent along would be the person looking after them, was very important to some of the older care users we interviewed. They also valued choosing when they received care (for example being able to choose what time they received the help they required to get up or to go to bed), and choosing what tasks would be done on a particular day. As one male recipient of Direct Payments put it:

> The advantages were that we weren't waiting for a home help who wasn't coming – for a start. [Or who] when they came, [said] 'I can't stop, because I've got somebody else to go to.' [Which meant that]

instead of us getting our three hours, we got an hour, or an hour and a quarter, or three quarters of an hour.... Being able to choose our own workers and decide how we wanted it done, what we wanted, when we wanted it done, and not when they wanted to come and do it. If there's something special we want doing, it's done for us. We'll say, 'don't bother vacuuming today, we'd like the cupboard done out.' This flexibility [means] – we've got control. Also, the point is that you're getting the same person all the time. Who wants 10 different people in 20 weeks? This was what we were getting. And they'd come in, and they didn't know where the vacuum cleaner is – so you've got to start all over again – training them, where things are.

In practice, care users' control over these matters was limited by the availability of suitable care workers, and by the skills, experience and attributes of the workers who cared for them. It was also affected by whether the care user employed the care worker directly or contracted with an agency to supply services. In the latter case, the degree of user autonomy was not necessarily any greater than when receiving routine services, since the older person involved would need to resolve issues and concerns with the agency rather than with the individual agency worker who attended them at home.

Some care users were acutely aware that their agreement specified an exact payment, and that this could not be varied without a formal SSD review. The services they could afford to purchase were also limited by the restrictions of the formal care needs assessment, and by the rules of the Direct Payment Scheme.

We asked the care users how they assessed risk when recruiting someone to work in their own home providing intimate care, and how they handled security issues, established a basis for trust, and assured themselves that the service they would receive was as dependable and flexible as they required. Here care users were aware that they had some protection through the procedures put in place by the SDPU (see above). There was also considerable emphasis on the personal qualities of any individual care workers who were specially valued. As one put it:

There is a very big difference between somebody who is with you 5 hours a day (Cath) and somebody who is with you 20 minutes, or something like that. They get up and go, and that's it, that's the end of it. But Cath is fantastic. She is very helpful and very encouraging in everything. She's a phenomenal woman.

Others explained that the Direct Payment arrangements made a difference to issues of trust and reliability:

> They have a key to our door. We're still in bed when they come. They open the door and start work. She won't start vacuuming until she hears me move. She knows I'm having a lie-in maybe. Then, when she hears me move, she asks, do I want a drink, breakfast . . .
>
> *Interviewer*: Did the home helps you had previously [before Direct Payments] have a key?
>
> Oh no – because they say they're coming on Tuesday, and you're stuck in all day on Tuesday, and then they don't come. Social Services think elderly people and disabled people are just sitting in the house, waiting for them to come, whether they come or not.

Although the relationships between care users and care workers could be extremely positive, even in our small sample, some of our interviewees had experienced difficulties in recruiting suitable people, or had chosen to dismiss a worker judged to be providing an unsatisfactory service. Others had recruited people already personally known to them, or who had been recommended by a friend or an existing worker whom they trusted. Those who chose the direct employment option, rather than the use of agency labour, found recruitment something of a burden, involving placing an advertisement, responding to phone enquiries, and interviews at the Job Centre.

As we have indicated, the UK Direct Payments Scheme is highly regulated. Users are required to set up separate bank accounts for all financial transactions within the scheme, and to handle contracts of employment, pay slips, holiday forms and sickness notes, as well as the documentation involved in advertising for and recruiting a care worker. The local SDPU, which had been set up to provide advice and support for care users, appeared to be effective in helping users manage the necessary paperwork, although accessing the scheme had been difficult for some. One user referred to the Direct Payments Scheme as 'the best kept secret' in the city. Another explained that the process of joining the scheme took some time and could be frustrating:

> We have only been doing it about 2 months and we are still in the depths of that. We are supposed to be having somebody to come out to talk to us about that [from SDPU]. She is coming out in about a month I think. She is on holiday I believe he said. We are waiting

for them to come to help us with these accounts that we are in a bit of muddle with, quite frankly. [At the moment] I write out one cheque. No, I write out two, I suppose. I pay Sally out of the SDPU account and I pay the agency out of the SDPU. We haven't yet discovered whether it covers it. At the moment it doesn't, I know we are in the red at the moment. But again, I am waiting for somebody to come out to help us with these accounts. We are doing our best to keep them.

Issues for care workers employed by older people through Direct Payments

The picture painted by the 15 care workers we interviewed was – even in our small study – highly variable. Even in the highly regulated scheme operating in the city where we conducted our research, and in the context of a local agency specifically tasked with supporting scheme users, care workers' experiences ranged from the very positive to the exploitative and intolerable.

Our interviewees included some care workers who were very contented with their employment arrangements and with the nature of their work, making very positive comments about feeling valued, praised for their dedication, and appreciated by those they cared for. One, who found her relationship with the care user very satisfactory, pointed out that the relationship rapidly became more than 'just a job':

> You become quite close to them because they trust you and you trust them. I would say you almost become like friends really. You are very important to them and they are to you of course.... Naturally, some you become closer to than others, but on the whole I think you don't want to let them down. That's very important.

For others there could be another side to the care worker experience of Direct Payments. Even working for an elderly care user via an agency could be problematic, as this care worker, who had recently stopped working for an elderly couple receiving Direct Payments, shows:

> They're a lovely couple, don't get me wrong, but my time was 5 [until] half 6, and many a night I didn't get [home until] half 7 – and it's only on (the same) road. If my time says a certain time, then I want to finish at that time. Unless they were sick – that would be

different. [It was] fixing things, and then wanting you to sit and talk
to them. More loneliness than anything else. It was, 'can you wash
my hair; do you mind if you can do this for me...' You know, all
just little things – but in my time. I did ring the agency, and said,
'Look, I don't mind being there, if there's an extra hour, or an extra...
I don't mind being there – but am I going to get paid for that extra?'
[The agency said they] were only getting payment for that hour and
a half.

Our interviews with care workers revealed a number of issues which
they considered affected their protection at work and their employment rights. It is emphasized that our sample included some who felt
their older employers were extremely considerate. The regulation of
the scheme and its administration via SDPU meant that basic rights
to holidays, sickness benefits and inclusion in the state national insurance scheme was normally covered. Beyond this formal protection,
the workers also included some whose care users insisted on paying
for extra holidays, or who had helped them with financial or other
matters in their personal lives. Some stressed that their conditions of
employment were considerably better than those they had experienced
previously when working for employment agencies or in residential
care homes.

Sometimes the relationship did not work out so well, however, and
care workers experienced treatment by their older employers which fell
below the standard acceptable in an employment relationship:

> I just left. I just couldn't put up with him any more, so I just left and
> I'm unemployed now... He wrote me a letter... He phoned me up
> and he just said, 'You're sacked!'
>
> *Interviewer*: So he sacked you, it wasn't a matter of you leaving?
>
> (Then) he wanted me back. He didn't really know what he wanted.
> I phoned him up and said, 'The doctor's signed me off work; I can't
> move.' I was laid in bed, and he said, 'Right, then you're sacked.'
> I said, 'but you can't just sack me like that, I've got a doctor's note
> which I'm sending to you', but he said, 'That's it, I don't want you
> any more!'

Others were very conscious of job insecurity. They pointed out that
their job was highly vulnerable, and that if the person they cared for
had to be admitted to hospital, or died, they could find themselves

without employment overnight, or in a situation of some confusion as to whether or not their labour was required. One of the interviewees explained:

> It is a very bad thing actually, because you do get clients ringing in suddenly and saying 'we don't need the service today.' Or maybe they just get taken into hospital – that happens a lot actually, and then you lose that work, don't you? Sometimes it can be for 2 or 3 weeks. It has also happened to me that I've been sent as 'cover' to someone's house, and they've said 'Oh, we didn't really ask for anybody.' But you've gone out there. Now actually the agency will pay you the mileage and say 'Well, you can claim for half an hour of your time' – but you're still losing 3 or 4 hours' pay, which you had anticipated, you see.

We were also struck by the casual, almost chance mode of recruitment into this type of work in some cases:

> I'd seen the advert in the corner shop. I came home one day, and I rang up and I couldn't get through, and then I let it go a little bit. Then I went up to the shops again and I saw the advert still in and I thought, 'I must ring that number; I must enquire what it is rather than just . . . you know, leave it.' So I did, and they asked me to go down – and that was sort of it. We hit it off straight away and I thought, 'Well, I can give it a go; see how I go, you know.'

Some care workers were able to describe their daily routine with their older care user in great detail. It was clear that for those without prior training, this work involved considerable learning 'on the job', and picking up from other care workers the best way of handling very intimate care tasks which could be heavy, awkward or potentially painful for the care recipient.

> There's always somebody else there with me, so I'm not on my own, which is a good thing with me being new. If I was on my own I'd be a bit [stuck] . . . unless I'd had some past experience, which I did have in the hospital. But it is a totally different thing in somebody else's house. So, basically we help them go to the toilet, help them with getting out of bed. I have to wash her on the bed. So you're turning her from side to side. And when you've done that, you've got to help her [dress]. She does try to help, as best she can. Then you've

got to put her socks on – you've got to be very careful because of her feet which are all bent over, and her legs are very sensitive around the knee joints. You have to support them with cushions because she can easily twist the ligaments. So you have to be really careful when you're doing that. At that point I shout the other lady in. She comes and helps me lift her into the wheelchair.

Some care workers were concerned about their health when working in the private homes of their employers. This included health risks arising from exposure to the care recipient's tobacco smoke, and from being expected to conduct procedures such as lifting and moving without another worker to assist them, or without aids such as a hoist or an adjustable bed. Some felt that, had they been employed through an agency or other employer, they would have been protected from such risks, and would have had someone apart from the individual employer to appeal to.

Another concern was that, although the SDPU had good arrangements in place to support care users, systems for supporting care workers who encountered difficulties, especially those in the direct employ of the older person, were very limited. Our interviewees included some who had resigned because they could not resolve disputes about pay, holidays, working hours and work tasks, and one who had felt personally harassed by her employer. There was also at least one case of summary dismissal (see above) and a case in which wages were withheld.

These employees had felt there was no-one they could rely on for effective support. Several care workers commented that 'they had no-one to turn to' when things went wrong, and no-one to ask for advice in dealing with a difficult client, whose behaviour was sometimes recognized as a feature of their disability or health situation. The establishment of trust and friendship in the caring relationship could also give rise to difficulties. One care worker explained that she came into work even when unfit through illness, because she knew her elderly employer would otherwise be unsupported, and several others reported doing unpaid overtime, completing unpaid tasks in their own homes (cooking, ironing, etc), and having to accept changes to working hours which sometimes put them under uncomfortable pressure.

The experiences of those we interviewed thus revealed both some major benefits, notably (but not only) for care recipients, and some significant disadvantages of the Direct Payments scheme as it operates with regard to older people. Given official determination to extend the scheme, and sluggish take-up in most parts of the UK, it is important that those features of the scheme that offer a way of improving on other ways of delivering services are given greater publicity. At the same time, those aspects that expose care users and care workers to greater risk than is the case under other arrangements need to be addressed in a systematic way. Our research suggests that it is when care workers are employed directly by an older person (rather than via an agency) that the risks to both parties are likely to be greatest. Additional protection, in the form of training and support schemes for care workers employed in this way, and further development of the advice and guidance available to care users involved in the scheme would seem to be important and necessary developments. Such enhancements will need to be funded from official sources to ensure that appropriate protection is available in all areas of the country. If in the formal arrangements for implementing the Direct Payments Scheme for Older People care is not taken to provide adequate protection and working conditions for care workers, it will prove impossible to attract sufficient labour of suitable quality to meet the expanding demand for domiciliary care.

Notes

1. Aged 65 and over for men and 60 and over for women.
2. 80 per cent of over 65s had help with domestic tasks from informal carers; 10 per cent relied on both informal and formal help; and 10 per cent relied solely on formal services (from GHS, cited in Wittenberg *et al.*, 2001).
3. *Minimum Income Guarantee* (MIG) topped up any existing income or benefits to a minimum level at the time of the research. Rates were higher for those who were disabled and lived alone or with another disabled person, for carers getting Carer's Allowance and for homeowners with mortgages or housing loans. The actual payment received depended upon individual circumstances, savings and income level, but the MIG did not take account of Disability Living Allowance, Attendance Allowance, Housing Benefit or Council Tax Benefits. About one-third of pensioner households received these low-income related benefits (DSS 1999, cited in Age Concern, 2001a). MIG was replaced with Pension Credit in October 2003, retaining many features of the MIG, but aims not to penalize those with modest savings who have saved for their old age (DWP, 2004).
4. The main *disability benefits* claimed by people over 65 are Attendance Allowance (AA) and Disability Living Allowance (DLA). These are claimed by about one-fifth of pensioners (Age Concern, 2001b). AA is paid to people who develop personal care needs after the age of 65 through illness or disability. It is tax-free, and paid at different rates depending on the care needed. In 2001, 1.29 million people claimed AA. Women comprised 71 per cent, rising to 82 per cent of those over 90 (DWP, 2001).
5. *Carer's Allowance* (formerly called Invalid Care Allowance) is a taxable benefit for informal carers who spend at least 35 hours per week caring. Informal

carers aged 16 and over can apply, and can include relatives, friends or neighbours. From October 2002, the upper age limit for qualifying for Carer's Allowance was removed. Prior to this, carers aged 65 and over could not apply for this benefit.

6. *Disability Living Allowance (DLA)* was introduced in April 1992. Available only to people who become ill or disabled before their 65th birthday, it continues after retirement age, while the claimant requires help (DWP, 2001). Like AA, DLA is not means tested and can be paid even if the claimant does not actually receive care. In May 2001, 519,300 people over 65 were claiming DLA, some 23 per cent of all DLA claimants (DWP, 2001).

7. These were also known as personal assistance support schemes (PASS), self-operated care schemes or independent living schemes.

8. Also termed care assistants, support workers, carers, facilitators or enablers.

9. British Council of Organizations of Disabled People.

10. Zarb *et al.* (1998) found that many of the third party schemes established before the 1996 Act, had slightly wider criteria than the legislation recommended.

11. Although Direct Payments are not means tested as such, Section 1(2b) of the 1996 Act states: 'If the payee satisfies the authority that his means are insufficient for it to be reasonably practicable for him to make up the difference [in the cost of providing care], the authority shall so adjust the payment to him . . . as to avoid there being a greater difference than that which appears to them to be reasonably practicable for him to make up.'

12. For example, all the participating authorities consulted in the PSI research included a charge to the user for overheads; recruitment costs; some holiday and sick pay; and an element to cover staffing in emergencies (Zarb *et al.*, 1998). Charging for community care services can not necessarily be based on the same criteria.

13. This issue was identified in the 1998 *Modernising Social Services* White Paper, the 1999 *Royal Commission* report on the funding for long-term care and the Audit Commission report on home care charges (Audit Commission report, May 2000).

14. Partly due to the *1968 Social Work Act* which made direct payments legal in Scotland.

15. National Centre for Independent Living

16. During 2003–4 (after our research was completed) the UK government made £4.5m available nationally to charities, through a Direct Payments Development Fund, to work in partnership with local authorities to 'encourage people to exercise choice and control through the use of Direct Payments'. The June 2004 announcement of successful bids in the second round of this scheme included six Age Concern agencies in different localities, together awarded almost £600,000 (Department of Health press release ref. 2004/0223).

References

Age Concern (2001b) *Pensioners' Incomes*, ref 0201, London: Age Concern.
Annual Business Inquiry (2002), Office for National Statistics, data from NOMIS.

Barnes, C. (1997) *Older People's Perception of Direct Payments and Self-operated Support Schemes*, Leeds: University of Leeds, BCODP Research Unit, School of Sociology and Social Policy.

Census of Employment/Annual Employment Survey (1991) Office for National Statistics.

Clark, H., Gough, H. and Macfarlane, A. (2004) *It Pays Dividends: Direct Payments and Older People*, Bristol: The Policy Press.

Dawson, C. (2000) *Independent Successes: Implementing Direct Payments*, York: Joseph Rowntree Foundation.

Community Care (Direct Payments) Act 1996, London: Her Majesty's Government, online at: www.hmso.gov.uk/acts/acts1996/1996030.htm.

Department of Health (1998) *Modernising Social Services*, Government White Paper, Cm 4169, London: The Stationery Office.

Department of Health (2000a) *A Quality Strategy for Social Care*, Consultation Paper, London: Department of Health.

Department of Health (2000b) *Community Care Statistics 2000: Home Help/Home Care Services, England*, London: Department of Health.

Department of Health (2000c) *Social Services Performance in 1999–2000: The Personal Social Services Performance Assessment Framework Indicators*, London: National Statistics.

Department of Health (2001) *Community Care (Direct Payments) Act 1996: (Revised) Policy and Practice Guidance*, London: Department of Health.

Department of Health (2001b) *Domiciliary Care: National Minimum Standards Regulations, Care Standards Act 2000*, London: Department of Health.

Department of Health (2004) *Department of Health Community Care Statistics 2003: Home Care Services for Adults, England*, London: Office for National Statistics.

DSS (1999) *The Pensioners' Incomes*, Series 1998/9, National Statistics 198.

DSS (2000) *The Pensioners' Incomes Series*, London: Department for Social Security, Analytical Services Division.

DWP (2001) *Disability Living Allowance, Attendance Allowance and Invalid Care Allowance: Disability Care and Mobility Quarterly Statistical Enquiry*, London: DWP, DWP Information Centre, Analytical Services Division.

DWP (2004) *The New Pension Credit: A Review of the Campaign to 2004*, London: The Pension Service.

Eborall, C. (2003) *The State of the Social Care Workforce in England*, vol. 1, Leeds: TOPSS England, WIU Report.

Hasler, F. and Zarb, G. (2000) 'Direct Payments and Older People: The Principles of Independent Living', *Research Policy and Planning*, 18(2), 7–12.

Hasler, F., Campbell, J. and Zarb, G. (1999) *Direct Routes to Independence: A Guide to Local Authority Implementation and Management of Direct Payments*, London: PSI/NCIL.

Jones, R. (2000) *Getting Going on Direct Payments*, Report prepared on behalf of the ADSS, Salisbury: Wiltshire County Council Social Services Department.

Kennard, M. (1999) *12 Month Evaluation of the Leeds Direct Payments Scheme*, Leeds: Leeds City Council Social Services Department.

Kestenbaum, A. (1996) *Independent Living: A Review*, York: Joseph Rowntree Foundation.

Lewis, J. and Meredith, B. (1988) *Daughters Who Care: Daughters Caring for Mothers at Home*, London: Routledge.

Low Pay Commission (2005) *National Minimum Wage Report*, Office for National Statistics.

Means, R. and Smith, R. (1998) *Community Care, Policy and Practice*, 2nd edn. Basingstoke: Macmillan, now Palgrave Macmillan.

Morris, J. (1993) *Community Care or Independent Living*? York: Joseph Rowntree Foundation.

Office for National Statistics (2000) *National Population Projections: 1998-based*, ONS series PP2 no. 22, London: The Stationery Office.

Office for National Statistics (2003) *Census of Population*, Crown Copyright.

Office for National Statistics (2004) *2001 Census Commissioned Tables*, Crown Copyright 2003.

Pearson, C. (2000) 'Money Talks? Competing Discourses in the Implementation of Direct Payments', *Critical Social Policy*, 20(4), 459–77.

Population Trends (2003) vol. 114, London: The Stationery Office.

Rainey, C. (1999) *Evaluation of Direct Payments Pilot*, West Sussex County Council. Derby: National Centre for Independent Living.

Royal Commission on the Long-Term Care for the Elderly (1999) *With respect to old age* – Research volume 3.

Speyer, J. (1998) *Making Direct Payments to People with Learning Difficulties*, unpublished report, Sheffield: VAS.

Ungerson, C (2004) 'Whose Empowerment and Independence? A Cross-national Perspective on "Cash for Care" Schemes', *Ageing and Society*, 24, 189–212.

Wittenberg, R., Pickard, L., Comas-Herrera, A., Davies, B. and Darton, R. (2001) *Demand for Long-term Care for Older People in England to 2031*, PSSRU/Health Statistics Quarterly 12, Winter 2001. London: ONS, The Stationery Office.

Yeandle, S., Gore, T. and Herrington, A. (1999) *Employment, Family and Community Activities: A New Balance for Women and Men*, Dublin: European Foundation for the Improvement of Living and Working Conditions.

Zarb, G. and Nadash, P. (1994) *Cashing in on Independence: Comparing the Costs and Benefits of Cash and Services*, Somercotes, Derbyshire: BCODP.

Zarb, G., Hasler, F., Campbell, J. and Arthur, S. (1998) *Implementing and Management of Direct Payment Schemes*, London: PSI.

7
Mixed Blessings: Long-term Care Benefits in Germany

Ulrike Schneider and Carlos Reyes

Flashback: Issues and Non-issues in the development of German policy on long-term care

Until 1995, public support provided to long-term care clients was entirely tax-funded and means-tested in Germany, with no access to benefits from the contribution-based social insurance system which is the defining feature of the German welfare state. Persons in need of care whose financial means were insufficient to meet their care needs were eligible for benefits from the social assistance scheme regulated in the *Bundessozialhilfegesetz – BSHG* (Federal Social Assistance Law) enacted on 1 July 1962 (Mager, 1999, p. 212).

Given the high financial cost of professional long-term care, a long-term disabling condition constitutes a serious poverty risk. Official statistics show that in 2001 the average monthly charge for institutional care – net of board and lodging – amounted to €1,565 (Statistisches Bundesamt, 2003a, p. 18), while the estimated monthly cost of home care services ranged from €390 to €1,450, depending on the care user's degree of disability (Stiftung Warentest, 2002, p. 73). This compares with an average monthly income of €1,953 of elderly couple households – €977 per head – in 1999 (Deutscher Bundestag, 2003).

Not surprisingly then, prior to the long-term care reform in the mid 1990s, most care users became financially dependent on relatives and/or had to draw social assistance benefits. The majority of beneficiaries were frail older people: about 80 per cent of older people living in nursing homes or in skilled nursing facilities depended on public assistance (Geraedts *et al.*, 2000, p. 376). This situation was thought to be inappropriate for people who had worked all their lives, paying taxes and contributing to the pension and health care system.

Net social assistance payments to long-term care clients amounted to €6.4bn in 1994. In Germany, social assistance is the responsibility of municipalities and the states (*Länder*). Therefore, the increase in long-term care spending over time was a major concern for already over indebted communities, and became a prominent issue in the debate about fiscal federalism (Karrenberg and Münstermann, 1999, pp. 194, 213; Seewald 1998, pp. 106–8; Statistisches Bundesamt, 1999, p. 10).

Against this background, the Kohl administration decided to establish a two-tiered system of long-term care in 1994. The first layer of protection consists of an employment related, contribution-based long-term care insurance (LTCI), while tax-funded social assistance remains a resource of last resort. Long-term care insurance was made mandatory for those who meet the criteria for membership in the statutory health insurance scheme. All other persons (with private health insurance coverage) now need to procure private long-term care insurance. At first, benefits could only be claimed by care users living in the community, but on 1 July 1996 coverage was extended to institutional care. About 90 per cent of the German population is now covered by the social long-term care insurance programme, with private insurance covering the remainder (Schneider, 2000, p. 9).

The stated goals of the 1994 reform were to: ease the financial burden of long-term care spending for the *Länder* and municipalities; reduce the risk of poverty for care clients; increase the supply of long-term care services; expand home- and community-based services; and to support informal caring.

Fiscal considerations rather than pressures from persons suffering from a long-term functional disability assumed primary importance in the shaping of Germany's new long-term care policy:

> It is only once certain institutions were affected by... demographic trends (in terms of rising costs and in terms of programmes being diverted from their initial purpose) that the problem became an issue for politicians. What the latter were responding to was the growing discontent not of the elderly and the care-givers but of the institutions which were thus put under pressure. (Morel, 2003, p. 23)

The 1994 reform effectively shifted long-term care spending in Germany from the states and communities to the social insurance system. The number of people supported with 'help for care' fell from 476,000 in 1994 to 246,000 in 2002, and net social assistance payments to long-term care clients declined from €6.6 bn in 1994 to €2.4 bn in 2002 (Statistisches Bundesamt, 2003b, pp. 38, 54).

The long-term care policy debate in Germany was also concerned with sustaining or supporting low-cost settings for the provision of care. This also explains some of the emphasis placed on home and community care. Home care has been assumed to be the care arrangement preferred by care recipients and their families, as well as a low-cost setting for care provision. There was, therefore, a consensus in the political arena on developing measures that prevent or delay institutionalization, such as improving access to, and quality of, home care services, and devising a variety of direct and indirect carer benefits (Deutscher Bundestag, 1993; Leitherer, 1997, pp. 396–7; Morel, 2003, p. 22).

Employment issues did not take centre stage in the debates surrounding the introduction of social long-term care insurance. One of the recurrent topics in the early 1990s concerned the harmful effects on the economy of widening the tax-wedge by raising employment-based contributions to fund the new long-term care insurance. Critics of the new long-term care scheme still hold that employment-based contributions work like a tax on labour, discouraging employment. On the other hand, the increase in public long-term care spending could be expected to augment employment in care-related professions. However, the official explanatory statements accompanying the government draft of the 1994 'Dependency Insurance Act' make no mention of positive employment impacts. It was only well into the process of enacting the law that this point was raised by a cabinet member. At this stage, government officials projected that the new provisions for long-term care would create some 150,000 jobs in the social services sector. This benefit in terms of job growth was an argument brought forward to support an increase in public spending on long-term care even in times of budget constraints (Hauschild, 1997, p. 37; Pabst, 1999, pp. 235 et seq.).

The political emphasis, however, was on establishing incentives for family caring. There is a common belief that women's increased labour force participation will diminish the capacity of families to provide unpaid care to relatives. Hence, the hope was that offering cash benefits would help underpin family care, because care recipients would pass parts of their cash benefits on to any family carer. In addition, beneficiaries were allowed to combine cash benefits and benefits in kind. As care needs increase, family caregivers may thus seek supplementary support from paid care workers, rather than giving up their caring role completely. This has meant that the specific design of the

German benefit system actually worked to limit rather than to foster employment growth in formal care. Moreover, little, if any, attention has been given to the impact of the benefit system on the employment–care nexus for family caregivers, most of whom are women. Those opposed to supporting informal care fear there will be additional pressures on women to give up work for care (Jenson and Jacobzone, 2000; Joshi, 1992).

Against this background, this chapter investigates the ways in which the benefit design in the German long-term care system affects employment. To this end, we briefly examine the main features of the social long-term care insurance scheme. One of the outstanding characteristics of the programme is the option for eligible persons to choose between, or to combine, cash benefits and benefits in-kind. This freedom of choice distinguishes the German LTCI from most other countries' long-term care systems. The conditions and outcomes of exercising this choice can be expected to affect substantially the employment impact of the programme, since the higher the share of beneficiaries opting for in-kind benefits, the higher the demand for professional care workers. The chapter, therefore, goes on to summarize findings on the choice and use of cash benefits, as compared with choosing benefits in kind. It then explores the relationship between benefit design and employment, and goes on to consider recent decisions to test case-managed systems of 'individual care budgets' and other current issues in the German long-term policy debate affecting long-term care benefits.

The mixed-benefit design of Germany's long-term care system

Institutional framework

The legal basis of the German long-term care scheme is the *Pflegeversicherungsgesetz – PflegVG* (law on long-term care insurance) codified as the eleventh book of the German social law book.[1]

To administer the system, the law established *Pflegekassen* (long-term care insurance agencies). These are independent but quasi governmental entities, which are managed under the aegis of statutory health insurance in order to achieve cost savings and to take advantage of existing expertise. The procurement of services for those beneficiaries who receive benefits in-kind is organized as a collective bargaining system at the regional level. Associations of care funds enter into negotiations with regional provider associations and local providers of social services about service fees. Providers include private, public or non-profit institutions, and agreements may also be reached with individual long-term care professionals (Mager, 1999, p. 213).

If a person in need of care is not eligible for benefits from the long-term care scheme s/he may still be eligible for social assistance benefits (benefits in kind and/or cash benefits). Municipalities are responsible for the procurement of home care services, while the districts or the *Länder* are responsible for securing access to institutional care, and both are granted by the social assistance schemes (Mager, 1999, p. 214). Accordingly, the *Länder* are supposed to introduce their own long-term care laws (*Landespflege-Gesetze*), which for the most part concern public funding for the development of care infrastructure.

Funding

The German long-term care scheme is financed through compulsory contributions, which are equal throughout Germany. From January 1995 they represented 1 per cent and since July 1996 1.7 per cent of gross earnings. Any rise in the contribution rate can only be determined by an act of parliament, and there is a fixed ceiling for the monthly earnings that are taken into account in calculating the insurance premium. The contribution base (*Beitragsbemessungsgrenze*) for 2004 amounts to monthly earnings of €3,487.50, with the maximum contribution set at €59.29 per month. The premium is shared equally between employers and employees, but the transaction is processed by the employer. In the case of pensioners, the premium is shared equally by the pensioner and his or her pension fund. The federal unemployment agency pays contributions on behalf of the unemployed. This arrangement is a typical Bismarckian design element. Employers originally objected to this approach, but were then offered compensation for sharing the contribution. This compensation consisted in eliminating a mandatory paid holiday (Penance Day) (Cuellar and Wiener, 2000, pp. 10–11).[2]

The system was originally set up as a pay-as-you-go system, where contributions made in each period should not exceed the expenditures in that same period. Current deficits will undermine this notion in the medium term.

Beneficiaries and eligibility criteria

The law (§14 and §15 SGB XI) states that persons are eligible for benefits granted by the long-term care insurance scheme if they have a mental or physical condition that results in a need for assistance with two activities of daily living (ADLs) for at least 90 minutes a day, and is expected to last for at least six months. In addition to help with ADL, prospective beneficiaries must also require help in some instrumental activities of daily living (IADLs) (Comas-Herrera *et al.*, 2003, p. 5).

ADLs refer to personal hygiene (bathing, using the toilet, shaving); eating (including food preparation); and mobility (getting in and out of bed, dressing, walking, standing, climbing stairs, leaving and returning home). IADLs refer to household activities such as shopping, cooking, cleaning, washing clothes, washing dishes and heating the home (Cuellar and Wiener, 2000, p. 12). The criteria are applied in the same way in assessments for benefits at home or for institutional care. There are, however, three eligibility categories, which vary according to the time required for care and the frequency of assistance needed (§15 SGB XI).

Additional 'help for care' benefits from the social assistance scheme are subject to means-testing. As shown in Table 7.1, the number of care clients who depend on social assistance has dropped considerably over time, following the introduction of LTCI in 1995.

Carers constitute a second group of LTCI beneficiaries. For two of the benefits offered – accident insurance and pension provisions (§44 SGB XI) – access is limited to those who meet the following eligibility criteria. Social security benefits are targeted to persons who provide

Table 7.1 Recipients of long-term care benefits, Germany 1994–2002

	Recipients of benefits from the social long-term care insurance (000s)			Recipients of 'help for care' social assistance benefits (000s)		
	All	*Home care*[1]	*Institutional care*	*All*	*Home care*[2]	*Institutional care*
1994	–	–	–	454	192	265
1995	1,061	1,061	–	373	88	286
1996	1,547	1,162	385	285	68	217
1997	1,661	1,198	463	251	66	185
1998	1,738	1,227	511	222	63	159
1999	1,819	1,275	544	247	58	189
2000	1,822	1,261	561	261	60	202
2001	1,840	1,262	578	256	62	194
2002	1,889	1,289	600	246	61	185

Note:
[1] Net of double entries;
[2] includes day/night care.
Source: Bundesministerium für Gesundheit und Soziale Sicherung (2001) and Statistisches Bundesamt (2003b, p. 38).

a minimum of 14 weekly care hours to LTCI beneficiaries (who are, by definition, substantially disabled persons) living in the community; who are not full-time employed (employed for less than 30 work hours per week) or retired; and who do not provide care on a 'gainful' basis (§19 SGB XI).

In 2000, some 530,000 informal carers – 93 per cent of whom were women – were eligible for pension provisions and accident insurance. Spending on these benefits amounted to €1.1bn in 2000. Take-up rates and expenditure on these types of carer benefits have recently been declining. In addition to these direct benefits offered to carers, cash benefits provided to care recipients are explicitly treated as an additional source of income to (family) carers. The legislation aimed to 'enable care users to express gratitude' to any (family) carer via cash gifts from the cash benefits received.

Benefits

Benefit design requires three basic decisions: about what services and providers to cover; what type of benefit to offer; and the degree of choice offered to beneficiaries. This section discusses the first design issue. Benefit types and choices available to beneficiaries are considered below.

The first benefit design issue relates to the range of services and providers covered. Service coverage can be narrow, focusing on help with the ADLs or on medical assistance. Programmes can also cover home modifications, assistance with transport or social support services (Freedman and Kemper, 1996, p. 139–140). LTCI covers a limited set of formal services, whereas coverage is broader in the case-managed welfare system. The emphasis in the menu of LTCI service benefits is on nursing and homemaking (the latter involves financial management and other services well beyond standard housework), rather than on housekeeping (help with standard housework) or social support. Health care comes within the remit of the sickness funds, but it is not always easy to distinguish between medical treatments for acute conditions and care provided because of a long-term disabling condition.

The German long-term care system provides benefits at three levels of dependency. Each dependency level represents a specific degree of functional limitation based upon the definitions of ADLs and IADLs mentioned above. The system is not designed to cover fully all costs related to long-term care, but to relieve some of the financial burden. Benefits are flat rate, and any additional care needed has

Table 7.2 Out-of-pocket payments for long-term care[1], Germany 1997 and 2002

Out-of-pocket expenses related to care	1997 (%)	2002 (%)
No out-of-pocket expenses	40.4	47.4
< 99 Euros	21.9	20.0
100–249 Euros	25.2	22.2
250–499 Euros	8.4	6.6
> 500 Euros	4.1	3.8
Total	100.0	100.0
n =	920	1,054

Note: [1] Households of LTCI beneficiaries living in the community.
Source: adapted from Runde *et al.*, (2003, p. 20).

to be met by family caregivers or has to be paid for out of pocket. Table 7.2 shows the percentage of households who report having out-of-pocket expenses for long-term care services in excess of the benefits received.

Since benefits are graded, the gap in coverage depends on the care recipient's degree of functional limitation, as well as on the specific care arrangement chosen. In the case of residential care, the German long-term care scheme differentiates between costs for board and lodging, investment costs and the actual cost of care services. Board and lodging is not covered under the LTCI. These so-called 'hotel costs' do not include costs resulting from building or modernizing nursing homes, which are treated as investment costs. The latter are partly financed by the *Länder* and partly by nursing home residents, while care expenses are co-financed by the long-term care insurance (see Comas-Herrera *et al.*, 2003, p. 25). Additional health related costs are be covered by health insurance (Mager, 1999, p. 240).

Benefits on a sub-national level resemble social assistance benefits and are, therefore, modest. In addition, they take into consideration any benefits obtained from other long-term care schemes, namely the federal long-term care insurance (Mager, 1999, p. 222).

The German LTCI offers benefits to persons in need of care (attendance allowances) as well as benefits to carers. The latter include: provision for substitute care (€1,430 covering 4 weeks of holiday); free training classes in nursing (*Pflegekurse*); further training (when resuming employment after a spell of informal care); pension coverage and accident insurance.

The monthly pension entitlement for one year of informal care currently ranges between €6.60 and 20€ (€5.80–€17.40 in the former East-German *Länder*); spending related to these carer benefits was €1.07bn in 2000 (6.4 per cent of total programme expenditure).

Special features of the German system: Abundance of benefit categories and choices

Freedman and Kemper (1996, pp. 131–3) distinguish four types of care benefits based on two basic characteristics of a benefit: (a) whether the benefit is provided in cash or in-kind; and (b) responsibility for determining the benefit (level). With regard to the latter dimension, models of consumer-direction assume that care clients are able to arrange care for themselves. Case-management, by contrast, is much tighter and leaves less room for choice about providers and care plans. This typology can be extended by looking at another dimension, namely (c) whether the benefit is directed at care clients or at carers. The potential spectrum of benefits from which to assemble a long-term care support programme then includes:

- 'Disability allowances' for care clients, which are cash benefits for unrestricted use by beneficiaries.
- 'Individualized cash benefits' directed at care clients, which involve case management.
- Standardized service entitlements, where the level of the benefit is fixed in the programme rules, leaving little discretion to beneficiaries or nurses.
- Managed service entitlements for care clients, where case managers or nurses determine the types of services to be used and the benefit level.
- Respite care, although provided in-kind to a care client, targeted to the carer and offering an opportunity to take a break from caring. Other carer benefits may include training for care or job training (especially after terminating a caring spell).
- Cash benefits to, or wages for, carers.

The benefit design within the German LTCI offers beneficiaries the opportunity to choose among four out of six of these basis benefit categories. The categories omitted are those involving case-management.[3] Benefits to care clients include in-kind benefits for institutional care, in-kind benefits for formal community-based services, a flat rate cash benefit paid to persons receiving home care, or a mixed benefit package. With the latter, benefits for formal community-based

Table 7.3   Long-term care insurance benefits (in € per month)

	Home care (cash benefits)	Home care (in-kind)	Day and night care (in-kind)	Nursing home care (in-kind)
Dependency level I	205	384	384	1,023
Dependency level II	410	921	921	1,279
Dependency level III	665	1,432	1,432	1,432

Source: §§ 36–45 SGB XI.

services and cash benefits may be combined. In instances where home care is not available to the extent needed, beneficiaries may also combine cash benefits or in-kind benefits for home care on the one hand, with day or night-care delivered outside the home (in institutions) on the other. The flat rate cash benefit is graded according to the three levels of disability as codified in the law, and amounts to €205, €410 or €665 per month (see Table 7.3). Beneficiaries who opt for cash benefits may spend them at their own discretion. In particular, it is up to them to pass on any of the benefits granted to any person providing care (Igl and Stadelmann, 1998; Reyes, 2003, p. 4; Skuban, 2000). In cases where different types of benefits are combined, the use of one type of benefit reduces the level of the other type of benefit chosen (i.e., there can be no accumulation of benefits).

This broad range of benefits may have been adopted to offer freedom of choice as well as with an instrumental rationale. By implementing a system that leaves the care user with a choice, a more optimal use of resources is assured. Furthermore, both in-kind and cash benefits have distinct and different advantages (Thurow, 1974). Overall, the design of the benefit system strikes a balance between consumer choice, accountability and cost-containment (Walker and Schwalberg, 1996, pp. 7 et seq.).

The German benefit system gives care clients the basic responsibility to decide upon the service mix used (the selection of caregiver and/or services), which means that they in fact choose between different degrees of involvement. Opting for a cash benefit implies full responsibility for one's own care arrangement. Care clients (and their informal caregivers) who select a combination of cash benefits and formal community-based services accept a certain degree of co-decision-making by care professionals and will have to adjust to their schedules. In an institutional care setting, there is little if any co-decision-making by care clients. To sum up: in the German system, clients' involvement in care plan determination is high, but beneficiaries may decide deliberately to forgo some of their discretion.

Care clients' choices relating to the type or mix of benefit they would like to use is likely to affect employment in the long-term care sector. The higher the share of beneficiaries opting for in-kind benefits, the higher the demand for professional care workers. At the same time, benefit choices can also be expected to have an impact on the employment decisions of family carers. Given the crucial role of benefit choices in determining the various outcomes of German long-term care policy, in the following section we will briefly summarize evidence on benefit choices and benefit use.

Empirical evidence on benefit choice and benefit use

Motives for the choice of cash benefits

In December 1995, shortly after the introduction of LTCI, Evers and Rauch (1996) conducted 12 interviews among elderly beneficiaries who had opted for cash benefits in order to investigate their choices and use of cash benefits. Further insight into the motives for choosing benefits was obtained in a 1996 representative survey of almost 3,000 LTCI beneficiaries aged 30 and older and their families (Runde *et al.*, 1996). This survey focused on attitudes towards the new long-term care insurance, on behavioural responses to the institutional setting and on the satisfaction of beneficiaries. Several questions addressed the specific features of cash benefits and service benefits. In what follows, we draw on both studies to highlight factors determining the choices LTCI beneficiaries make between cash benefits and benefits in kind.

Relative attractiveness of in-kind and cash services

Evers and Rauch (1996, pp. 32 et seq.) assume that a strong preference for family care, combined with the actual availability of relatives who may provide such care creates a predisposition for cash benefits. The results of the 2002 Eurobarometer study show that preferences for family care are indeed strong in Germany. Asked about how they would deal with the emerging care need of an elderly parent living alone, roughly a third of respondents made reference to formal care, whereas just under two-thirds thought in terms of family care (European Foundation for the Improvement of Living Conditions, 2004, p. 75).

Experienced family carers appear to be quite confident in their own caring capacities and rely on their family doctor for additional support.

According to Evers (1997, p. 514), rather than selecting services in-kind, care clients tended to consult their general practitioners in case of need. Home visits by the doctor are covered – in an open-ended way – by sickness funds. Hence, family carers may simply feel no need to consult home care agencies.

Also, from the perspective of care recipients (and their families) formal home care services cannot fully substitute for family care, which is usually based on long-standing interpersonal relationships. Runde *et al.*'s study (1996, p. 77) shows that 67 per cent of beneficiaries drawing in-kind benefits, and 41 per cent of those who were using home care services, thought that 'having in kind services delivered to one's house by strangers' and experiencing a lot of change in the provider's personnel is a disadvantage of service benefits.

The traditional preference for family care in Germany has shaped public policy towards long-term care. As a result, support for developing community-based care services was only moderate prior to the 1994 long-term care reform. In the mid 1990s, clients and their families still faced shortages or deficiencies in certain services (i.e., day or night care) and certain low-level support services were not covered by LTCI. The supply of attendance services and social support services was still limited at this time, and there is still much room of improvement ten years into the programme's operation. In services for people with dementia, for example, only about 6 per cent of the 12,300 registered social service providers in the community offer a basic support arrangement (Röber, 2004, p. 5). Attendance time is not adequately covered by LTCI, so it is not profitable for home care providers to include this type of support in their range of services (Deutscher Bundestag, 2001, p. 1; Evers, 1997, p. 514). However, recent legislation linked to the Dependency Insurance Act (*Pflegeleistungs-Ergänzungsgesetz* (PflEG)) has increased coverage for people suffering from dementia or other persons requiring general supervision (see below).

A fair number of care clients 'sample' community-based services following a release from hospital, because the sickness funds cover post acute home health services. According to experts in the field, who have been interviewed in conjunction with the 1995 pilot study of LTCI beneficiaries, care clients tend to be discontented with these services (Evers, 1997, p. 513). Home health services are experienced as inflexible in terms of the type of help offered and also with respect to the scheduling of visits. Furthermore, they are characterized by frequent changes in the staff delivering services to out-patients. It is reasonable to assume that negative experiences from early incidents of hospitalization – which may occur even before the onset of a long-term limiting health condition – contribute to negative images of formal care services.

On the other hand, the households of beneficiaries who use in-kind benefits apparently come to value these services. Care clients and their families appreciate that 'with service benefits, the care recipient is less dependent on relatives', as declared by 61 per cent of beneficiaries using the mixed-benefit and 68.3 per cent of those using services based in the community only (Runde *et al.*, 1996, p. 80). The same households also acknowledge that in-kind benefits provided by home care agencies 'allow time savings', which is considered an advantage by 90 per cent of the mixed-benefit households and by 69 per cent of households in the service-benefit group (Runde *et al.*, 1996, p. 79).

The study by Runde *et al.* also shows that only one in two households that have selected a cash benefit, and one in three households receiving a combination of cash and service benefits, perceive cash benefits as a 'personal and regular income for carers' (Runde *et al.*, 1996, pp. 73 et seq.). This corroborates the findings from Evers and Rauch (1996, p. 36) that money was not a factor that initiated family care in the first place, but rather was a benefit which went with it. Against this backdrop, cash benefits appear to make little difference for the interrelated decisions about employment and caring by potential family carers. Furthermore, cash benefits do not seem to have changed the character of family caring in a way that brings it closer to formal employment.

In 1995, the majority of households applying for LTCI benefits had already established a care arrangement some time previously. They stuck with family caring and welcomed the new benefits as a way of sustaining the established arrangement. More and more, care clients and their families now take first-time decisions on care arrangements, and may assess the advantages and disadvantages of each benefit category in a different way (Evers, 1997, p. 512, note 9). This is, however, still to be fully established through further empirical investigation.

Change in the use of long-term care benefits over time

Table 7.4 displays the actual take-up behaviour of LTCI benefits over the past eight years. In the first year of operation, the overwhelming majority of beneficiaries selected cash benefits (83 per cent) or a combination of cash and service benefits (7.7 per cent). Only a small minority of beneficiaries opted for in-kind benefits. The share of beneficiaries using benefits in-kind has gone up since then – an effect which is partly accounted for by the extension of LTCI coverage to institutional care in 1996 (Runde *et al.*, 2003; Simon, 2003).

Table 7.4 Beneficiaries of the social long-term care insurance by type of benefit chosen (percentages)

	Benefit					
Year	Cash benefit	In-kind benefit	Combined-benefit	Day/night care	Institutional care	Institutional care (homes for disabled people)
1995	83.0	7.7	7.7	0.2	–	
1996[1]	60.4	6.8	8.7	0.2	22.7	0.4
1997	56.3	6.9	9.1	0.3	24.6	2.2
1998	53.6	7.5	9.6	0.4	25.2	3.2
1999	52.0	8.1	10.2	0.5	25.7	2.9
2000	50.7	8.5	10.3	0.5	26.3	3.0
2001	50.0	8.4	10.5	0.6	26.7	3.0
2002	49.6	8.4	10.4	0.7	27.0	3.1
2003	49.0	8.6	10.3	0.7	27.3	3.2

Note: [1] Second half of the year, as benefits for institutional care were introduced on 1 July.
Source: Bundesministerium für Gesundheit und Soziale Sicherung (2001).

Spending on cash benefits fell by 4.9 per cent between 1997 and 2001, whereas spending on combined-benefits and spending on benefits in-kind (care in the community only) increased by 28 and 29 per cent, respectively. There are two possible interpretations of this trend: an increase in the use of in-kind services could be indicative of how family care arrangements respond to a deterioration in the care recipient's condition. In this case, community-based services work in effect to stabilize ongoing informal care arrangements. Interestingly, the increase in the use of in-kind benefits and mixed-benefits is highest for beneficiaries with the lowest level of disability. So care needs seem to have increased for a fair share of beneficiaries in this group who have not been grouped into a higher disability – and thus benefit – level. Yet, the increase in services can also be seen as a sign of an 'erosion of informal care' (Simon, 2003, p. 224) and overstressed carers. The latter explanation is the more plausible when the increase in nursing home transitions is taken into account (Simon, 2003, p. 225). Recent developments thus point to an increase in the use of in-kind benefits which is likely to increase employment in the long-term care industry.

Long-term care benefits and employment

Employment is related to provisions for long-term care in several ways. First, there is the potential impact of different funding regimes on aggregate employment. Alternatively, the effects of overall programme spending or benefit design on employment can be assessed; this is the focus of the present section. In what follows, we look first at the impact of social long-term care insurance on employment in the social services sector. We also explore the impact of benefits on the employment of family carers. More specifically, we then discuss whether cash benefits can establish employer–employee relations between care clients and family carers in private households, which are in any way comparable to employment contracts or paid jobs elsewhere. A further question concerns the impact of benefit design in the German LTCI on the supply of the labour of family carers.

Employment growth in the social services sector

Public procurement of long-term care services on behalf of those who claim in-kind benefits creates a direct link between programme expenditure and demand for care professionals. Moreover, the demand for social services – and thus for workers who deliver these services – increases if beneficiaries decide to top up the level of services covered by insurance through private out-of-pocket spending. In some instances, recipients of cash benefits may decide to use (part of) the cash transfer on community-based services.

Figure 7.1 shows the development of employment in social services (excluding hospitals) from the introduction of the German LTCI in 1995 until 2000. The chart shows five lines, each representing the number of employees in different categories of social services employment. Employment figures for registered (hospital) nurses, (hospital) nurse aides and nurse practitioners show the highest increases in absolute terms. The number of registered (hospital) nurses employed in social services nearly doubled from 66,000 in 1995 to 112,000 in 2000. The employment of nurse practitioners shows similar expansion; it rose from 169,000 in 1995 to 282,000 in 2000. Both figures show a relative increase (69.7 and 66.9 per cent, respectively). The employment of (hospital) nurse aides grew by 44.4 per cent, from 36,000 in 1995 to 52,000 in 2000.

There is lower absolute growth in employment in the case of homemakers and housekeepers, where the number of employees rose from 20,000 in 1995 to 33,000 in 2000 and 13,000 in 1995 to 19,000 in 2000, respectively. Uncertificated housekeepers (*Haushaltshilfe*) offer support with standard housework, while certified homemakers (*HauswirtschafterInnen*) assist with the household's financial management and other services, going well beyond standard housework. Homemakers receive at least 36 months of vocational training.

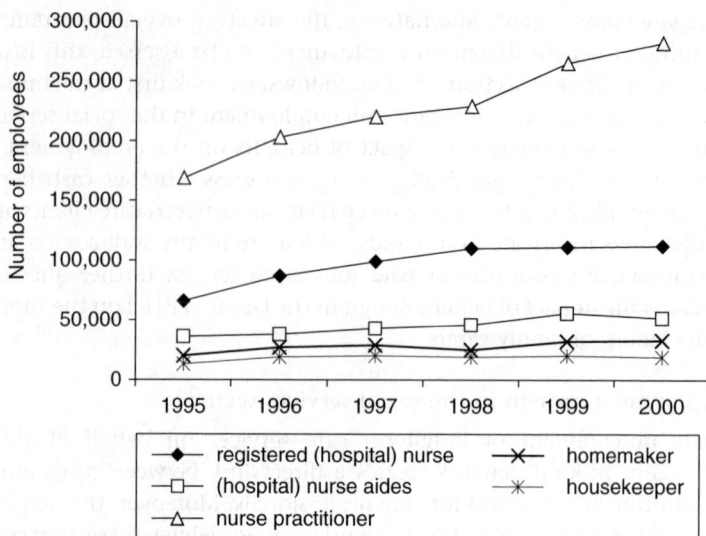

Figure 7.1 Employment growth in social services[1] in Germany 1995–2000
Note: [1] excluding hospitals
Source: Bundesministerium für Gesundheit und Soziale Sicherheit (2001, p. 162).

The difference in rate of growth may arise from the more essential or indispensable service provided by registered (hospital) nurses, (hospital) nurse aides and nurse practitioners, compared with the services delivered by homemakers and housekeepers. The type of care the homemakers provide may be a more essential type of care, closer to the essence of care, while housekeepers help to run errands or perform other tasks that are more related to the household than to the person in need of care. This distinction is consistent with the categorization of help needed into support with ADLs on the one hand, and the less essential IADLs on the other, as posited by the German LTCI (Cuellar and Wiener, 2000, p. 12). IADLs represent additional services that may be more easily provided by informal carers, and are thus less likely to be bought from professional providers.

On an aggregate level, employment in social services (excluding hospitals) increased by 63.8 per cent, from 304,000 employees in 1995 to 498,000 in 2000. The Social Report 2001 (Bundesministerium für Gesundheit und Soziale Sicherheit, 2001, pp. 161–2) attributes the creation of almost 200,000 jobs in social services to LTCI. To what extent the benefits provided under the German LTCI scheme account for this job expansion cannot be stated more precisely. Other factors, such as the out-of-pocket payments made by LTCI beneficiaries or persons who did not qualify for LTCI benefits at the start, may also be driving this employment growth. Certainly, LTCI played an important part in this job creation, as out-of-pocket expenses for long-term care services remain low (Runde *et al.*, 2003, p. 20). However, to what extent employment in the long-term care sector would have developed without the introduction of LTCI remains an open question. It is very difficult (if not impossible) to measure the truly distinctive impact of the 1994 legislation.

The benefit levels within LTCI have not been adjusted since the Dependency Insurance Act was passed. As a result, the real value of benefits has been constantly eroding, since prices for professional care medication and auxiliaries are rising. Findings from two representative surveys of LTCI beneficiaries in 1997 and 2002 show that out-of-pocket spending has not compensated for this loss in the value of the benefits received (Runde *et al.*, 2003, p. 20). The proportion of households reporting out-of-pocket expenses was actually 7 percentage points lower in 2002 (52.6 per cent) than in 1997 (59.6 per cent). Furthermore, just 8 per cent of LTCI beneficiaries spent additional money on home care services. Only households with monthly net income of €2,500 or more displayed a higher share (18.6 per cent) of beneficiaries with out-of-pocket spending on services based in the community. This group may be responsible for the slight increase in employment among homemakers and housekeepers. Taken together, there appears to be no 'crowding-in' effect of public long-term care benefits in terms of additional private care expenses which would support and stimulate employment growth in the care sector.

Benefit design and the employment of family carers: A new formalized 'worker status' for family carers?

The German long-term care scheme does not include care allowances. However, the cash benefits which form part of the benefit package for care clients can be passed on to family carers. Hence, there is at least the potential for a systematic and stable exchange of cash for family care. Taking account of the pension benefits for high-intensity carers and the premiums paid into accident insurance on their behalf, LTCI provisions seem to transform unpaid household labour into low paid, yet nevertheless paid employment. At a second look, however, the 'jobs' created in the realm of family households, have

Table 7.5　Calculated hourly wages for family carers providing home care

	Care intensity (hours per month)	Cash benefit (€)	Hourly wage (€)
Dependency level I	45–89	205	4.55–2.30
Dependency level II	90–149	410	4.55–2.75
Dependency level III	150–240	665	4.40–2.77

Source: Adapted from Pabst (1999, pp. 237 et seq.); based on §§15 and 37 SGB XI.

little else in common with regular jobs. There are striking differences in terms of wages, job security and access to social security (Pabst, 1999, pp. 237 et seq).

Even assuming that the full amount of the cash benefit is passed on to the family carer, the imputed hourly wage rate is very modest. Table 7.5 shows the range of wage rates for all levels of disability. A person caring for an LTCI beneficiary with the lowest level of disability, for example, would have to spend at least 45 hours of care per month on informal care (equivalent to 90 minutes per day – §15 SGB XI). At a benefit level of €205 per month, this hypothetical wage amounts to €4.55 per hour. With the care intensity increasing to just below the threshold for obtaining a level II benefit, the hourly wage rate reduces to €2.30 per hour.

Second, family carers who meet the eligibility criteria for obtaining social insurance benefits only gain pension and accidental injury coverage. No contributions are made on their behalf regarding unemployment, health or long-term care insurance. Furthermore, the level of pension entitlement that is acquired through specializing in family care is negligible. The monthly pension entitlement for a full year of informal caring currently amounts to €6.60–20.00 (€5.80–17.40 in the former Eastern-German *Länder*).

Finally, the payment is not something paid family carers can rely on, as they will be deprived of their earnings as soon as the dependent person opts for a different type of benefit for home care, moves into a nursing home, or dies. The 'employment' status of the family carer is thus highly precarious.

In summary, cash benefits have no positive employment impacts for informal carers. On the contrary, the mere existence of a cash benefit available to dependants which can be passed on to family caregivers may discourage family carers – predominantly women – from entering the labour market or from continuing in paid employment. Furthermore, the entitlement criteria for carer benefits limit the number of hours that can be spent in paid work.

Benefit design and the employment–caring nexus for family caregivers

A variety of empirical studies have investigated whether there is a statistically significant association between decisions taken about caring on the one hand, and the labour supply decisions of potential carers on the other hand. Here we summarize findings from several recent studies, before investigating the moderating role of long-term care benefits in the relationship between informal care and employment.

A recent analysis based on 1994 and 1996 data from the European Household Panel (ECHP) looked at women aged 45 to 59 who had been employed at least once in the period under consideration (Spieß and Schneider, 2003). This shows that women tend to reduce their weekly working hours once they assume a new caring responsibility or when the intensity of caring increases. For women in northern Europe, and hence in Germany, it is the change in care status that is negatively related to working hours. The working hours of women in southern Europe tend to vary with changes in the intensity of care. The latter finding points to the fact that women in southern Europe have less opportunity to share care responsibilities with other relatives or care professionals.

A study based on the German ECHP data, again focusing on women, who provide some 80 per cent of informal care, estimated the opportunity cost of informal care in terms of foregone earnings (Schneider, 2000). The analysis distinguished between earnings lost by working age women who were currently not employed and by women in paid employment. The loss in gross yearly earnings was estimated at €1,890 for those who were employed as well as caring, or an equivalent of €2.56 per hour of informal care provided. Female carers who were not participating in the labour market lost €6,136 per year (or €6.14 per hour of informal caring).

Several factors shape the relationship between caring and employment (Carmichael and Charles 1998). The cost of caring for a dependant draws on the household's budget, potentially causing household members to take up or remain in employment (the 'income effect'). In addition, time spent out of the home offers a way of recovering from the emotional and physical stress associated with caring (the 'respite effect'). Both factors may have a positive effect on the likelihood of employment and/or on the number of hours worked per week. On the other hand, carers' time budgets are limited, so additional hours of caring compete with leisure or with time spent in paid employment (the 'substitution effect').

Studies for Britain confirm that the likelihood of employment is influenced more by income and respite effects than by the substitution effect. However, the substitution effect affects the number of working hours (and hence earnings) in a negative way. The effects vary by gender, by care intensity, and by the care experience. Caring reduces the odds of employment by 12.9 per cent for men and by 27 per cent for women. Furthermore, men are more likely to combine full-time employment with caring than women. Interestingly, there are threshold effects such that providing more than 10 hours of care per week reduces the likelihood of employment, and providing more than 20 weekly hours of care has a noticeable effect on earnings. British employees providing more than 20 hours of informal care per week earn some 10 per cent less per hour than colleagues who do not face caring responsibilities. Carmichael and Charles also found the negative impact of caring on earnings to be lower for those employees with more experience of caring, which they interpreted as learning to cope with time pressure (Carmichael and Charles, 2003a, 2003b).

In summary, caring has been found to have a negative impact on the labour supply decisions of family carers. These effects seem to be shaped by the institutional background at the country level (Spieß and Schneider, 2003). There are several factors at work which partly countervail: income and respite effects on the one hand, and a substitution effect on the other. The relative strength of these factors varies by gender, care intensity and experience of caring. Against this background, how do we judge the potential impact of the specific design of long-term care benefits in Germany on the labour supply of informal carers?

In terms of the income effect, a cash benefit option reduces both the odds of combining caring and employment and the number of working hours of those who do. There is a reduced care-related need to earn income. In addition, pressures on women to assume the traditional housekeeping and caring roles and to forgo employment opportunities could be backed up by the cash option and social security benefits for caregivers (Evers, 1997, p. 517; Pabst, 1999, p. 238).

The eligibility criteria for carers' access to pension coverage completely exclude full-time employment for the carer. Family carers are not supposed to spend more than 30 hours per week in gainful employment. At the same time, access to pension benefits is limited to carers who provide at least 14 hours of care per week. If the threshold effects identified for British carers apply to German carers – more than 10 hours of caring for an impact on the odds of employment and more than 20 hours for an impact on earnings – these criteria would damage the employment opportunities of family carers.

At the same time, the existence of a mixed-benefit option and improved access to services in the community could strengthen the respite effect and mitigate time pressures (the substitution effect). However, more than 70 per cent of working family carers providing care to LTCI beneficiaries support a person who draws cash benefits only (Runde *et al.*, 2003, p. 34). The benefit chosen could be indicative of the fact that community-based services do not meet the specific demands of the carer (i.e., in terms of scheduling or location). Also, as explained above, in most cases beneficiaries and their family carers jointly decide on the type of benefits to be claimed. The care client may judge the pros and cons of in-kind benefits differently from his or her carer. According to Runde *et al.* (2003, p. 34), there is no statistically significant relationship between a carer's employment and the type of benefit used. However, such a relationship may emerge if working hours rather than employment status are examined, and if occupational status is controlled for. Further empirical research is needed on this point.

Mixing up the mix? Current issues in Germany's long-term care debate

Possible future adjustments – An overview of the political discussion

Since 2000 the German long-term care system has been operating in deficit. Deficits totalled approximately €400 m in 2002 and €500 m in 2003. This was partly because of reduced contributions made by unemployed people. Previously, annual deficits could be covered by the financial surplus accumulated in earlier years. The Kohl administration set up the system with a built-in surplus by allowing insurers to collect contributions from January 1995, but only paying out benefits for home or ambulant care from April 1995 (and for stationary care from July 1996). This financial reserve is expected to cover the deficits until 2006 only.

The margin for measures capable of reforming the system is slender. Currently employers and employees contribute 1.7 per cent of gross earnings to the system. Higher contributions would increase non-wage labour costs and probably worsen the general labour market situation.

However, following a decision by the supreme court, the government has decided to increase contributions by 0.25 percentage points for childless insurants aged 24 to 65 from January 2005. Other solutions range from moving to a tax-funded system or merging health and long-term care insurance, to abolition of the system as a whole (Meyer-Timpe, 2003; *Süddeutsche Zeitung*, 2003).

The current debate on reform of the German LTCI also affects changes in the benefits permitted by the system. There has been considerable political pressure on LTCI administrators to adjust benefit levels to current revenues. Meyer (2003, p. 321) found that the medical assessment of a care user's degree of functional limitation by the LTCI is influenced by budget pressures. One indication for budget-oriented benefit allocation is that in the past the overall amount of care approved (measured in minutes) has been growing along with the revenues (see Simon, 2003, p. 228).

Preventing or delaying transitions into institutional care is considered an effective cost containment strategy. To this (and other) end(s), recent reform of the long-term care legislation has opened the door for a variety of pilots which include the use of case-managed care budgets, which are currently being tested in seven regions in Germany.

Individualized, case-managed care budgets

One strategy, which takes financial concerns into account, as well as contributing to the empowerment of care clients and the quality of care, is to increase the coverage and supply of low-level support services. These services seem to meet the needs of care clients with mental health problems, who need supervision and attendance rather than support with performing the activities of daily life. Since long-term care insurance made no provisions for this group of care clients until very recently, attendance had to be provided by family carers. Emotional stress and time pressures are likely to be factors prompting the move of care users into nursing facilities, which are costly places for providing the low-level care needed (Deutscher Bundestag, 2001, p. 17).

A recent legislative amendment to the 1994 legislation (*Pflegeleistungs-Ergänzungsgesetzes – PflEG*) permits pilot activities (§8 Abs.3 SGB XI) which develop the German long-term care system, including individualized care budgets (*Personenbezogene Pflegebudgets*) (Schmidt, 2004, p. 134). It has also introduced additional cash benefits (€460 per month) for beneficiaries suffering from dementia or who need supervision for other reasons. Use of these benefits is subject to different rules than the use of standard cash benefits, and may involve case-management

(Deutscher Bundestag, 2001, p. 18 et seq.), and it is these innovations which we now discuss, together with their potential employment impact.

From September 2004, seven regions in Germany[4] have been testing a new case-managed benefit, in a project running for five years which is being evaluated. Individual care budgets offer a case-managed benefit in addition to cash benefits, benefit packages for community-based services or in-kind benefits for institutional care. The level of the benefit will be equal the value of in-kind benefits for community-based care, ranging from €383 per month for beneficiaries with the lowest degree of functional limitations, to €1,432 for beneficiaries with the highest level of dependency.

Recipients of cash transfers under this programme may spend their benefit on social services, but cannot pass the benefit on to a family carer. They have a wider choice of providers and services than recipients of in-kind benefits. Beneficiaries in the pilots may buy services from an agent who is not a contracted partner of a care fund. The benefit can also be used to purchase services that are not specifically related to help with ADL. Case-workers will advise beneficiaries on their choice of services, and will offer support in the contracting process. They may help in assessing the quality of services offered or purchased and will also secure accountability. A concern is that no funds should be channelled into the grey economy. The association of care funds is spending €8 m on this pilot over the next four years (o.V. 2004; Arntz and Spermann, 2004, pp. 12 et seq.; Deutscher Bundestag, 2001, p. 17).

Individualized care budgets can be tailored to the needs of care recipients, and give beneficiaries a higher spending capacity than recipients of the standard cash benefit. However, the extra resources are not targeted towards family carers, but channelled into community-based services. Proponents of this type of benefit hope to achieve the empowerment of care clients as service providers improve their customer focus in response. The effectiveness of individual care budgets thus depends crucially on the ability of care clients and their families to shop for services. Counselling is considered essential in securing the quality and accountability of this type of cash benefit (Arntz and Spermann, 2004, pp. 12 et seq.; Schmidt, 2004, p. 135).

The new care budget for persons with special attendance needs creates an incentive for home care agencies to develop new types of (low-level) support services and seeks to relieve family carers from some care demands (Deutscher Bundestag, 2001, pp. 16 et seq.). Since 1 April 2004, LTCI beneficiaries with a substantial need for supervision can claim €460 per year for additional care services as specified by the law or in state specific legislation (day care, night care, low-level support). While home care agencies have not yet adjusted their range of services accordingly, temporary employment agencies have entered the market, offering, for example, support in running errands (Röber, 2004, p. 6).

Commenting on the draft of the *Pflegeleistungs-Ergänzungsgesetz*, policymakers stressed that their primary aim was to improve the care infrastructure, and that an alternative was simply to increase the level of cash benefits. Some strings are, therefore, attached to the use of the new cash benefit. The 'attendance budget' may not be spent on additional in-kind benefits of the type included in the standard package of in-kind benefits, and provided by the contract partners of the care funds. This means the care funds cannot absorb the additional programme funds by merely charging extra for difficult working conditions. However, traditional providers of home care services may develop and deliver new types of attendance services.

Both measures rely on ring-fenced funding to improve the coverage of long-term care insurance while simultaneously increasing the efficiency of the long-term care system and developing the care infrastructure in the community. They stimulate job growth in low-level support services, but may also slow employment growth in home care services and in institutional care.

The annual cost for a household that formally employs a home helper on a 'mini-job basis' can be used to estimate the maximum effect of the pilot on low-paid employment in private households. If the home helper works 50 hours per month (11.6 hours per week) for an hourly wage rate of €8, the annual cost to the employer (including flat-rate social insurance contributions and a Christmas allowance) amounts to some €5,500.[5] Spending €1 bn on this type of benefit, and assuming that case-management and administration would claim 10 per cent of this budget, would create some 164,000 'mini jobs' in the households of beneficiaries. Current spending on cash benefits is around €8 bn per year; the pilots have a yearly budget of €2 m.

Conclusion

Germany can look back on ten years' experience of its long-term care insurance scheme. Many of its initial goals were met (Cuellar and Wiener, 2000, p. 9). The legislation covers almost 100 per cent of the German population, who now have to provide for long-term dependency in one way or another. The number of recipients benefiting from the LTCI scheme is rising steadily, reaching a total of 1.8 million bene-ficiaries in 2002. Services can be provided to disabled persons in all age groups, preventing unnecessary fragmentation of long-term care protection. There are now fewer recipients of social assistance benefits among frail and elderly people, reducing heavy budgetary pressures on communities responsible for granting social assistance benefits ('help for care'). Contributions to the LTCI could be kept at 1995 levels. The exploding costs of institutional care and other care services have been restrained by budget oriented benefit allocation, and by not adjusting benefit levels in line with inflation. Yet this cost containment comes at a price for programme effectiveness; recently the number of care users dependent on social assistance has been increasing again. The poverty risk is particularly high among care users receiving institutional care. One in three care users living in a nursing home or skilled nursing facility depends on social assistance (*Süddeutsche Zeitung*, 2003).

The potential impact of the new German long-term care policy on employment in the social services sector is dependent on total programme expenditure and on the level of individual benefits. In this chapter we have investigated the major factors guiding the way German LTCI beneficiaries make choices between cash benefits and benefits in kind. This deserves particular attention, because, as we have indicated, the pattern of benefit choice and use limits the extent to which programme spending translates into employment growth in professional care.

The freedom of choice between the different benefits of the German LTCI enables persons in need of care to receive a benefit mix that closely suits their needs. In the early years of the programme, longstanding traditions and attitudes towards family obligations seem to have guided the benefit choices of care users and their families. Hence, cash benefits met with a strong private orientation in long-term care (Evers, 1997, p. 517). As most beneficiaries opted for cash benefits or a combination of cash and in-kind benefits, the full potential employment impact of the long-term care legislation was not realized. Much programme spending was absorbed in private households and thus did not benefit the labour market for care professionals, homemakers or housekeepers.

However, there have been distinct changes in the relative use of in-kind and cash benefits over time, with more and more households opting for in-kind services (or combinations of cash and in-kind bene-fits). This trend could be indicative of the fact that the care needs of beneficiaries have been increasing. It may also signal greater accept-ance of professional care services in the population. Nevertheless, cash benefits remain the preferred choice of persons in need of care. In 2003, 49 per cent of beneficiaries still received cash benefits only, and some 10 per cent combined cash benefits and community-based services.

Benefits in kind have a direct impact on employment in the social services sector, but are for budgetary reasons, less welcome to the LTCI administrators. Cash benefits, particularly in the German case, have a weaker influence on employment. One reason for this is the unregulated use of cash benefits by beneficiaries. Cash benefits may flow directly into the households' general budget without any spending on care. They may also be used to compensate informal long-term carers. Furthermore, cash benefits offer lower coverage compared with in kind benefits.

The difference in the levels of cash and in-kind benefits has helped to keep spending on long-term care under control, because most beneficiaries opted for cash benefits. A decade after introduction of long-term care insurance, willingness to provide informal care remains high, just as policymakers had hoped (Evers, 1995, p. 25). Despite the introduction of long-term care schemes to keep families – in fact mainly women – caring was a policy objective.

The design of carer benefits in the German LTCI scheme makes combining informal care and participation in the formal labour market rather difficult, and tends to reduce the participation of women in the labour market. Even taking into account the fact that cash benefits to beneficiaries (care allowances) may be passed on to informal carers, there is limited scope for creating employment in the households of care users. Informal carers are in a disadvantaged position compared with formal carers, as their payment is up to the care user and their (fictitious) hourly wage rate is considerably lower. Social insurance coverage is also lower than for formal carers (Pabst, 1999, p. 238).

Case-managed care budgets, as recently introduced, may have a stronger impact on the labour market. Although these too are cash benefits, they may create employment at the lower end of the labour market, because their use is controlled and they cannot be used to compensate family carers. Demand for household help or support with other simple tasks (instrumental activities of daily living) fuelled by case-managed care budgets thus may increase demand for low skilled labour.

In conclusion, the full impact of benefit design decisions on the outcomes of the German long-term care insurance remains under-researched. This applies to the employment effects of long-term care insurance, largely neglected in the original benefit design, but which could, in practice, be significant. Further empirical research is needed to highlight the impact of the design of long-term care insurance on employment in social services, and on the labour supply decisions of informal carers.

Notes

1. 11. *Buch des Sozialgesetzgebungs buches*, SGB XI hereafter.
2. In Saxony contributions are fully paid by the employees, since the state parliament refused to give up a public holiday.
3. However, if a beneficiary is eligible for 'help for care' benefits, he would confront some element of case-management as well.
4. Annaberg, Erfurt, Kassel, Marburg-Bidenkopf, München, Neuwed, Unna
5. Authors' estimation based on http://www.400-euro.de/400/haushaltshilfe. html

References

Arntz, M. and Spermann, A. (2004) 'Wie lässt sich die gesetzliche Pflegeversicherung mit Hilfe personengebundener Budgets reformieren?' *Sozialer Forschritt*, 53(1), 11–22.

Bundesministerium für Gesundheit und Soziale Sicherung (2001) *Sozialbericht 2001*, Bonn: Bundesministerium für Gesundheit und Soziale Sicherung.

Carmichael, F. and Charles, S. (1998) 'The Labour Market Costs of Community Care,' *Journal of Health Economics*, 17(6), 747–65.

Carmichael, F. and Charles, S. (2003a) 'Benefit Payments, Informal Care and Female Labour Supply', *Applied Economics Letters*, 10(7), 411–15.

Carmichael, F. and Charles, S. (2003b) 'The Opportunity Costs of Informal Care: Does Gender Matter?' *Journal of Health Economics*, 22(5), 781–803.

Comas-Herrera, A., Costa-Font, J., Gori, C., di Maio, A., Patxot, C., Pickard, L., Pozzi, A., Rothgang, H. and Wittenberg, R. (2003) *European Study of Long-Term Care Expenditure: Investigating the Sensitivity of Projections of Future Long-term Care Expenditure in Germany, Spain, Italy and the United Kingdom to Changes in Assumptions about Demography, Dependency, Informal Care, Formal Care and Unit Costs*, Report to the European Commission, Employment and Social Affairs DG, London: London School of Economics Health and Social Care.

Cuellar, A. E. and Wiener, J. M. (2000) 'Can Social Insurance for Long-term Care Work? The Experience of Germany,' *Health Affairs*, 19(3), 8–25.

Deutscher Bundestag (1993) *Gesetzentwurf der Fraktionen CDU/CSU und F.D.P. Entwurf eines Gesetzes zur sozialen Absicherung des Risikos der Pflegebedürftigkeit (Pflege-Versicherungsgesetz - PflegeVG). Bundestags-Drucksache 12/5262*, Bonn: Deutscher Bundestag.

Deutscher Bundestag (2001) *Gesetzentwurf der Fraktionen SPD und BÜNDNIS 90/DIE GRÜNEN. Entwurf eines Gesetzes zur Ergänzung der Leistungen bei häuslicher Pflege von Pflegebedürftigen mit erheblichem allgemeinem Betreuungsbedarf (Pflegeleistungs-Ergänzungsgesetz - PflEG). Bundestags-Drucksache 14/6949 vom 24.09.2001*, Berlin: Deutscher Bundestag.

Deutscher Bundestag (2003) *Schriftliche Fragen mit den in Woche vom 24. Februar 2003 eingegangenen Antworten der Bundesregierung. Bundestags-Drucksache 15/512, vom 28.02.2003*, Berlin: Deutscher Bundestag, 41–2.

European Foundation for the Improvement of Living Conditions (2004) *Quality of Life in Europe. Health and Health Care in an Enlarged Europe*, Luxembourg: Office for Official Publications of the European Communities.

Evers, A. (1995) 'Die Pflegeversicherung. Ein mixtum compositum im Prozeß der politischen Umsetzung', *Sozialer Forschritt*, 44(2), 23–8.

Evers, A. (1997) 'Geld oder Dienste? Zur Wahl und Verwendung von Geldleistungen im Rahmen der Pflegeversicherung', *WSI Mitteilungen*, 50(7), 510–18.

Evers, A. and Rauch, U. (1996) *Geldleistungen in der Pflegeversicherung – Motive und Mittelverwendung bei Personen, die im Rahmen des Pflegeversicherungsgesetzes die Geldleistungsalternative in Anspruch nehmen. Dezember 1995 – Mai 1996*, Pilotstudie gefördert durch die Hans-Böckler Stiftung, Düsseldorf, mimeo.

Freedman, V. A. and Kemper, P. (1996) 'Designing Home Care Benefits: The Range of Options and Experience', In Freedman, V. A. and Kemper, P. (eds), *From Nursing Homes to Home Care*, Binghamton: Haworth Press, 129–48.

Geraedts, M., Heller, G. and Harrington, C. A. (2000) 'Germany's Long-Term-Care Insurance: Putting a Social Insurance Model into Practice', *The Milbank Quarterly*, 78(3), 375–401.

Hauschild, R. (1997) *Politische Ziele und Beschäftigungswirkungen der Pflegeversicherung – Resümee nach zweieinhalb Jahren. Konsequenzen der Pflegeversicherung für die Pflegeberufe: eine Tagung der Friedrich-Ebert-Stiftung und der Senatsverwaltung für Arbeit, Berufliche Bildung und Frauen*, 17 September 1997. Berlin.

Igl, G. and Stadelmann, F. (1998) 'Die Pflegevorsicherung in Deutschland', in Igl, G. and Stadelmann, F. (eds), *Soziale Sicherung bei Pflegebedürftigkeit in der Europäischen Union*, Baden-Baden: Nomos, 37–49.

Jenson, J. and Jacobzone, S. (2000) *Care Allowances For the Frail Elderly and their Impact on Women Care-Givers*, OECD Labour Market and Social Policy Occasional Paper No. 41.

Joshi, H. (1992) 'The Cost of Caring', in Millar, J. (ed.), *Women and Poverty in Britain in the 1990s*, New York, London, Toronto: Harvester Wheatsheaf, 110–25.

Karrenberg, H. and Münstermann, E. (1999) 'Gemeindefinanzbericht 1999. Steuerpolitik '99 – Nicht gegen die Städte', *der Städtetag*, 52(4): 151–240.

Leitherer, S. (1997) 'Allgemeines zum Leistungsrecht', in Leitherer, S. (ed.), *Handbuch Sozialversicherungsrecht. Band 4. Pflegeversicherungsrecht*, München: Beck, 389–430.

Mager, H.-C. (1999) 'Pflegesicherung in der Bundesrepublik Deutschland', in Mager, H.-C. (ed.), *Pflegebedürftigkeit und Pflegesicherung in ausgewählten Ländern*, Opladen: Leske and Budrich, 207–47.

Meyer, D. (2003) 'Eine Prognose zum zukünftigen Bedarf in der stationären Altenhilfe', *Zeitschrift für Sozialreform*, 49(2), 313–33.

Meyer-Timpe, U. (2003) 'So jung und schon ein Pflegefall', Hamburg: Die Zeit, 27 March.

Morel, N. (2003) 'Providing Coverage Against New Social Risks in Bismarckian Welfare States: The Case of Long-term Care', Paper prepared for the ESPAnet inaugural conference 'Changing European Societies – The Role for Social Policy', 13–15 November. Copenhagen.

Pabst, S. (1999) 'Mehr Arbeitsplätze für Geringqualifizierte nach Einführung der Pflegeversicherung? Beschäftigungswirkungen des SGB XI im ambulanten Bereich', In *WSI Mitteilungen*, 52(4), 234–40.

Reyes, C. (2003) *European Portability Rules for Social Security Benefits and their Effects on the National Social Security Systems*. Working Paper No. 9. Vienna: Department of Social Policy at the Vienna University of Economics and Business Administration.

Röber, M. (2004) 'Anspruch und Wirklichkeit des Pflegeleistungs-Ergänzungsgesetzes (PflEG)', *informationsdienst altersfragen*, 31(3), 4–7.

Runde, P., Giese, R., Kerschke-Risch, P., Scholz, U. and Wiegel, D. (1996) *Einstellungen und Verhalten zur Pflegeversicherung und zur häuslichen Pflege. Ergebnisse einer schriftlichen Befragung von Leistungsempfängern in der Pflegeversicherung*, Hamburg: Universität Hamburg/Arbeitsstelle für Rehabilitations- und Präventionsforschung.

Runde, P., Giese, R. and Stierle, C. (2003) *Bericht: Einstellungen und Verhalten zur häuslichen Pflege und zur Pflegeversicherung unter den Bedingungen gesellschaftlichen Wandels. Analysen und Empfehlungen auf der Basis von repräsentativen Befragungen bei AOK-Leistungsempfängern der Pflegeversicherung*, Hamburg: Universität Hamburg/Arbeitsstelle Rehabilitations- und Präventionsforschung.

Schmidt, R. (2004) 'Personenbezogene Budgets. Neue Impulse in der häuslichen Langzeitpflege', *Blätter der Wohlfahrtspflege*, 151(4), 134–6.

Schneider, U. (2000) *The Economics of Informal Care. Theory and Evidence for Germany*, Hannover, mimeo.

Seewald, H. (1998) 'Ergebnisse der Sozialhilfe- und Asylbewerberleistungsstatistik 1996', *Wirtschaft und Statistik*, 1998(6), 96–110.

Simon, M. (2003) 'Die Ausgaben- und Leistungsentwicklung der Pflegeversicherung in den Jahren 1997 bis 2001', *Sozialer Fortschritt*, 2003(9), 221–230.

Skuban, R. (2000) *Die Pflegeversicherung – Eine kritische Betrachtung*, Wiesbaden: Deutscher Universitätsverlag.

Spieß, K. C. and Schneider, U. (2003) 'Interactions Between Care-giving and Paid work Hours Among European Midlife Women, 1994 to 1996', *Ageing and Society*, 23(1), 41–68.

Statistisches Bundesamt (1999) *Statistik der Sozialhilfe. Ausgaben und Einnahmen 1998*, Beiträge in 1000 DM. Arbeitsunterlage. Bonn: Statistisches Bundesamt.

Statistisches Bundesamt (2003a) *Pflegestatistik 2001*, Pflege im Rahmen der Pflegeversicherung. Deutschlandergebnisse, Bonn: Statistisches Bundesamt.

Statistisches Bundesamt (2003b) *Sozialhilfe in Deutschland 2003*, Entwicklung, Umfang, Strukturen. Presseexemplar. Bonn, Statistisches Bundesamt.

Stiftung Warentest (2002) 'Geld für die Pflege. Gut gepflegt', *FINANZtest*, 2002(12), 66–74.

Süddeutsche Zeitung (2003) 'Pflegeversicherung wird in Frage gestellt', München: *Süddeutsche Zeitung*.

Thurow, L. C. (1974) 'Cash Versus In-kind Transfers', *American Economic Review*, 64(2), 190–95.

Walker, G. and Schwalberg, R. (1996) *Payment for Family Caregivers: Balancing Consumer Choice and State Program Objectives*, Washington, DC: AARP Public Policy Institute.

8
Consumer-direction in an 'Ownership Society': An Emerging Paradigm for Home and Community Care in the United States

Sharon M. Keigher

Facing rapid population ageing in the next three decades, the United States expects its population aged 65 and over to grow from 12 per cent today to 20 per cent by 2030. Rather than prepare for population ageing, the Bush administration claims that 'social security is broken and needs total reform', and advocates diverting part of social security contributions into private investment accounts. Barely disguised in this discussion of social security in the USA are fundamental disagreements over future expectations of government, the meaning of dependency, the necessity of care itself, and how services might be delivered better, more humanely, and less expensively for tax payers. Like other developed countries, the US is testing out a new paradigm about choices over care in later life – moving a long way from the Fordist model of impersonal bureaucratic and standardized care delivery that has characterized institutional and home care for the past four decades, and towards a more personalized, flexible, humanized and privatized model which aims to give consumers more alternatives and more control.

This chapter describes the main features of that emerging paradigm, consumer-directed care, by reviewing recent demographic and policy developments in the USA in relation to changes in the need for and availability of formal and informal care. It examines some of the dilemmas embedded in the new politics of long-term care choice, and highlights some of the challenges that may result from making 'choice' and private preferences the bases of public policy on long-term care.

The demographics of increasing care demand and limited public policies

In the USA, long-term care refers to providing assistance and services to people of any age who have chronic physical or mental illness or disabling conditions that limit their ability to perform the basic activities of daily living (ADLs), such as toileting, bathing and dressing. Of the 31.4 million Americans aged 65 plus living in the community, about 14 per cent (4.4 million) have long-term functional disabilities requiring ongoing help from others. About 2.3 million need help with one or more ADLs, while 2.2 million need help only with the instrumental activities of daily living (IADLs, such as cooking, shopping or going outside the home.) Almost another one million older people are severely cognitively impaired by various forms of dementia (ASPE and AOA, 1998, p. 15). Since functional disabilities increase with old age and are more common among women, an ageing population is expected to increase significantly the demand for basic long-term care; by 2030 one in five Americans will be over age 65 (Summers and Ihara, 2004).

It is important to note that alongside these developments, the rate of nursing home use by older people has declined over the past two decades (although the disability levels of residents have increased). In 2002, just 5 per cent of older people resided in nursing homes, while another 2 per cent were living in community housing with some services, but 93 per cent remained in the community in their own homes. In fact, less than a quarter of older people with functional disabilities – about 1.4 million people – reside in nursing homes at any given time, while 4.2 million live in their own homes and communities, even at higher levels of disability. Of the latter group, 1.6 million older people with severe disabilities (i.e., 3 or more ADL dependencies or severe cognitive impairment) are able to remain in the community in their own or a relative's home (ASPE and AOA, 1998, p. 14), where 96 per cent of them receive some assistance from informal unpaid caregivers, and two-thirds rely entirely on such caregivers.

Besides being less functionally disabled than a generation ago, today's older Americans also have more financial resources with which to purchase care, since a much larger proportion of them are financially secure than in the past. In 1965, when Medicare began covering all older people with medical insurance, 35 per cent of them were living in poverty. But in the ensuing four decades, that level has gradually declined to 10 per cent (see Figure 8.1). Older people's socio-economic security (and that of their adult children) greatly improved after 1965

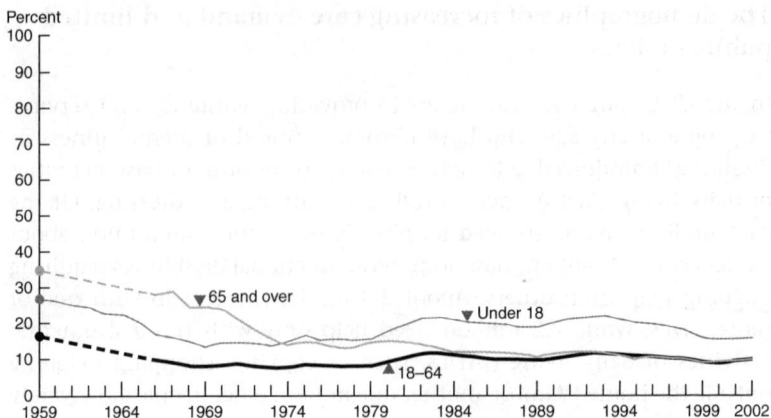

Figure 8.1   Poverty rate of the population, by age group, 1959–2002

Source: Federal Interagency Forum on Aging-Related Statistics (FIFARS) (2004) *Older Americans 2004: Key Indicators of Well Being*, Washington, DC: US Government Printing Office, p. 12.

as a result of Medicare (government health insurance for older people), Medicaid (state-federal health coverage for all on low incomes) and the indexing of Social Security pension levels to the cost of living.

The need for a place in a nursing home is typically precipitated by a sudden change – loss of social support or of family care, the onset of illness and/or functional disability, or precipitous loss of financial resources. State aid through Medicaid for nursing home care is highly means-tested, and is available outright to only the poorest 10 per cent of older Americans. (Other older people are ineligible for Medicaid unless they have to spend their incomes to the poverty level every month on high medical expenses.) Moving into a nursing home is the usual way older people 'spend down', since the high cost of such care exhausts the average older person's income and assets within a year or two; in most states Medicaid then picks up all costs. A mix of private and public financing supports nursing homes, each funding source strategically limiting its exposure for payment by denying eligibility, and limiting the scope, use and duration of the services it covers. Many policies combine to deter individuals from using nursing homes.

On the other hand, community-based services and residential alternatives to nursing homes are developing rapidly as private market demand for them grows, technological advances facilitate these choices, and more people with disabilities express interest in choosing and controlling their own use of them (Summers and Ihara, 2004, p. 1). This privatization trend is at the heart of today's long-term care and the new politics of choice and control.

Spending on long-term care

In 2002, national spending on long-term care (both nursing homes and community services) was almost $180 billion. Medicaid paid for the largest share of this, covering $83.7 billion, or 47 per cent of all long-term care spending. Out-of-pocket spending by consumers and their families was the second largest share at $37 billion, or 21 per cent of total long-term care spending. Medicare, the universal health insurance for the older people, was next with 17 per cent. Private medical and long-term care insurance accounted for 10 per cent, and other private and public sources financed the remainder (Summer and Ihara, 2004). Thus about a third of long-term care expenses are currently borne by private sources.

The majority of long-term care spending has traditionally gone to nursing homes, but as government sources absorb an ever increasing share of all nursing home costs, an important shift in long-term care priorities was occurring quietly during the 1990s. In 1992, 85 per cent of long-term care spending was for nursing homes, and only 15 per cent for home and community care paid for by Medicaid, Medicare, the Older Americans Act,[1] and local governments. By 2002, the proportion of Medicaid long-term care spending for nursing homes had declined from 85 per cent to 70 per cent, while home and community care spending had increased to 30 per cent – nearly $25 billion (Summers and Ihara, 2004, p. 2). As state and federal officials sought innovative ways to limit their fiscal obligations for long-term care, there has been some effort to bring even more 'balance' to the states' long-term care systems. Policy in the last decade has been to increase community-based resources with funds saved by constraining and even reducing the supply of costly nursing home beds.

The economics of care supply: legitimizing home care and acknowledging who does it

Fifty-two million Americans (31 per cent of the population aged 20 to 75) provide informal care to a sick or disabled family member or friend.

About 37 million help family members and 15 million help friends, and 8 per cent of these provide help to more than one care recipient. (ASPE and AOA, 1998, p. 5). Of older people with functional disabilities who continue to reside in the community, 96 per cent receive at least some assistance from informal caregivers. Those older people at the greatest risk of moving into nursing home care (those with three or more ADL disabilities) tend to live with others, receiving an average of 60 hours of informal care per week, supplemented by 14 hours of assistance from paid helpers. About half of this group use paid care support. The 4 per cent of disabled older people who live alone with high levels of disability receive much more paid care (56 hours per week) than informal care (about 29 hours per week). (ASPE and AOA, 1998, p. 17). It is nevertheless the case that only about one-third of disabled older people with long-term care needs use any formal home care services of any type, with just 5.4 per cent relying entirely on paid helpers. On average, disabled older people who live alone are less severely disabled, receive fewer hours of total assistance per week, and receive more hours of paid help per week than those living with others.

The provisions of the long-term care system are largely in the hands of the states, which determine (within federal guidelines) the level and type of disabilities that qualify individuals for Medicaid (the largest public payer for such services), whether and under what circumstances to provide home care services, and the type and amount of services to provide. Medicaid varies considerably from state to state; in addition, most states also spend their own general revenues to supplement Medicaid's coverage.

The mixed financing of this long-term care delivery system complicates the tracking of changes in the 50 states, because 'care supply' actually means a different mix of resources in each state. A 'worker shortage' generally means a shortage of registered nurses, but can also refer to lower-waged nursing assistants, personal care workers, and personal attendants.[2] When examined closely, however, care 'shortages' also reflect demographic transformations affecting the whole population.

Most state Medicaid programmes have traditionally contracted with home health care agencies to provide home care to older and disabled adults. While consumers may have had a choice among available agencies, they often had little say in who provided the services, or even when they came, since most agencies only sent care workers to their clients' homes on week days. Consumers typically received assistance when it was available, rather than when they actually needed or wanted it. For many people needing help with getting in and out of bed, eating, or toileting, this has meant getting up late in the day, having meals at odd times, going to bed before the sun sets, and going without services at weekends.

Consumer-directed care and Direct Payments: the US form of 'routed wages'

In 1981, federal budget legislation gave state Medicaid programmes more discretion in providing services to aged, disabled and developmentally disabled people living at home in their communities. Medicaid 'waivers' could be granted to states that created additional home and community services by reducing nursing home use. Gradually these waivers became the main source of funding for states using Medicaid for home and community-based services.

States' traditional welfare programmes had also created individualized arrangements for delivering personal care under Medicaid. These flexible programmes developed incrementally, in response to political pressure from organizations of disabled people seeking more independence. In the early 1980s the Independent Living Movement actively advocated Medicaid 'consumer-choice' programmes. These grew quickly, employing care workers (sometimes called Personal Assistant Services) for non-elderly adults with physical disabilities. In some cases, these policies allowed payment to family caregivers. Some were only available to impoverished recipients who lived in remote locations, who spoke languages other than English, who had family members on public assistance, or who were difficult for formal state and voluntary agencies to serve. States with county-based social service systems (e.g., California and Wisconsin) had for years allowed Medicaid consumers to select a care worker they already knew, who the county paid directly; the eligibility of care workers and payment methods were county decisions which varied throughout the state. Traditional welfare programmes also allowed payment to family caregivers, sometimes in lieu of public assistance. These family members' eligibility for payment, however, varied greatly from state to state; usually spouses could not be paid, since the disabled person's eligibility for Medicaid was contingent upon the whole family's poverty.

In the early 1990s, consensus began to develop around the need for more flexibility in care programmes for disabled consumers who could be allowed to hire and manage their own workers and even pay them themselves. The terms 'consumer-direction', and 'direct-payment' emerged to describe personal assistance for mobile consumers and in-home care for homebound persons with disabilities. This coincided with states' gradual adoption of voucher systems for a variety of other services, such as child- and foster-care (similar to the 'cash option' in care). Government vouchers for childcare were granted, contingent on co-payments levied according to family income, with which a parent could choose among licensed and unlicensed providers.

In 1998, the federal government, with private foundation support, launched a national pilot to thoroughly test the use of cash benefits for Medicaid consumers by enabling them to purchase their own personal and attendant care. Operating under another Medicaid waiver, the 'Cash and Counseling Demonstration and Evaluation' was initiated in three states – Arkansas, Florida and New Jersey – to test the feasibility of operating a consumer cash benefit. Throughout 2005 an extensive evaluation assessed how well this worked.

Over time, 'Consumer-Directed Care' has evolved into programmes of services offering maximum choice and control to disabled persons needing help with daily personal care activities, particularly adults eligible for means-tested public benefits (Medicaid). Offering a variety of arrangements for managing the care and payment of workers, the idea is to permit users to choose their preferred services, their own schedule of when and how services will be delivered, and by whom, among professionals, other trained workers, neighbours, friends, and family members, the services are actually provided (Simon-Rusinowitz *et al.*, 2005).

Paying family caregivers

Since older consumers seem to prefer receiving care from familiar helpers, an important aspect of consumer control is being allowed to pay family members for providing care. A 1985 study of all 50 US states found that 35 states paid some relatives to provide home care, under certain circumstances. Medicaid payments for personal, in-home care for disabled, low-income aged persons had existed unevenly in some states for decades (Linsk *et al.*, 1988). Other states had initiated family caregiver payments through Medicaid waivers. Federal Medicaid regulations had always allowed states to cover personal care, but these rules were variously interpreted as disallowing payment to family members and to uncertified providers.

Research on payments to family caregivers since 1985 has described: the extent of such payment programmes and their features (Burwell, 1986; England *et al.*, 1989; Gerald, 1993); the attitudes of administrators and policy makers about family payments (Linsk *et al.*, 1992);

consumer-directed homecare approaches, including family providers (Sabatino, 1990); family payments as an incentive to caregivers (Biegel, 1986); and an evaluation of specific programmes (Whitfield and Krompholz, 1981)

The Cash and Counseling Demonstration (CCD) and Evaluation Project,[3] is exploring these questions in-depth with the benefit of a rigorous quasi-experimental design (Mahoney *et al.*, 2000). Preliminary telephone surveys of disabled Medicaid consumers found good support for paying family caregivers; 90 to 92 per cent of potential participants indicated they would be interested in a consumer-directed 'cash option' under Medicaid, because it would enable them to 'hire whomever you want to provide services, even a friend or relative' (Mahoney *et al.*, 2004). Follow-up focus groups also liked the option of hiring relatives or friends, although reactions were mixed about doing so. A few had concerns about a lower level of professionalism from family members, and whether relatives could deal comfortably with provider–client conflicts. Most, however, liked the idea of paying a friend or relative who was already helping with personal care needs, feeling such persons would know their special needs, likes and dislikes better. African-American and Hispanic consumers especially liked the idea of hiring a relative or friend of their own ethnicity (Simon-Rusinowitz *et al.*, 2005).

The CCD is testing one of the most unfettered forms of consumer-directed services – offering Medicaid consumers in Arkansas, Florida and New Jersey a cash allowance and information services in lieu of agency-delivered care. CCD clients can use their cash benefit to purchase personal care services, assistive devices, or home modifications that best meet their individual needs. Information services include assistance with handling employment tasks such as hiring, training and managing workers, as well as cash management and payroll responsibilities. In theory, consumers who shop for the most cost-effective providers may then (through such savings) have funds to purchase additional services (Kapp, 1996).

Research in the three states has found almost all CCD group recipients used the allowances to hire workers, usually relatives or acquaintances. This accesses a source of assistance usually unavailable to traditional agencies, since these caregivers are motivated primarily by their relationship with the consumer, rather than by employment as a care worker. However, treatment group consumers in all demonstration states had difficulty hiring workers if they did not have a relative or friend to hire (Phillips and Schneider, 2002). This suggests the potential value of friends and family as an alternative labour pool for home care, and the need for programmes like CCD to facilitate linking quality workers with care recipients who may not have access to friends or family who can provide care (Harris-Kojetin *et al.*, 2004).

The Bush Administration easily incorporated the CCD project into its New Freedom Initiative,[4] and in 2003–04 initiated a plethora of other federal initiatives to eliminate barriers to community living by enhancing consumer choice in care planning in a variety of services. Besides CCD, the Real Choice Systems Change pilot demonstration grants are funding Nursing Home Transitions, along with Personal Assistance Services, Money Follows the Person, Quality Assurance/Improvement, and broader systems change grants, with over 22 states participating in these initiatives so far. A collaborative clearinghouse website (www.hcbs.org) provides up-to-date information on these activities in the states receiving federal support. In late 2004, ten new state pilot demonstrations were added to the CCD programme by replicating or expanding on the CCD model.

Policy development: How two different state models affect consumers

Two different forms of consumer-direction described below illustrate some different ways that consumer discretion has been implemented. California's 30-year-old In-Home Supportive Services programme is compared with Arkansas' new Independent Choices programme to show how state policies have developed over time, and how provision of care is allocated and monitored.

California

California's county-operated In-Home Supportive Services (IHSS) programme, in operation since the 1970s, serves over 200,000 frail and disabled persons statewide, of whom 62 per cent are over age 65. The largest Medicaid funded 'consumer-directed care' programme in the US, this programme was the subject of a great deal of policy research in the late 1990s, as federal interest grew in designing 'consumer-direction' and 'direct-payment' approaches. A federal grant to researchers at UCLA[5] permitted a large-scale evaluation of the programme, encompassing the perspectives of both consumers and providers (Benjamin *et al.*, 1998).

That 1997 evaluation found that about half of the consumers in the programme hired relatives, and a quarter hired friends. Those hiring relatives tended to be older, less educated and more likely to come from ethnic minorities than other consumers in the programme. On average, consumers hiring relatives felt more security and less risk, had more choice about how their services were delivered, and had equal or greater satisfaction with their care than those cared for by non-relatives. They also received more hours of service, and had better health outcomes than those served by non-relatives. Consumers hiring relatives and friends also felt closer interpersonally to their workers and rated them as more reliable than workers who were unknown to them when hired (Benjamin *et al.*, 1998).

California's programme has some uniquely positive features. Its Medicaid and Aging programmes operate autonomously, with partial funding from the local counties (as they are in New York and Wisconsin). Since Medicaid disallows the hiring of spouses and parents of children who are minors to provide personal care, the state and counties use their own revenues to pay spouses and parents for care work. Worker payments are authorized by the consumer and IHHS, and paid directly to the care worker. County employees assess consumers' needs and determine how many hours of care per week to authorize.

Counties also set the wage rates and, in recent years, pressure from California trade unions has led to the establishment of 'Public Authorities' in several counties to govern the programme. These boards, composed of equal numbers of consumers, care workers and government officials, negotiate with the county, state and trade unions representing workers to determine the annual wage scales. They guarantee certain worker benefits, including health insurance for all those working at least 20 hours per week, and establish quality standards for acceptable care. Registries in local areas serve as information and resource centres, assisting both consumers and workers to find each other. Transparency in the governance mechanisms of these Public Authorities has opened up the whole system to public oversight and increased workers' wages and benefits in counties with especially high costs of living.

Arkansas

Arkansas' Independent Choices Program, the first cash and counselling programme implemented in the federal demonstration states, began enrolling participants in December 1998. Like most states, Arkansas' State Unit on Aging and its Medicaid programme had traditionally contracted with private home care agencies (both for-profit and voluntary) to deliver personal care. Consequently, residents who needed personal assistance had had little choice in how, when, and by whom their services would be provided until the CCD programme created options.

When first introduced in Arkansas, Independent Choices encountered some bureaucratic and political hurdles. In many counties there was some resistance from the traditional provider agencies since each anticipated losing clients to the new programme. State officials and programme managers facilitated the CCD implementation. Interested participants were placed in a pool to be randomly assigned to either the Independent Choices programme or to the control group receiving traditional agency-provided services. A nurse and a social worker using a standardized instrument to determine the number of hours of care each individual required assessed each applicant's needs during a home visit.

Between December 1998 and 2002, 1,004 applicants were randomly assigned to the consumer-directed (experimental) group that got the 'cash option', and another 1,004 received traditional services. The latter clients (the control group) were given a list of home health care agencies they could contact directly to obtain services, or, if currently receiving services, could continue to use their previous agencies.

The experimental, consumer-directed group received monthly allowances and the responsibility for procuring their own care worker. They could hire whomever they wanted (except a spouse). The number of care worker hours in the client's new or existing care plan determined the amount of the monthly allowance; the average monthly benefit for these consumer-directed clients averaged $320 per month (Simon-Rusinowitz *et al.*, 2005).

The consumer-directed group also had choices in how to handle the cash they received. They could use fiscal intermediaries (at no charge) to handle book-keeping and payroll services on their behalf. Alternatively, counsellors were available (also at no charge), to provide advice and support in creating a plan for cash management, recruiting and hiring workers. Counsellors approved the cash management plans, and monitored them to protect against fraud and abuse. Consumers could receive the monthly payment directly as an electronic funds transfer to their bank account, and, if they had family members, loved ones, or friends willing to provide the care they required, they could spend the funds on other necessities as they saw fit. This allowed consumers to use their funds to modify their homes or vehicles, or purchase household appliances (microwave ovens, washers and dryers) to help them live more independently, although few clients actually did this. Evaluation of the CCD has thus far found consumers in the Cash Option significantly more satisfied than those in traditional services.

The impact of consumer-directed care delivery on care workers

While gerontologists have been strongly interested in family caregivers for over two decades, concern is now growing about the supply, quality and work–life balance of long-term care workers. This extends to the question of whether consumer-direction offers a higher quality experience for workers, and, in turn, for consumers. Benjamin's study of the California IHHS includes a comparison of outcomes for consumers cared for by consumer-directed workers and agency-employed workers (Benjamin and Mathias, 2004)

A slightly different analysis compares paid care workers who were *family members or friends* with *workers not previously known* to the consumers. This comparison raises issues about family boundaries, and the utility of quality standards and external oversight. Three hundred and sixty five telephone interviews with agency workers and 253 with consumer-directed workers (a 62 per cent response rate) explored workers' experiences of stress versus satisfaction from their work under the two care models. Workers rated their felt stress from concerns about client safety when left alone, client behaviour issues, the worker's own emotional state, getting along with the client, and the clarity of work roles. They also rated their satisfaction with work roles, their own performance, career advancement opportunities, and the independence and flexibility they felt.

Significant differences were found on 9 of 10 variables. Agency workers were less likely to have a high school education, but more likely to have care work experience. Consumer-directed workers tended to have some college education and were more likely to have another job than the agency workers; they cared for fewer clients, but their clients tended to need more help with ADLs and more service hours than did the clients of the agency workers. (Counties had financial incentives to assign more severely impaired clients to the less-costly consumer-direction model.)

For most workers, under both models, the consequences for work–life differences were relatively modest. Agency workers were somewhat insulated from worries about the consumer's safety when they were not there, so were more able to leave their work 'at work'. By contrast, consumer-directed workers had been serving the same recipient longer than agency workers, were more likely to live with or near the recipient, to assist with a wider range of tasks and to provide additional help without pay. These differences reflect the consumer-direction workers' personal commitment, as well as the blurred boundaries between employee and familial roles. Consumer-directed workers cannot easily recast familial and friendship relationships into 'detached' or 'professional' ones (Benjamin and Matthias, 2004, p. 485).

Differences between the two cohorts on worker satisfaction were also small. Agency workers received better wages, benefits, and training than consumer-directed workers, but most still received no fringe benefits; only 39 per cent had health insurance, 37 per cent had sick leave, and 37 per cent received paid vacation leave. Agency workers lived farther from their clients and had to travel to 3 to 4 clients' homes per day. Not surprisingly, they had more scheduling and travel difficulties than the consumer-directed workers. Consumer-directed workers, on the other hand, were more satisfied by their interpersonal relationship with the client and the flexibility they had in performing tasks, control factors in long-term care work known to reduce work-related stress (Bowers and Becker, 1992). Consumer-directed workers also generally received more individualized training. Benjamin and Matthias conclude that there is little difference in outcomes between the two types of workers in terms of satisfaction and stress.

Ethnicity and race, however, were stronger predictors of satisfactory outcomes than either the consumer-direction or agency model. White workers reported more positive perceptions of their roles than Latinos or Asian workers, whereas Asian and Black workers were more positive about the career benefits associated with their jobs. Benjamin and Matthias conclude that external, professional oversight mechanisms are less necessary to assure quality in consumer-directed care, partly because most of such care is personal and supportive, rather than medical. They argue, along with Doty *et al.* (1996) and others, that recipient, family and worker judgements are central to monitoring quality (Benjamin and Matthias, 2004, p. 487).

Differences between home care work done for elders paying privately and Medicaid consumers

Some fuzzy assumptions underlie national discussion of consumer-direction, cash options, and direct payments. Since so few disabled older people living at home are sufficiently low-income to qualify for Medicaid, for most disabled older adults this model is essentially a privatized, commodified verbal contract, in which a care receiver simply pays a care worker for their help; home care is a distinctly 'private good'. Historically, such private domestic service has ranged from slavery and indentured servitude to 'tending', 'sitting', or 'private duty nursing'.

Its modern iterations legitimate an independent, self-employed person entering another person's private domestic space to provide instrumental, physical, and/or emotional assistance or care, under the sole direction of the individual they serve or their representative. This 'private good' – care – may be given voluntarily (without compensation), or by independent entrepreneurs, who often develop close relationships with their clients (Morris *et al.*, 1998).

Research in Wisconsin in the late 1990s examined worker issues in consumer-directed care arrangements from yet another angle. Exploring independent care work in the 'grey market' in one large city, qualitative interviews explored consumers' and workers' perspectives on the characteristics of successful independent care arrangements (Keigher 1999a; Keigher and Luz, 1997). Focusing on the financial, social and physical distances between the elderly consumers, their families, and the workers they hired, the study highlights the implications of such interpersonal distance for power dynamics, intimacy, respect and communication.

Studies of several states have highlighted attractive features of direct payments and independent workers under Medicaid Personal Care: consumer control and satisfaction (Doty *et al.*, 1996; Keigher and Murphy, 1992); particular benefits to minority and immigrant beneficiaries (Benjamin, 1999); and advantages for part-time and female workers with families, other employment, or other obligations. The long-term care insurance industry features the private hiring of care workers as a desirable option for older disabled individuals, especially those without children or who prefer not to be cared for by their children (LifePlans, 1999). Such insurance provides qualified disabled beneficiaries a term benefit, a certain amount of money per day or week with which beneficiaries can purchase their own care.

Keigher's research examined 40 'cases', drawn to allow comparison of consumers in two existing independent consumer-directed care arrangements. The first were private arrangements in which disabled elderly consumers simply selected and paid one or more self-employed care workers to care for them. The second were subsidized arrangements whereby independent workers (all unrelated to the client) were identified and selected by low-income, disabled older people on Medicaid and paid by the county to provide a specified type and amount of care. This programme pays many more relatives and friends than unrelated 'strangers', but this study examined only unrelated workers.

Extended interviews were conducted separately with the stakeholders in each 'unit' – the disabled older consumer, the family caregiver (where there was one), and the care worker; care workers were interviewed a second time 6 months later to learn what had changed since the first interview and to identify the particular interests, needs and values of each of these interdependent 'stakeholders'.

Nearly half of the subsidized consumers were African-American, as was only one of the 20 privately paying older people. The subsidized consumers were younger (mean age 78.3 compared with 83.3), less likely to have children or other informal care, had higher needs for medical and financial assistance (partly reflecting the medical and financial criteria of the subsidy programme), and were more likely to need total care. The privately paying consumers, on the other hand, who were far more financially secure, received fewer hours of care per day and, though older than those in the consumer-direction subsidy programme, were more likely to be living alone (see Keigher (1999b) for more details on consumers).

The independent workers expressed commitment to providing good care within their own limits, and a strong preference for independent employment, rather than work for an agency or nursing home. Experienced workers negotiated with consumers and/or their families to create a good situation for themselves and their client(s). This gave them satisfaction and adequate compensation to make their effort, time, and emotional energy worthwhile, including when and how much to work (full or part-time). Some independent workers had learned the job by working in a nursing home, caring for members of their own families, or simply by doing what needed to be done. But motivated, capable workers, especially the African-Americans, faced disadvantages in this labour market. Often relying on word of mouth to find new clients, and lacking reliable transport, many had difficulties finding and reaching the outlying homes of affluent paying clients who offered reasonable wages.

Of the 41 workers in the sample, the biggest problem with being 'self-employed' was that compensation rarely, if ever, included fringe benefits. Some private clients paid only cash, avoiding both taxes and social security contributions. Beyond this, workers received no insurance coverage for occupational injury, unemployment, sick leave, and most importantly, health insurance. Twenty-five per cent had health insurance privately or through their husbands' employment, but 45 per cent had no private health insurance. If they were injured, they depended instead on means-tested medical assistance (Medicaid), or on the county medical indigent programme. (Fifty-seven per cent of the subsidy workers were in this latter group or had no health insurance of any kind.)

Nor were these healthy workers. Ranging in age from 22 to 75, the mean age of the private workers was 56, and of the subsidy workers 46.

Many had no private health insurance because they had 'pre-existing' medical conditions, so could not qualify. Within 6 months of their interviews, one worker had died of cancer, two had begun dialysis, two had given birth, and several had been treated for chronic debilitating illnesses: lupus, diabetes, a suspected brain tumor, Krohn's disease, lyme disease, depression and alcoholism. Many had high levels of personal debt or bankruptcy due to their own, or their children's medical bills, which they had been paying for many years.

Federal welfare reforms being implemented during late 1996 and 1998 were flooding entry-level jobs in long-term care with unskilled, poorly educated women with little work experience. Required to work 40 hours per week to receive the new Temporary Assistance for Needy Families benefit, they received a flat $673 per month, regardless of their family size. Care worker turnover rates began increasing immediately, while wages stagnated or declined.

Assessed by county care managers, all consumers in the subsidy programme received 'medically necessary' or 'medically-related' care, a requirement for using Medicaid funds for personal care. Consequently, while both subsidy and privately paid workers did 'housework' and 'provided companionship', only the privately paid workers were paid for doing housework and providing companionship, allaying the loneliness, confusion and isolation of older people living alone, and assuring their safety. Since the privately paid workers were older, they were also less physically capable of heavy lifting, bathing and other personal care tasks.

Workers in the subsidy programme generally had tight work schedules, due either to the needs of their own children and families, or other jobs. One-third relied entirely on public transport, or went by bicycle or on foot to their clients' homes. About half of all the workers lived in the city's most racially segregated, dangerous inner city, where drug trafficking and gang violence are a daily threat. Few could safely get to work early in the morning, stay at work after dark, or work all night. One of the hardest expectations to meet was 'to arrive on time' for their clients, since many took long bus rides, making several changes, or hitched rides with others to work. Fewer than half had their own cars, which limited control over their arrival times. Transport problems featured highly for those who had left by the time of the second interview.

Reflections on the impact of consumer direction on workers

Consumer-direction of long-term care is a promising development in American home and community care, apparently compatible with the USA's steadfast valuing of independence, personal responsibility, and free choice. However, it cannot be successfully implemented without adequate support (including funding) for all three stakeholders in these intimate, long-term home care relationships (Keigher, 2000, p. 158).

The move towards consumer control was initiated by organizations of younger disabled people seeking independence, often from their own parents. Their advocacy established myriad arrangements for independent living with supportive, proximate personal assistance when needed. Such persons often require live-in assistance, and consumer-direction policies have facilitated the individualized creation of such arrangements. More than half of disabled older people appear to have relatives and/or friends who may provide care, some of whom will qualify for reimbursement under Medicaid.

These arrangements, however, are quite different for frail disabled, lonely and resource poor older people in later life. The CCD pilots described in this chapter are beginning to identify significant differences between familiar peers and family caregivers, and the independent care workers who are strangers to them who may be available to provide care. The latter group have personal needs of their own, often raising children and caring for other dependants; they typically receive marginal wages and very few benefits. And to complicate relationships further, older people who are without family or friends often have very significant socio-emotional needs, and may need more assistance than one independent care worker can provide, especially when the older person is extremely resource poor.

The challenge for self-employed care workers today is earning a living wage. Workers often have difficulty putting together sufficient numbers of clients and jobs to accrue 30 to 40 work hours per week, and enough income to purchase health insurance if the employer offers a group plan. Few communities have registries or cooperatives for matching workers and consumers, and even when mechanisms exist to match them up, workers are not paid for their travel time and expenses. Some disabled consumers capably manage their own workers, sometimes scheduling several throughout a week with a variety of complex schedules. Some even have 'back-up coverage' if a worker is ill, or cannot come at the scheduled time. But other consumers, and/or their family caregivers, find the task of arranging all this simply too great.

Immigrant labour, particularly from Mexico and Central America, is already filling some of the USA's needs for care workers. Employed throughout most entry-level employment in the US economy, the number of foreign-born workers in the USA has increased by 72 per cent since 1990, while the total population has increased by only

18.6 per cent. Foreign-born persons are now 34.2 million, or 12 per cent of the US population, up from only 8 per cent 15 years ago. And 23 per cent of foreign-born women work as 'household and service workers' (compared to only 16 per cent of native-born women), generally concentrated in the largest cities. Unfortunately, immigration policy is highly hypocritical. Where employment of undocumented workers is accepted, the labour market is characterized by the presence of workers willing to accept the very lowest wages; local labour markets often respond by exploiting all workers.

As older adults come to depend upon disadvantaged labour, 'because it is all they can afford', they become unintentional accomplices to labour exploitation, as well as prey for unscrupulous workers. While consumer-direction or self-managed care seems incompatible with regulation, impoverished consumers living alone do not have the resources to hold fiduciary responsibility for workers, especially those who are also on very low-incomes and need full-time work. On the other hand, immigrant workers are an available group likely to fill these roles, for whom training and networking services would be useful if immigration provisions could better legitimize their roles.

Conclusion: Correcting the projected 'care deficit'?

Consumer-direction and direct payments to independent workers are becoming an integral part of the rapidly changing American eldercare system. Public–private partnerships and 'private market solutions' (which users purchase privately) are developing throughout the USA's network of ageing services. Given the improved level of private resources available to older Americans today, these public–private provisions seem inevitable. The US government is today loathe to create (much less to finance) universal programmes for any age-group. It seems fair that individuals who can afford to should pay for their own care, perhaps even until their assets are exhausted.

On the other hand, the free market momentum stimulated by the Bush Administration's New Freedom Initiative, and 'Ownership Society', seeks to privatize decision-making processes even within publicly funded programmes (Keigher, 1999b). Indeed, emerging hybrid programmes (public–private partnerships) are giving middle- and upper-income individuals more choices, while little concern is raised about the concomitant erosion of means-tested government services for older people on low-incomes. Social security with universal coverage has taken on great importance, because today, 'among older Americans in the lowest two-fifths of the income distribution, Social Security accounts for 83.5 per cent of aggregate income, and public assistance accounts for another 11 per cent' (FIFARS, 2004). The 40 per cent of older people who live alone, are not homeowners, and whose only income is from social security, are highly vulnerable.

It seems certain that home care will continue to consume an increasing share of public long-term care funding, simply because the market demand for it will grow so much faster than demand for nursing home expansion. The US has reallocated 15 per cent of total long-term care spending away from nursing homes and into home and community-based services in the past 13 years alone, a shift widely lauded for 'rebalancing' the care systems in the states. Unfortunately, there is little assurance that the individual efforts that have been encouraged to provide care out of compassion for loved ones, will receive much relief overall. At age 85 plus, 19 per cent of older people are in long-term care facilities, and another 7 per cent in community housing with services (FIFARS, 2004, p. 54). There may be no cost-effective way, other than with means-tested 'routed wages' or allowances, to deliver this much care throughout whole communities.

Fundamental to discussion of elderly consumers' well-being must be assurances that workers caring for older people can live decently – that such work earns sufficient income and health insurance to provide workers with security as well. The first necessity, for workers as well as for older consumers, is protection against potentially destabilizing catastrophic health care costs. Unfortunately, the US shows no sign of planning realistically for this essential aspect of the coming age wave.

Notes

1. Dr S Keigher is a Professor of Social Work at the Helen Bader School of Social Welfare, University of Wisconsin-Milwaukee, 2400 E. Hartford Ave., Milwaukee, WI 53201, USA.
2. In this discussion, all those working directly with older consumers are referred to as 'care workers'.
3. This project involved a collaboration between the Robert Wood Johnson Foundation and the US Department of Health and Human Services.
4. This project was a collaboration between the Robert Wood Johnson Foundation, the Centers for Medicaid and Medicare Services, and the Aging, Disability and Long-Term Care unit of the Office of the Assistant Secretary for Planning and Evaluation, US Department of Health and Human Services.
5. University of California, Los Angeles.

References

ASPE and AOA (DHHS Office of the Assistant Secretary for Planning and Evaluation and the Administration on Aging) (1998) *Informal Caregiving: Compassion in Action*, Washington, DC: US Department of Health and Human Services.

Benjamin, A. E. (1999) 'A Normative Analysis of Home Care Goals', *Journal of Aging and Health*, 11(August), 445–68.

Benjamin, A. E. and Matthias, R. E. (2004) 'Work–Life Differences and Outcomes for Agency- and Consumer-Directed Home-Care Workers', *The Gerontologist*, 44(4), 479–88.

Benjamin, A. E., Matthias, R. E. and Franke, T. M. (1998) *Comparing Client-directed and Agency Models for Providing Disability-related Supportive Services at Home*, Los Angeles: University of California, Los Angeles, School of Public Policy and Research.

Biegel, D. (1986) *Family Elder Care Incentive Policies: Final Report of the Pennsylvania Department of Aging*, Pittsburgh: University of Pittsburgh, Center for Social and Urban Research.

Bowers, B. and Becker, M. (1992) 'Nurse Aides in Nursing Homes: The Relationship Between Organization and Quality', *The Gerontologist*, 32(3), 360–6.

Burwell, B. (1986) *Shared Obligations: Public Policy Influences on Family Care for the Elderly*, No. 55-83-0056, Cambridge, MA: SysteMetrics.

Doty, P., Kasper, J. and Litvak, S. (1996) 'Consumer-directed Models of Personal Care: Lessons from Medicaid', *Milbank Memorial Fund*, 74, 37–409.

England, S. E., Linsk, N. L., Simon-Rusinowitz, L. and Keigher, S. M. (1989) 'Paid Family Caregiving and the Market View of Home Care: Agency Perspectives'. *Journal of Health and Social Policy*, 1, 31–53.

FIFARS (Federal Interagency Forum on Aging-Related Statistics) (2004) *Older Americans 2004: Key Indicators of Well Being*, Washington, DC: US Government Printing Office.

Gerald, L. (1993) 'Paid Family Caregiving: A Review of Progress and Policies', *Journal of Aging & Social Policy*, 5(1/2), 73–89.

Harris-Kojetin, L., Lipson, D., Fielding, J., Kiefer, K. and Stone, R.I. (2004) *Recent Findings on Frontline Long-Term Care Workers: A Research Synthesis 1999–2003*, Institute for the Future of Aging Services, Association of Homes and Services for the Aging, Office of Disability, Aging, and Long-Term Care Policy, Washington, DC: OASPE

Kapp, M. (1996) 'Enhancing Autonomy and Choice in Selecting and Directing Long-term Care Services', *Elder Law Journal*, 4(1), 55–97.

Keigher, S. (1999a) 'Feminist Lessons from the Gray Market in Personal Care for the Elderly: So What If You Have to Spend Your Own Money?' in Neysmith, S. (ed.), *Critical Issues for Future Social Work Practice with Aging persons*, Columbia University Press.

Keigher, S. (1999b) 'The Limits of Consumer-directed Care as Government Policy in an Aging Society', *Canadian Journal of Aging*, 18(2), 182–210.

Keigher, S. (2000) 'The Interests of Three Stakeholders in Independent Personal Care for Disabled Elders,' *Journal of Health and Human Services Administration*, 23(2), 136–60.

Keigher, S. and Luz, C. (1997) *Common Stakes in Homecare of the Elderly: A Pilot Study of Milwaukee's Gray Market in Independent Care*. Milwaukee: School of Social Welfare, UW-Milwaukee and the Helen Bader Foundation.

Keigher, S. and Murphy, C. (1992) 'A Consumer View of a Family Care Compensation Program', *Social Service Review*, 66(2), 256–77.

LifePlans (1999) *Long-Term Care Insurance Claimant Study*, Report to Department of Health and Human Services and Robert Wood Johnson Foundation.

Linsk, N., Keigher, S. and Osterbusch, S. (1988) 'State Policies Regarding Paid Family Caregiving', *The Gerontologist*, 28(2), 204–12.

Linsk, N. L., Keigher, S. M., Simon-Rusinowitz, L. and England, S. E. (1992) *Wages for Caring. Compensating Family Care of the Elderly*. New York: Praeger.

Mahoney, K. J., Simone, K. and Simon-Rusinowitz, L. (2000) 'Early Lessons from the Cash & Counseling Demonstration and Evaluation', *Generations*, 24(3), 41–6.

Mahoney, K., Simon-Rusinowitz, L., Loughlin, D. M., Desmond, S. M. and Squillace, M. R. (2004) 'Determining Personal Care Consumer's Preferences for a Consumer-directed Cash and Counseling Option: Survey Results from Arkansas, Florida, New Jersey, and New York Elders and Adults with Physical Disabilities', *Health Services Research*, 39(3), 643–64.

Morris, R., Caro, F. G. and Hanson, J. E. (1998) *Personal Assistance: The Future of Homecare*, Baltimore, MD: The Johns Hopkins University Press.

Phillips, B. and Schneider, B. (2002) *Moving to Independent Choices: The Implementation of the Cash and Counseling Demonstration in Arkansas. Final Report*, Princeton, NJ: Mathematica Policy Research Inc.

Sabatino, C. P. (1990) *Lessons for Enhancing Consumer-directed Approaches in Home Care*, Washington, DC: American Bar Association Commission on Legal Problems of the Elderly.

Simon-Rusinowitz, L., Mahoney, K., Loughlin, C. M. and DeBarthe Sadler, M. (2005). 'Paying Family Caregivers: An Effective Policy Option in the Arkansas Cash and Counseling Demonstration and Evaluation', *Marriage and Family Review*, 37(1/2): 83–105.

Summers, L. L. and Ihara, E. S. (2004) *State-funded Home and Community Based Services Program for Older People*, Washington, DC: AARP Public Policy Institute.

Whitfield, S. and Krompholz, B. (1981) *The Family Support Demonstration Project*, State of Maryland, Office on Aging.

9
Conclusion: Dilemmas, Contradictions and Change

Clare Ungerson and Sue Yeandle

In the opening chapter of this book, we briefly introduced some of the themes that each of the chapters raise. In this conclusion we discuss and analyse these themes, and present a framework for understanding the variation in cash-for-care arrangements that exists between different welfare states and, in the example of the USA, between states within the same federal system. We also consider how far cash-for-care schemes are sustainable: many of them, in particular the French, German, Dutch and UK schemes, are subject to considerable recent and ongoing reform, suggesting that this innovation in social care is at an early stage in its development, and that there are within it some as yet unresolved dilemmas.

Origins of the schemes

One feature of the development of the 'cash-for-care' schemes described in this collection is that most of them developed during the 1990s.[1] It was during that decade that the ethos of consumerism, dominant in the 1980s in the more conventional marketplace of goods and commodities, began strongly to influence the way in which social and health services were delivered. The view that the 'end users' of a wide range of services delivered by and through the professional practice of doctors, nurses, social workers and others should be 'empowered' in relation to these professionals was signalled by the term 'modernization'. 'Modern' social services were those in which consumers were enabled to make their own choices, including choices between different services, and/or between differentially priced but similar services. In theory, the outcome optimized their own preferences. As the British Prime Minister Tony Blair put it in 2004, in relation to the modernization 'project': 'we are proposing to put an entirely different dynamic in place to drive our public services: one where the service will be driven not by the managers but by the user.' (Speech by the British Prime Minister, July 2004, cited in Department of Health, 2005.) Cash-for-care schemes such as those described in this book are a logical development of consumerism: as the recent Green Paper on the future of social care for adults in England states:

> People at the centre of assessment have the opportunity to choose what services and support they think would best meet their needs. The services and support chosen might be different from the services that the formal care system has on offer, and we want to create a mechanism that will allow individuals to keep control and choice over their situation and the support they actually receive. In talking to people who use services and to carers, it is clear that direct payments give people that choice and control, and we think that this is a mechanism that should be extended and encouraged where possible. (Department of Health, 2005, paras 4.21 and 22)

Thus 'choice', 'empowerment' and 'autonomy' – all terms describing social democratic values with which it would be difficult to quarrel within the framework of western capitalist culture – constitute the central ideological underpinnings of cash-for-care schemes.

At the same time there has been in play in all these countries a rather more pragmatic value which has not been made so explicit – cost containment. One of the overarching motivations for the development of home care (often referred to in the UK as 'community care') is the belief that care delivered in the homes of care users is cheaper and more cost efficient than that delivered in residential settings. The basis for this view is complex and not fully elaborated, but one key dimension is that the 'hotel' costs of living and accommodation are largely covered by care users themselves: their accommodation costs, and their current expenditures on food and heating, can legitimately be taken as resources which individual care users, rather than the welfare state, provide for themselves.

Second, policies designed to support care users in remaining in their own homes can tap into the nexus of affect and obligation that surrounds our understandings of 'home', household', 'family' and 'kin'. It is thus assumed that informal carers will often emerge to provide additional, unpaid, care services. As the chapters on Germany and Austria make clear, a key objective of the long-term care insurance policy instituted in these two countries in the 1990s was to promote social care delivery in people's homes, rather than in the existing and relatively expensive and medicalized residential care sector. Other nations, such as Italy, have promoted commodified care schemes partially to promote care delivery at home in a context where residential care, particularly for older people, was underdeveloped. In all these countries, informal care has been perceived as an important source of both low cost and 'cost-free' caring labour. Cash-for-care schemes thus act as a particularly useful element in a portfolio of social care policies designed to support and retain people in their own homes.

Home care is also widely viewed as a generally welcome form of social care delivery. While part of its attraction for governments is undoubtedly concerned with 'squaring the circle' (Bonoli *et al.*, 2000), it is commonly presented as a way of satisfying established consumer preference, since there is considerable research evidence that older and disabled people wish to stay in their own homes for as long as possible (Royal Commission on Long-Term Care, Research Volume 2, 1999).

A further way in which cash-for-care schemes promote cost containment is by permitting the 'employment' of relatives. Here the schemes function as a method of embedding and retaining informal care (and indeed can operate as a means of generating additional informal care that would otherwise not be forthcoming). In this case the attraction is that cash-for-care schemes both enlarge the pool of labour available to care, and ensure that the additional labour in that pool can be secured at very low cost. This embedding and enlarging process seems to work particularly well where some forms of social protection, for example pension and other social security rights for kin 'employed' as carers, are retained within the scheme, enabling the opportunity costs of 'paid' informal care (primarily foregone wages in the conventional labour market) to be reduced for the care giver/worker. Thus cash-for-care schemes can act as an additional incentive encouraging informal carers to move from the conventional labour market into a more hybrid form of care and work in the domestic domain, as seen in our examples from Germany and Austria.

Further forms of cost containment arise as overhead costs are shifted away from welfare state agencies and on to individual care users. This enables the state to reduce two types of costs: employment costs and organizational (bureaucratic) costs. By eliminating the costs of recruitment, because in cash-for-care schemes the individual care user becomes responsible for finding their own labour, the state immediately reduces one set of employment costs. In most cases the public purse also avoids the costs of: training new staff and running regular refresher courses (e.g., in manual handling skills); security checks (including criminal record checks in the UK); line and performance management (including regular supervision and team meetings); staff development; and sickness or other absence.

Where care users become the hirers and firers of their own labour, they also become, in theory, the micro managers of employment risk. This enables public agencies to pass their risk management costs on to the care user as well. Indeed, when they feel at risk, care users can respond merely by activating their control of the employment process. This contrasts with the options available to social service agencies which, faced with a consumerist and potentially litigious operating environment, have to manage risk through elaborate and expensive quality assurance procedures. In domiciliary care these procedures are not only expensive but are also inherently insecure, since this type of care has to be delivered on a one to one basis within the privacy – and invisibility – of the domestic domain. This provides yet another reason for putting the very person who can observe the quality of care at close and continuous quarters – the care user – at the head of the employment process, by giving them the resources to become the fully fledged 'employer' of their own caring labour.

A further element in the development of these types of scheme, and one which has been particularly powerful in the USA and in the UK, has been the presence, within the political process, of strong lobbies of disabled and older people promoting the values of autonomy and agency (using the term 'independent living'). 'Independent living' is here used in two senses: it is an ideology (closely associated with the social, as opposed to the medical, model of disability) which has formed the basis for liberationist policies and research epistemology (Barnes and Mercer, 1997; Morris, 1991; Oliver, 1996; Shakespeare and Corker, 2002) and it is the founding idea behind the practical policy of providing cash for care so that disabled people can live independently while directly employing their own personal assistants (Morris, 1993). It is in the latter sense that the politics of disability are most relevant to the promotion and maintenance of cash-for-care schemes. It is significant that in Britain the recent government Green Paper on the future of social care for adults in England is entitled *Independence, Well-being and Choice* and, as the quote from it at the beginning of this section indicates, that the British cash-for-care scheme, known as Direct Payments, is at the core of policy development in this area. The link between 'independence' and cash for care has thus become part of the discourse of social care analysis, and reflects the success of the disability lobbies (especially in the UK) in promoting that linkage.

There are, then, some important dominant strands in the development of cash-for-care schemes – in particular, consumerism and its associated term of 'empowerment', cost containment, the use of cash-for-care schemes to shift the locus of care to home and community and from state to individual, and the power of the disability lobbies to link the notion of 'independence' to the direct employment of personal assistance through the use of cash for care. These origins provide the foundations for the construction of all the cash-for-care schemes studied here, although, as the chapters in this book make clear, the precise architecture of each cash-for-care scheme as it emerges in its national context is highly variable.

National and local variations

One of the original ideas of the *Shifting Boundaries* project on which many of these chapters are based was that difference in the macro aspects of policy construction of cash-for-care schemes would impact on the micro configuration of care relationships. In many respects our data has borne this out (Ungerson, 2004; Ungerson, 2006; Ungerson and Yeandle, 2005). On the basis of the empirical data emerging from our five-country study, we have shown that there are considerable national differences in the type of labour that is recruited, in the amount of time over which care tasks are delivered, and in the nature of the affective and contractual relationships that pertain between care users and care providers. We have explained these differences, at least in part, as arising from the organization and structure of the cash-for-care schemes, and as influenced by certain contextual factors (outlined in more detail below) that impact on the configuration of commodified care relationships and on the emotions contained within them (Ungerson, 2006).

In many ways these differences are not surprising. The original selection of the countries included in the *Shifting Boundaries* project was based on two main ideas: first, that there would be differences in the micro care relationship, depending on whether or not the scheme allowed for relatives to be paid, and thus in some sense, 'employed' by care users; and, second, that there would be differences contingent on how far the scheme was regulated. By 'regulation' we meant both monitoring, by outside bodies, of the quality of care, and protection, through social security systems and employment law, for the care workers involved. From our analysis we developed a diagrammatic representation of these two dimensions: the employment of relatives, and regulation/non-regulation. We named this the 'cross of routed wages' (see Figure 9.1).

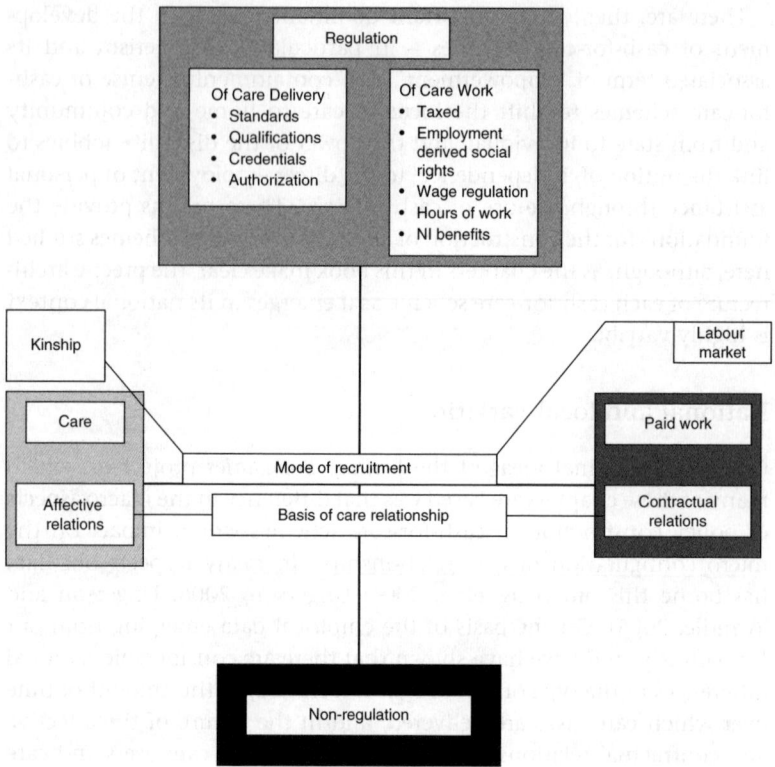

Figure 9.1   The 'cross' of 'routed wages'

The four quadrants in Figure 9.1 describe the type of labour that will typically be recruited, depending on the scheme.

For example, one can expect, in the top left hand quadrant, to find a scheme where workers are recruited through kin networks rather than via the conventional and formal labour market, but where, at the same time, the caring labour that emerges is heavily regulated by an outside body. In the lower right hand quadrant, are found schemes where there is very little or no regulation, but where workers are recruited in the conventional labour market, which can include the illegal labour market. In the upper right hand quadrant we locate schemes that are both heavily regulated and that recruit in the conventional labour market, while in the lower left hand quadrant are schemes that allow the 'employment' of relatives – or of anyone else for that matter, since they are totally unregulated.

This schematic representation became our framework for interpreting the data from the five countries initially involved in the *Shifting Boundaries* project. We identified five different models of cash for care, which related to the particular schemes that we found in the national systems studied (see Figure 9.2). The location of particular models in this figure

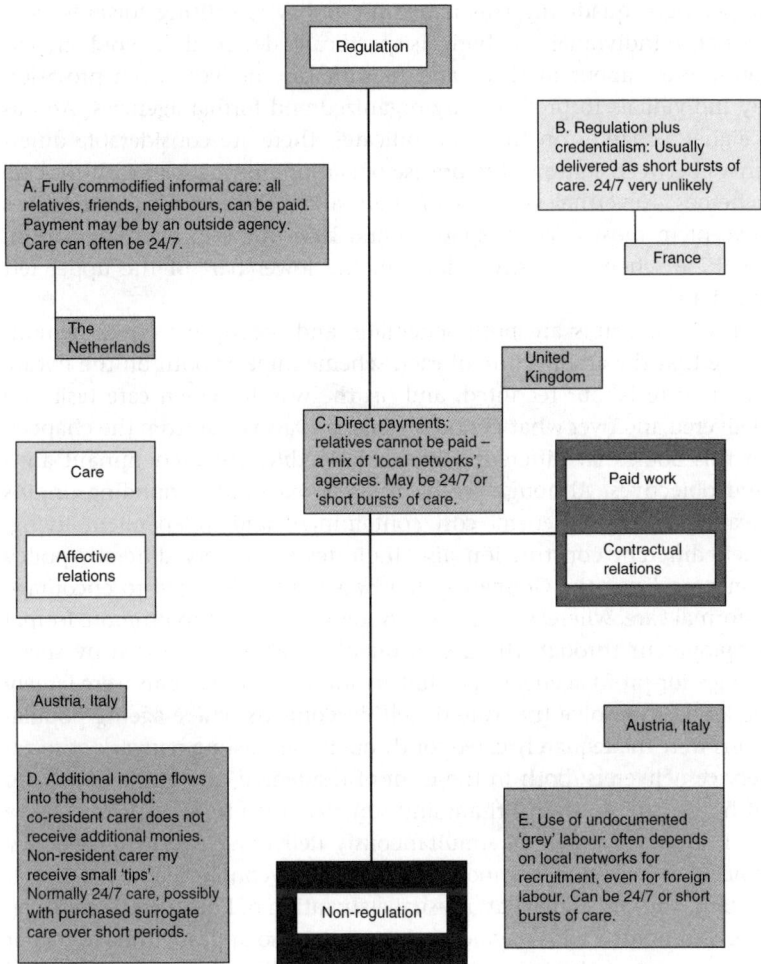

Figure 9.2 Schemes for organizing 'routed wages': types of payment and time availability

indicates how far they allowed for the employment of relatives, and how far they were regulated by external bodies.

The additional countries described in this book – Germany and the USA – can also be positioned in the figure. Germany belongs in the lower left quadrant, indicating that, as in the Austrian and Italian schemes, the cash in effect enters the household and is used in an unregulated manner. However the German scheme, as described in Schneider and Reyes' chapter, has begun to move towards the upper right quadrant. This is because policy is shifting towards case-managed individual care budgets specifically designed to avoid encouraging grey labour markets, and to shift care delivery from provision by individuals to provision by organized and formal agencies. And as Keigher's chapter on the USA indicates, there are considerable differences between states in the precise operation of American cash-for-care schemes. Nevertheless, most of them allow the payment of relatives (except in most cases of spouses) and have some form of regulation, so these schemes mostly belong in the lower part of the upper left quadrant.

These diagrams are both schematic and descriptive. They demonstrate that the architecture of each scheme impacts both on the nature of the care labour recruited, and on the way in which care tasks are delivered and over what period of time. It is also clear from the chapters in this book that different schemes have different predominant aims and objectives. Although we have discerned similar founding origins relating to consumerism, cost containment and independent living, their different construction also indicates some very different policy concerns. Thus the German system was largely designed to encourage informal care, whereas the French system has sought to promote formal employment through the use of qualified labour employed by social service for-profit agencies. The Italian and Austrian systems were largely designed to resolve the 'care deficit' in contexts where ageing populations were inadequately cared for through the existing network of social service deliverers, both in the form of residential care and in the form of home care. In both Britain and America, cash-for-care policies have been seen as capable of simultaneously delivering two general policy objectives – consumer empowerment and cost containment. The Dutch system, with its somewhat unusual elaboration of bureaucratic management combined with payment of relatives, also appears to have had at its core a set of objectives that include the political recognition of, and considerable compensation for, the unpaid work of care by informal carers. However, as the Dutch chapter makes clear, this strong support for informal carers is vulnerable when new governments with different ideas about family solidarity, and about how that solidarity should underwrite low-cost care, come into office.

Our comparative analysis of the cash-for-care schemes discussed in this book raises some key issues about the care of older people. Before exploring these, it is important to note that once a scheme is in place, it gives rise to a politics of defence – by those who gain from the scheme as it has been set up – and of attack, from those who consider there are also losses. Thus in the Dutch chapter we are made aware that a scheme that contains the possibility of considerable generosity towards care givers can come under attack when it seems not to be fulfilling its cost-containment objectives. At the same time, strong lobbies of care users and their carers respond in defence (and their views are well represented by the authors of the chapter on the Netherlands in this book).

Are these policies sustainable?

Any innovation in policy inevitably raises questions about its sustainability. In the case of cash-for-care schemes, there are strong reasons, in the work reported here and elsewhere, for thinking that they do fulfill certain key objectives of modern welfare states, including both consumer empowerment and some degree of cost containment. These factors probably ensure that cash-for-care schemes will remain in place for some time. However they also introduce some quite radical notions about care delivery. These make them vulnerable to strong criticism, and indeed give rise to some internal contradictions which may lead, in the future, to some changes. This might in turn decrease their cross-national variability.

The first issue they raise concerns the quality of care, and whether or not there should be some form of professional monitoring of process and outcome. Most of the schemes considered in this book, including and especially those that allow or encourage the payment of relatives, have at their core an idea that care delivery by kin, or by friends or other people selected by care users themselves, is (at least) 'good enough' care, and that at best it is far preferable to care rationed, organized and delivered by professionals. These schemes thus run counter to another trend within social care – namely the management of risk through the accreditation and professionalization of frontline care workers. A backlash against this development is not (yet) evident, although there are signs that it may grow. As suggested in the chapter on Germany, care users may increasingly be given case-managed individual budgets.

These would ensure that professional case managers become much more closely involved in the end use of the monies made available to care users. The very recent proposal in the UK Green Paper on adult social care (Department of Health, 2005) that there should be case-managed 'individualized budgets', running alongside the existing Direct Payments scheme, seems very closely to follow the German experiment with case-managed budgets. Furthermore, as the Italian and French chapters show, there is, in all these countries, an increasing awareness that allowing consumers total 'choice' as to whom they employ means there are no controls of any kind on the quality of caring labour, or on the outcome in terms of the quality of care delivered. The idea that risk and vulnerability can both be satisfactorily controlled through the hiring and firing practices of individual employers is increasingly, by implication, under debate. In all the countries considered, attempts to bring professionalization and training into these non-collectively organized intimate relationships can be observed. Thus in Germany and France, new policies designed to promote the deployment of care labour through the medium of organized and publicly accountable care organizations have emerged, while Italy and the UK have seen the development of training courses and minimum qualifications for care workers (but in the UK there is currently no policy pressure to promote the training of personal assistants employed directly by care users).

A second issue arises in those schemes that allow the payment of relatives on a generous scale, as in the Dutch scheme and some schemes in the United States. Here, in certain forms of domestic labour identified as 'care', it is becoming legitimate for biologically and biographically related individuals to be paid for the tasks of care they deliver to their kin. The fact that spouses are often excluded from these payments – again in the United States, but also in France – demonstrates the fuzziness and doubt that often surround those schemes that commodify previously unwaged informal care. Through marriage, spouses are seen as subject to a set of moral (and possibly contractual) obligations to care, which are considered to be stronger and more explicit than those that apply to other kin, including daughters and daughters-in-law. Given trends towards divorce and cohabitation rather than formal marriage, it is not clear how long this view can prevail. The British example, which originally expressly forbade the payment of relatives and co-residents (and still now allows it only in special circumstances), shows that a much wider notion of the availability of unpaid care via kinship can also determine the architecture of particular schemes. Policy makers keen to avoid 'deadweight' expenditure may try to ensure, as in the UK, that public expenditure cannot be used to pay for care work that would be undertaken anyway, without any financial remuneration.

The debate about whether or not relatives can be paid to care needs to be set in the context of the wider processes of individualization and atomization that have occurred in the late twentieth and early twenty-first centuries. Payments to relatives to care, for example the direct employment of a daughter by a disabled mother, conflict with those notions of family solidarity and shared norms of obligation that were prevalent following the two world wars of the twentieth century (and which endure in some contemporary cultural contexts). While part of a very wide reaching debate, these issues are likely to be discussed both in terms of values and beliefs and on pragmatic grounds specific to the aims and objectives of each particular cash-for-care scheme. For example, those who support the payment of relatives may argue that this helps address the difficulty of recruiting and managing care workers through the conventional labour market. They may even add, as the chapter on the United States indicates, that it reflects a strong preference, especially among the poor, for engaging close relatives and familiar peers in delivering caring labour.

Any aspect that makes a scheme more palatable to individual care consumers and which fits closely with their preferences is likely to increase take-up. This point may be of particular interest in the UK, where the employment of relatives is currently made very difficult in the Direct Payments scheme, but where take-up remains extremely low, particularly among older care users. It may also be argued that paying relatives helps in the development of culturally appropriate care for ethnic minority groups. Here we can expect the payment and 'employ-ment' of relatives to continue to be debated and renegotiated. It is possible to envisage some form of political trade off, between those seeking to increase take up and the attractiveness of the scheme to care users, and those pursuing cost-containment goals and charged with avoiding 'deadweight' costs. In resolving these matters it can be expected that national and local politics will continue to be prominent, and thus that variations between national and, in federal systems, state schemes will continue.

Policy change may also arise in response to concerns among policy makers and social care professionals about how far schemes facilitate the recruitment and employment of 'grey' labour. Grey labour drawn from undocumented migrant workers is likely to be particularly controversial. Policy makers may be indifferent to the employment of such labour, which constitutes a pool of workers who are relatively cheap and (due to housing difficulties of their own) often willing to provide care on a co-resident and 24/7 basis. Both the Italian and Austrian chapters in this book suggest that in these countries government is relatively insouciant about the strong presence of undocumented migrant labour within the caring work force. On the other hand, grey labour has been the focus of attention in both EU and some national political debates, and raises issues of tax evasion, unfair wage competition, and the development of a body of workers lacking social protection, pension entitlements and, in the USA, access to health care. There may be trade offs here between short-term expediency and long-term deficits, and tensions between those ministries responsible for delivering care to an ageing population and those charged with attending to fiscal probity and revenue maximization. These tensions are built into many of these schemes, and are likely to lead to national level political debates which may lead to future policy change.

Finally, governments and electorates will face the important question of the cost of cash-for-care schemes, and of how they can be funded. As we indicated in the introduction to this book, many of the schemes have been developed as part of a portfolio of measures to contain or reduce the aggregate costs of social care. They are expected to do this through the encouragement of social care rather than health care, through promoting home care rather than residential care, and (in those schemes which permit it) by enlarging the supply of care workers through the payment and 'employment' of informal carers. As many of our contributors point out, the social care provided through these schemes is relatively cheap mainly because the workers employed in a highly labour intensive industry are on very low wages and have very limited, if any, social protection. Their low rates of pay arise from the construction of personal and social care as 'unskilled', with the need for training and credentials downplayed. Yet the discourse about care and 'skill' is undoubtedly shifting towards a different understanding of the trainable skills of care, and our evidence (and other empirical data) draws critical attention to the way cash-for-care schemes encourage the exploitation of very vulnerable labour (Anderson, 2000; Ehrenreich and Hochschild, 2003). If caring labour and care work come to be more highly evaluated – and there are many good reasons why they should – there will be important consequences. Trade unions representing care workers, social care professionals seeking to promote the quality of care outcomes, and educators responsible for extending training opportunities, will all take up the refrain of the need to upskill care. The commodification of care and the introduction of the cash nexus into the household and kin network will then need to reflect the way in which paid care in the conventional labour market is slowly becoming a more skilled and better paid occupation. These processes will contribute to a rise in aggregate wages and the costs of care work, both within and beyond the household, will inevitably increase.

How are these additional costs of care to be funded? As some of the chapters in this book point out, there are three main fund-raising options: compulsory long-term care insurance schemes, both organized by the state and through compulsory private insurance; general taxation; and payment at the point of use (commonly called, in continental Europe, 'co-payments' or, in the UK, service charges). All three methods raise important political and economic issues. Any system of funding which raises personal taxation is likely to be very controversial. In the UK, for example, the 1999 Royal Commission on Long-Term Care's recommendation that there should be free personal care funded through general taxation was rejected on grounds of cost by the UK government (Royal Commission on Long-Term Care, 1999). Proposals that social care should be funded by compulsory long-term care insurance have also proved politically impossible in the UK, where both New Labour and Conservative parties are extremely wary of any proposal that would increase the perceived personal tax burden. As the chapters in this book indicate, governments are increasingly turning to co-payments to fund at least part of social care. But co-payments are themselves not without controversy. They can act as a deterrent to take-up and, if means tested, are a disincentive to save during a working lifetime. These cash-for-care schemes thus highlight the difficulty of funding social care in the context of ageing populations and accredited and upskilled care workforces. The likely outcome is that governments will continue to try to promote *both* informal care *and* qualified care: the former to satisfy increased demand from an ageing population, the latter to satisfy the politics of care 'upskilling'. The internal contradictions of this approach are likely to prove very difficult to sustain, and in consequence the funding of social care will continue to be highly problematic in all developed welfare states.

Further variations

Other contextual factors are also likely to drive variation between schemes and to be subject to change. These are also likely to impact on the nature and quality of the care relationship. As the Austrian, Italian and USA chapters demonstrate, the availability of 'grey' labour, and whether or not that labour largely consists of international migrants, will be a variable that depends on geographical propinquity to economies with much lower labour costs, the permeability of international borders, and the effectiveness of regulatory systems in policing that potential labour supply. Even in countries with large supplies of 'grey' labour (whether local or global), there will be internal variations between regions and between urban areas and their rural hinterlands. As the Italian chapter indicates, the availability of this insecure and easily exploitable labour can be used to drive down the overall remuneration of care work and to reinforce the predominant view that care work is an unskilled, low status activity. It can also be a means of further stigmatizing those who work in the sector.

A second contextual factor, applying to different countries and to different parts of those countries, is the nature of the national and local labour markets for care work. This in turn impacts on the ease with which care users can hire and fire their own caring labour. Two factors are likely to determine this pool of labour: first, the unemployment rate in the local labour market, and, second, the availability of other types of occupation in which those (especially women) with relatively low levels of skill and educational achievement can find employment. Both these factors are subject to national and local determinants: for example, in the Netherlands care work is rather better paid than work in other low paid sectors predominantly occupied by women, in contrast to the competition, in the UK labour market, from large supermarket employers and others who are able to pay somewhat more for the low skilled labour they require than can usually be earned by those performing the highly responsible and onerous tasks of personal care (Yeandle *et al.*, forthcoming, 2006). Difficulty in recruiting labour is likely to have knock-on effects on care users' ability to 'hire and fire', which will limit achievement of the objective of care user empowerment, and may act as a barrier to take up. There are nevertheless temptations, in those countries with large migration flows and relatively easy availability of low paid female labour, to support schemes which are unregulated, and to continue to 'turn a blind eye' to well established illegalities and risks to both care users and care workers.

The chapters in this book, in particular the UK chapter, demonstrate that, while one can make generalizations about the type of labour likely to emerge within the architecture of a particular scheme, the actual outcome of care work configuration is very variable between employers.

In other words, individual 'employers' appear to put together their own 'package' of caring labour which, within a context of what labour is locally available, is highly variable. Some people employ large numbers of people who work for them on a shift basis, others employ one person; some employ people who share a similar culture and language, others employ those with whom they have little in common. In the empirical data derived from the *Shifting Boundaries* project (described and published elsewhere), we have also noted that some 'employers' are engaged in a relationship with their care workers that is both intimate and very long term, whereas others are more likely to have 'employees' who are short term and with whom they have a 'cool' and task orientated relationship (Ungerson, 2006). This variability in the configuration of the care relationship and the numbers and type of care workers 'employed' is, in our view, a sign that one of the main objectives of these types of scheme is working effectively. Even within the generalizations that we have linked to particular funding regimes, some care users are apparently able to mobilize an element of choice as to the organization of their personal care. In that sense, cash-for-care schemes are indeed a form of empowerment for care users.

Having considered the factors that determine variability in national care schemes and the ways in which they might be driven to change given the tensions embedded within them, we now turn to some of the other issues raised by the chapters in this book, particularly those that apply to the nature of employment in the care work sector and the future of long-term care delivery.

Into the future

Among the many unresolved issues contained within this mode of care delivery, where care users directly employ their own care givers, is the question of how that care work is – and should be – organized. As the contributions in this book demonstrate, within cash-for-care systems there are essentially three types of care organization: commodified informal care delivered by kin, where the 'organization' occurs within the domestic domain and operates within the politics of kinship obligation; paid care organized on an *ad hoc* basis, where care users recruit and manage their own labour; and paid care organized by outside agencies, which provide care services as and when needed, (usually) on a for-profit basis. The chapters on France and Germany demonstrate that in some systems there are strong policy incentives to promote the latter form of organization. In France, agencies are regarded as a means of promoting formal paid employment which can be visible to the fiscal authorities; in Germany the use of formally organized labour is regarded as a form of quality control. However, as we have already pointed out, the difficulty with this development is that the employment of more expensive labour via for-profit agencies increases costs. This will pose difficulties both for governments facing long-term care funding crises, and for individual consumers many of whom will find well paid qualified caring labour unaffordable. Even where users can afford agency workers, they may only be able to employ them for very short hours. From the empirical evidence in the *Shifting Boundaries* study, we know that some users of cash-for-care schemes prefer to employ individuals who work only for them, working for longer hours than they could afford if they had to rely on workers employed by a social care organization. The same can be true of care workers, some of whom prefer to care for single individuals over long periods, rather than to get caught up in what has been described in our data as a 'conveyor belt' of care.

These developments mean that the trend towards providing cash rather than services to care users, via the welfare state, is leading both to a polarized policy position on the nature of care work and, at the same time, to a polarization of care work itself. In some welfare states, the policy position appears to be to try to develop a qualified care workforce while simultaneously trying to maintain or enlarge both the workforce providing informal care, and a waged workforce which draws primarily on unskilled labour. Recent developments in the UK are typical of this bipolarization of policy. Here the policy aim appears to be both to develop a system for controlling the quality of care (for example by the imposition of minimum standards of qualification via the Care Standards Act, 2000) and, at the same time, keeping the aggregate costs of care work relatively low by a continued emphasis on informal care and, perhaps, turning a blind eye to the development, in some metropolitan areas, of an invisible labour market of care work largely filled by casually and informally employed 'unskilled' care workers. At the heart of this somewhat contradictory stance is a debate about whether 'care' is, or is not, skilled work. The policy message speaks increasingly of the need for care workers to receive training, and of the risks involved in devolving the invisible and responsible work of personal care within the domestic domain to untrained workers. Yet this rhetoric is not applied to the work of informal carers who are assumed, through the operation of affect, to deliver the high quality care to their individual 'loved ones' which paid care workers need to be trained to deliver to strangers. The assumption that informal care necessarily arises from relations of affect, and that affect automatically gives rise to quality care, is questionable. The evidence that care is generated as much by a sense of the 'proper thing to do' or 'duty' as by love is considerable (Finch, 1989; Finch and Mason 1992; Ungerson, 1987), while the assumption that affect necessarily leads to quality of care has also been questioned (see, for example, Twigg and Atkin (1994) on 'engulfed carers'). In our view, governments wishing to credentialize care work on grounds of quality control, at the same time as they encourage the continued use of informal care, are promoting contradictory policies. If extensive and relatively unsupported and untrained informal care is accepted and promoted, this in itself serves to undermine the notion that care work is essentially a skilled task for which training must be undertaken. With ageing populations ahead, and cost containment policy shifting responsibility for the care of older people away from the expensive health care sector and towards the currently much cheaper social care sector, a policy that promotes or permits the development of free or low cost care is bound to be attractive. But such free or low cost care is almost certainly untrained.

Given these contradictory policies, the labour market for care work is likely to remain polarized, between paid and credentialized workers working for agencies and the statutory sector, and much more casually or intimately employed labour working for individual care users. While accepting that many unpaid informal carers provide devoted care of exceptional quality, it must be acknowledged, as the USA chapter points out, that many of these individually employed care workers will be poor and unprotected, themselves working for other poor and unprotected and highly vulnerable older people. These will be invisible relationships, and just as with informal care, they will be difficult, if not impossible, to monitor. Both workers and users will be unprotected in these caring relationships and the health and safety regulations that apply to organized care workers will not be applicable. In other words, two different worlds of care work are likely to develop. In the first of these worlds, care labour will be increasingly professionalized, and will be accessible to those who can afford it, or who are able, through particular forms of frailty and recognized need, to muster the resources of the welfare state to gain entry to these services. Protection for these vulnerable users, and decent working conditions for care providers, will, in these relationships, begin to prevail. In the second of these worlds, there is likely to be poverty on both sides of the care relationship, along with lack of protection and support, and invisibility. If this happens, two types of care labour market will run alongside each other, used by different types of 'employers' – a polarization and inequality of caring circumstances that bodes ill for social justice as a whole.

All the chapters in this book have referred to the dominance, in the care work labour market, of female labour. This is inevitable while care work is regarded as relatively unskilled and is closely associated with notions of nurturant femininity. Once organized care work becomes credentialized, however, an occupational hierarchy for organized care work is bound to emerge. Upskilled, better paid and stripped of its essentialist 'feminine' qualities, it is possible that the very strong female predominance in this segment of the labour market will decline: men too will enter this form of paid employment, perhaps through qualifications acquired through higher and further education, and will gain entry to its upper echelons. Meanwhile, as we have argued above, another less organized labour market will co-exist, encouraged by the features of some of the cash-for-care schemes described in this book. We expect this latter labour market to remain female dominated. Moreover, where schemes encourage or allow for the employment of unregulated or undocumented migrant labour, caring labour will draw disproportionately on women from minority ethnic groups who find their employment opportunities severely constrained.

It is essential that governments and others responsible for developing an architecture of social care capable of meeting the challenging demands of the twenty-first century address these complex issues. Increased demand for home care will arise in the coming decades not only from the much larger population of very aged people, but also from rising numbers of sick and disabled younger people, since better healthcare increases their longevity and survival rates too. It is likely that governments and their citizens will want social care arrangements that enable unpaid informal caring to continue – but it is very important that governments explore whether this is best done through effective supportive services, enabling unpaid care to be possible alongside participation in employment, rather than through paying those who care unpaid to take on even more caring responsibility as paid care workers, or encouraging them to give up their prior paid work to enter this hybrid form of work and care.

This book has revealed considerable variation in the way cash-for-care schemes have developed, but has found no single blueprint that can be advocated as without disadvantages, or indeed as the best scheme so far available. Reflecting on all the evidence gathered here, we can only stress that these schemes will not, and cannot, offer governments a panacea for the difficult problems they face in developing good quality social care. Insofar as cash-for-care systems achieve flexible, responsive care delivery at the time and place that care users prefer, they will meet with the approval of those requiring care. But if they develop this at the expense of exploiting or marginalizing those who deliver that care, or even of pressurising into care work those unwilling to provide it or unprepared for what it involves, cash-for-care systems will risk falling into disrepute and contributing to, rather than removing, the inequalities in social care that confront us.

We hope this book will act as a stimulus to the extensive debate that all the states studied here need to have about how to resource, design and deliver the quality of social care that vulnerable people in our populations deserve.

Note

1. Only in the USA did a federal (and a handful of state schemes) start earlier, and then only in relation to disabled veterans, reflecting a policy of compensation for the personal aftermath of the Vietnam War.

References

Anderson, B. (2000) *Doing the Dirty Work?: The Global Politics of Domestic Labour*, London: Zed Books.

Barnes, C. and Mercer, G. (1997) *Doing Disability Research*, Leeds: Disability Press.

Bonoli, G., George, V. and Taylor-Gooby, P. (2000) *European Welfare Futures: Towards a Theory of Retrenchment*, Cambridge: Polity Press.

Department of Health (2005) *Independence, Well-being and Choice: Our Vision for the Future of Social Care for Adults in England*, Cm 6499, London: Stationery Office.

Ehrenreich, G. and Hochschild A. R. (eds) (2003) *Global Woman: Nannies, Maids and Sex Workers in the New Economy*, London: Granta Books.

Finch, J. (1989) *Family Obligations and Social Change*, Cambridge: Polity Press.

Finch, J. and Mason, J. (1992) *Negotiating Family Responsibilities*, London: Routledge.

Morris, J. (1991) *Pride against Prejudice: A Personal Politics of Disability*, London: Women's Press.

Morris, J. (1993) *Independent Lives: Community Care and Disabled People*, Basingstoke: Macmillan, new Palgrave Macmillan.

Oliver, M. (1996) *Understanding Disability: From Theory to Practice*, Basingstoke: Macmillan, new Palgrave Macmillan.

Royal Commission on Long-Term Care (1999) *With Respect to Old Age: Long Term Care: Rights and Responsibilities*, Cm 4192, London: Stationery Office.

Shakespeare, T. and Corker, M. (eds) (2002) *Disability/postmodernity: Embodying Disability Theory*, London: Continuum.

Twigg, J. and Atkin, K. (1994) *Carers Perceived: Policy and Practice in Informal Care*, Buckingham, Open University Press.

Ungerson, C. (1987) Policy is Personal: Sex, Gender and Informal Care, London, Tavistock.

Ungerson, C. (2004) 'Whose Empowerment and Independence? A Cross-national Perspective on "Cash for Care" Schemes', *Ageing & Society*, 24(1), 1–24.

Ungerson, C. (2006) 'Care, Work and Feeling', in Pettinger, L. *et al.* (eds), *A New Sociology of Work?*, Oxford, Blackwell.

Ungerson, C. and Yeandle, S. (2005) 'Care Workers and Work–Life Balance: The Example of Domiciliary Careworkers', in Houston, D. M. (ed.), *Work-Life Balance in the 21st Century*, Basingstoke: Palgrave.

Yeandle, S., Shipton, L. and Buckner, L. (forthcoming 2006) *Challenges in Meeting Demand for Domiciliary Care*, Sheffield: Centre for Social Inclusion, Sheffield Hallam University.

Index